THE ASSOCIATION FOR SCOTTISH LITERARY STUDIES

NUMBER FOUR

POEMS BY ALLAN RAMSAY
AND ROBERT FERGUSSON

THE ASSOCIATION FOR SCOTTISH LITERARY STUDIES

GENERAL EDITOR—MATTHEW P. MC DIARMID

POEMS BY ALLAN RAMSAY
AND ROBERT FERGUSSON

EDITED BY

ALEXANDER MANSON KINGHORN

AND

ALEXANDER LAW

ROWMAN AND LITTLEFIELD

TOTOWA, NEW JERSEY

First published in the United States 1974
by Rowman and Littlefield, Totowa, N.J.

Introduction, Textual Notes and Glossary
© 1974 A. M. Kinghorn and A. Law

Library of Congress Cataloging in Publication Data

Kinghorn, Alexander Manson, comp.
  Poems by Allan Ramsay and Robert Fergusson.

  (Association for Scottish Literary Studies.
[Occasional papers] no. 4)
  Bibliography: p.
  1. English poetry—18th century. I. Law, Alexander,
joint comp. II. Ramsay, Allan, 1685–1758. III. Fergusson,
Robert, 1750–1774. IV. Series.
PR1215.K48   821'.5'08   73–22361
ISBN 0–87471–501–6

Printed in Great Britain

CONTENTS

INTRODUCTION   vii

Notes   xxx
Select Bibliography   xxxiii

POEMS BY ALLAN RAMSAY

Elegy on Maggy Johnston, who died Anno 1711   3
Elegy on John Cowper, Kirk-Treasurer's Man, Anno 1714   7
Elegy on Lucky Wood in the Canongate, May 1717   10
Lucky Spence's Last Advice   13
Familiar Epistles between Lieutenant William Hamilton and
    Allan Ramsay
      Epistle I (Hamilton)   17
      Answer I (Ramsay)   20
      Epistle II (Hamilton)   22
      Answer II (Ramsay)   26
Horace's Odes
    Horace to Virgil, on his taking a Voyage to Athens   28
    To the Phiz an Ode   30
    An Ode to Mr. Forbes   32
    Horace: Book I, Ode V   33
    Horace: Book I, Ode VI. To His Grace John, Duke of
      Argyle   34
The Vision   35
My Peggy is a young thing   40
The Gentle Shepherd, A Pastoral Comedy   42
The Monk and the Miller's Wife: A Tale   105
Songs
    Polwart on the Green   112
    Up in the Air   112
    I'll never leave Thee   113
The Widow   115
The Marrow Ballad   116

POEMS BY ROBERT FERGUSSON

The Daft-Days 121
Elegy, On the Death of Scots Music 123
The King's Birth-Day in Edinburgh 125
Caller Oysters 128
Braid Claith 131
Hallow-Fair 132
Elegy, On the Death of Mr David Gregory, late Professor of
    Mathematics in the University of St Andrews 136
An Eclogue 137
The Lee Rigg 141
Auld Reikie, A Poem 141
To the Tron-kirk Bell 151
Mutual Complaint of Plainstanes and Causey, in their Mother-
    tongue 153
The Rising of the Session 157
Ode to the Bee 159
The Farmer's Ingle 161
The Ghaists: A Kirk-yard Eclogue 165
On seeing a Butterfly in the Street 169
Hame Content. A Satire. To all whom it may concern 171
Leith Races 174
Ode to the Gowdspink 179
To the Principal and Professors of the University of St Andrews,
    on their superb treat to Dr Samuel Johnson 181
The Election 184
Elegy on John Hogg, late Porter to the University of St Andrews 188
The Sitting of the Session 191
To my Auld Breeks 193
Horace, Ode XI. Lib. I. 195
The Author's Life 196
On Night 196

NOTES

Poems by Allan Ramsay 197
Poems by Robert Fergusson 201

GLOSSARY 210

INTRODUCTION

We have brought together in this volume a collection of the poems of Allan Ramsay and Robert Fergusson that, we hope, is representative of their best and most typical work. With two exceptions, both from Fergusson, our selection has been made from their Scots poems, chosen not only because they are Scots but also because they are their authors' best. Students of the eighteenth-century revival in Scots poetry – a revival that was to initiate a series of revivals, in the Scots verse of Robert Burns, James Hogg, Robert Louis Stevenson, Hugh MacDiarmid, and in the Scots dialogue of Walter Scott, John Galt and Lewis Grassic Gibbon – will find here basic material for their study, printed authoritatively and with the minimum of interference.

Ramsay's activities as poet and editor link the late mediaeval with the modern phases of literary Scots. He and Fergusson were among the first to rehabilitate the native language for use in comic and serious poetry, following its neglect throughout the seventeenth century. In this context he who knows only Burns lacks the necessary historical perspective, yet, although Burns in well-known passages declared his debt to Ramsay and Fergusson, it is only within recent years that critics, aided by reliable texts, have been able to examine in detail the extent and nature of his indebtedness.

The texts published here are, by kind permission, based upon the Scottish Text Society's editions, in which the present editors and the series editor have provided textual variants, detailed notes, and full commentaries. In this book we have supplied Ramsay's footnotes to certain poems, regarding these as an integral part of his poetic statement, but otherwise explanatory matter has been abbreviated or modified from that given in the standard editions.

Ramsay and Fergusson like Burns confront the reader of today with unfamiliar language. Ramsay furnished his collected *Poems* of 1721 and 1728 with simple glossaries, and there is also a short glossary at the end of Fergusson's 1773 volume of *Poems*. But these are insufficient for modern needs, Fergusson's verse being particularly wide and accurate in its Scots range. This volume therefore includes a glossary of Scots words and phrases used by both poets: in some instances Ramsay's definitions, which have a historic flavour of their own, are given.

The selection of poems to give a just balance, and to provide readers with an opportunity for a fair estimate of the talents of our two authors, presented a difficult problem. Ramsay lived to be nearly seventy-four; Fergusson died at twenty-four. Ramsay's verse fills three volumes of the Scottish Text Society's series; Fergusson's is contained in one. Much of Ramsay's most characteristic work is by its very nature diffuse; Fergusson's expression tends to be brief, pointed, technically polished. The Fergusson poems chose themselves without much difficulty, and we think that we have included all his best work, but Ramsay posed problems. We decided that we should print the whole of 'The Gentle Shepherd' because Ramsay's reputation owed so much to it, because it is interesting as a 'realistic' pastoral, the acting of which was for many years popular in Scotland, and because it can still convey a delightful sense of community. The other poems of Ramsay included here are nearly all from his earlier works. Inevitably there are notable omissions, and one editor at least regrets that it has not been possible to give 'An Epistle to Mr James Arbuckle of Belfast', if only for Ramsay's description of himself:

> *Imprimis* then, for tallness I
> Am five foot and four inches high:
> A black-a-vic'd snod dapper fallow,
> Nor lean, nor overlaid wi' tallow.
> With phiz of a Morocco cut,
> Resembling a late man of wit,
> Auld-gabbet *Spec*, wha was sae cunning
> To be a dummie ten years running.

Allan Ramsay the Elder was born on 15 October, 1684[1] in Leadhills, a lead-mining village in Lanarkshire, some 46 miles from Edinburgh. He was the younger son of a Scots father and an English mother. The references in several of his poems to the Earl of Dalhousie, chief of the Ramsays, as 'My Chief, my stoup and ornament', appear to be purely poetical and there is no evidence that he was related to that noble family. His father died when he was a baby, and his mother married again. Young Allan attended the parish school of Crawfordmoor, but we do not know how long he spent there or what he learned. His mother died in 1700, and his stepfather sent him to Edinburgh, where he became apprenticed to a wig-maker. He was eventually enrolled as a master wig-maker, and practised his skill in a shop probably in the Grassmarket of Edinburgh. In 1712 he married Christian Ross, by whom he had at least five children. The eldest, Allan, became the well-known portrait-painter:[2] his early training was largely due to his father's encouragement of his artistic gifts. It is likely that the poet himself had some ability in drawing, and he maintained a lifelong interest in the graphic arts.

In his late twenties Ramsay began to write verse in English, and helped to found a group calling itself the Easy Club[3] consisting of young men of literary interests. In the political climate of Edinburgh in the years after the Union of Parliaments of 1707, such a club could hardly avoid being strongly nationalist and even Jacobite in its sympathies. Ramsay shared these sympathies but naturally was mainly concerned with the literary and social interests of the members. The club provided a congenial atmosphere in which verse might be composed and criticised, and it was there that he was first encouraged to write poetry in Scots. The members took the names of older writers, Ramsay being known as Isaac Bickerstaff after the character in Steele's *Tatler*, but it was decided to change over to Scottish names and he became 'Gavin Douglas'. The last records we have of the Easy Club are of 1715, by which time Ramsay was already established in Edinburgh as a promising man of letters. The poems he published before 1721 were collected in the subscribers' edition he produced, printed by Ruddiman, in that year. The volume contains about eighty poems, of which about half were in English and in the style popular then in London. The Scots poems were written in a mixture of Scots and English of which the proportions varied from an obtrusively Scots vocabulary at one extreme to a slight admixture of Scotticisms at the other. As he stated in his Preface, many of the spellings were Scots, though the words were English, and in his view "the idiom or phraseology" was Scots whatever form the spelling took. In fact, pure vernacular – pronunciation, of course, was Scots – was mostly employed in comic or burlesque poems.

From 1718 Ramsay's poems are described on their title-pages as published by "the Author at the *Mercury*, opposite to Niddry's Wynd", and it is clear that Ramsay gradually gave up wig-making in favour of bookselling. His shop, finally situated "at the East End of the Luckenbooths", right in the middle of Edinburgh, became a meeting-place of men interested in literature,[4] and it was there that he established a circulating library, apparently the first in the British Isles.[5] He became a well-known figure in the cultural life of Edinburgh and its neighbourhood, and the familiar friend of men like Sir John Clerk of Penicuik, the scholar and lover of the arts; Lord Somerville, friend of the theatre; and Sir Alexander Dick, distinguished doctor and patron of the arts. In 1729 Ramsay helped to found a school of drawing and painting, called "The Academy of St. Luke": in that year, too, his son Allan, then aged 16 and also a member of the new Academy, made his first known attempt at a portrait from the life, taking his father as subject.

In 1724 Ramsay issued the first of five volumes of *The Tea-Table Miscellany*, a collection of songs in which Scots songs intended to be sung to traditional tunes were given prominence: though he did not treat old folk songs in the way that modern scholars approve, and though he often put eighteenth-century words and phrases in place of simpler words or of words that had been lost, he deserves full credit for directing the attention of scholars and patriots to the existence of these old songs. He attempted something similar for the older Scots poetry in his two-volume work, *The Ever Green*, first published in 1724, which brought to a more general audience many of the mediaeval Scots poems preserved in the Bannatyne Manuscript. The Preface of this collection is, however, best appreciated as a manifesto or defence of Ramsay's modern Scots poetry – "that natural Strength of Thought and Simplicity of Stile our Forefathers practised" . . . "Their *Images* are native, and their *Landskips* domestick; copied from those Fields and Meadows we every Day behold" . . . "There is nothing can be heard more silly than one's expressing his *Ignorance* of his *native Language*".

The pastoral play, *The Gentle Shepherd*, appeared in 1725, in the form reproduced in the present volume, and a ballad-opera version followed in 1729,[6] when the popular interest in Scots songs generated by Ramsay's own publications helped to give it additional attraction. In 1728 his second collection of poems came out, like its predecessor in a subscribers' edition printed by Ruddiman. Four further volumes of *The Tea-Table Miscellany* (1724–37), *Fables and Tales* (1722–30) and *A Collection of Scots Proverbs* (1737), based on an English compilation made by James Kelly in 1721, complete the list of Ramsay's main published works. He continued to write poetry, but much of it remained unpublished or was left to appear posthumously.[7]

Ramsay's most ambitious civic venture took place in 1736, when he opened a theatre in Carrubber's Close. This brave endeavour had a short life, for the theatre had to close under the provisions of the Licensing Act of 24 June, 1737, which forbade the performance of plays for gain outside London![8] This Act was used by the Edinburgh Presbytery to close the theatre, but he fought back vigorously and the process dragged on for two years. He suffered financial loss when the project finally had to be abandoned. Poems written during this period and personal correspondence express his anger at the hypocrisy of the 'unco guid'.[9]

About 1740 Ramsay retired from active business and built an octagonal house,[10] still standing, known as the Goose-Pie, on Castlehill. As a man of leisure he lived what he liked to regard as a Horatian life, with his friends and his books. His wife died in 1743, and his own long and apparently healthy life came to an end on or about 7 January, 1758. He lies buried in Greyfriars Churchyard.

Four portraits of Ramsay exist: two were painted by his friend John Smibert in 1717 and 1720, the second of which was used for the frontispiece engravings in the subscribers' volumes; one, done in oil in 1723, is by William Aikman; the fourth is the chalk drawing made by his distinguished son, now in the Scottish National Portrait Gallery.[11]

Most of the works of Ramsay selected for this edition come from his 1721 collection of *Poems* and are early compositions, representing the best of his experiments in Scots. 'The Gentle Shepherd' and some of the others appeared in his 1728 and 1729 collections of *Poems*, and only 'The Marrow Ballad' (1738) is of later date. The Elegies and 'Lucky Spence' are among his earliest work, displaying a realism and comic description that made Ramsay a popular Edinburgh figure. 'The Vision' appeared in *The Ever Green* of 1724 and expresses the resentment that he and his friends felt towards the 1707 union of the parliaments. Representative stanzas have been offered here, because they have great spirit, illustrating his most important motivation as a writer, patriotism. 'The Monk and the Miller's Wife', described by Lord Woodhouselee, one of Ramsay's most notable biographers and editors,[12] as a work which "would of itself be his passport to immortality as a comic poet", at least invites comparison with the similar tale sometimes attributed to William Dunbar, *The Freiris of Berwik*. Our choice includes some of Ramsay's versions of Horace's *Odes* which, though not 'translations', are good illustrations of the Scotsman's strengths and weaknesses as delineator of the small precise image. By trying to render Horace in Scots he was seeking to show the capacity of the native language as

Gavin Douglas had done two centuries before when he translated Virgil's *Aeneid*, and as Fergusson considered doing when he contemplated a Scots version of the *Georgics*. Ramsay's adoption of Douglas's name when a member of the Easy Club emphasises his early allegiance to the patriotic aims of the great translator. Besides collecting old Scots songs in *The Tea-Table Miscellany* Ramsay wrote songs himself, and we have included some of these as well as those he wrote for 'The Gentle Shepherd'.

His English poems, unrepresented here, are actually more numerous than his Scots ones. Indeed, it is not always easy to decide whether a given poem is English or Scots. In the Preface to *Poems* 1721 he sought to defend his selective use of Scots by saying that in certain of the completely anglicised poems:

> . . . all their Difference from the others is only in the bibliography of some Words, such as *from* for frae, *bold* for bauld, and some few Names of things; and in those, tho' the Words be pure English, the Idiom or Phraseology is still Scots.[13]

But for the poet the "Difference" was vital. The two poems to which he refers in this paragraph, 'The Morning Interview' and 'Content', are unimpressive imitations of his most frequently followed English model, Pope. The former is a dull derivative of *The Rape of the Lock*, and concerns the forenoon visit of a *beau* to his mistress. The background, which achieves no poetic identity, is vestigially Edinburgh and the verse can only be said to exhibit a competence in Augustan poetic diction.

Ramsay suited his style to his matter. Less dignified subjects were most fully dealt with in Scots. In the 'Lucky Spence' poem Ramsay, like Villon in certain stanzas of *Le Testament*, is talking through the mouth of a brothel-keeper and his words recall the original sound of Mistress Spence's crude ironies:

> Cleek a' ye can be Hook or Crook,
> Ryp ilky Poutch frae Nook to Nook.

This is not to say that he did not write seriously in a Scots idiom; a poem like 'Keitha: a Pastoral', an elegy on the death of the Earl Marischal's daughter, is cast in a conventional form but demonstrates his ability to sustain an overwhelmingly Scots vocabulary throughout a poem of one hundred lines. 'Keitha' and poems such as 'Wealth, or the Woody' and 'The Prospect of Plenty' anticipate 'The Gentle

Shepherd' in combining a classical English vocabulary with vernacular Scots in a serious context.

But the best Ramsay is the comic Ramsay of the elegies, epistles, tales and old-style songs. With the first three categories especially the reader feels that he is one of a small audience to whom the poet is delivering his verses, inviting enjoyment of topical references, absurd recollections, innuendoes and shafts of irony, such a circle, in fact, as the Easy Club must have provided when the earliest of these poems were written. His informative footnotes explaining the 'backgrounds' of Maggy Johnston, Lucky Wood, Lucky Spence and John Cowper would not have been needed by his companions of the Easy Club, and were added when he prepared his collection for a wider audience. Ramsay plainly enjoys the sound of his voice and these poems seem part of an older oral tradition. This becomes very clear when his flowing, careless, sometimes almost slap-dash style is considered alongside that of Fergusson, careful, controlled, planned, the work of a 'makar' comparable with Robert Henryson and William Dunbar.

In comparison, Ramsay's enthusiasm for language was untutored, a fundamental difference well illustrated by setting any of his Horace versions against Fergusson's single example of the same. The younger poet had an academic training in Latin, whereas Ramsay had to depend on translations and advice; had he comprehended the subtleties of his model more fully his confidence might have evaporated. Yet in these imitations and in 'The Gentle Shepherd' he preceded Thomson and the two Wartons in giving a clear impulse to eighteenth-century nature poetry, so that in this respect, as also in his literary antiquarianism, his adaptations of old songs, and the general reference of his writings to 'the folk', he has a place in the early history of the romantic revival.

The *Ever Green* and *Tea-Table Miscellany* collections had many shortcomings judged by modern editorial standards but they were both pioneer works, inspired by the will to re-assert a national identity seemingly lost or soon to be lost. The *Tea-Table Miscellany*, which stressed Scots as distinct from foreign melodies, was aimed at an audience which prided itself both on its Scots culture and on its urbanity; in these volumes Ramsay supplied new words to traditional tunes and gave the latter a fresh lease of life as vehicles for the communication of natural humour and unaffected sentiment. The songs which he wrote himself vary a great deal, but the lyric 'My Peggy is a young thing', which opens 'The Gentle Shepherd', is exactly suited to his rustic romance, his cottar-house comedy. The other songs chosen for inclusion here show Ramsay writing simple singable Scots very much in the folk tradition.

Of his talent for comic narrative, the epistolary correspondence with William Hamilton of Gilbertfield, the author of a version of Hary's *Wallace*, provides a particularly apt illustration. He found the six-line stanza – he was the first to call it 'Standart Habbie' – an easy medium for the wit and technical amusement of the poetical exchanges. Hamilton and Ramsay shared a common language, almost a code in some respects, grounded in mutually shared memories and an emotional *rapport*. With Hamilton he is indulging in the homespun colloquy that most delighted him. Time and change have worked against him here, but a later audience can still understand something of the game that is being played and even catch its spirit at moments, such a moment as this:

> *Quisquis vocabit nos* Vain-glorious,
> Shaw scanter Skill, than *malos-mores*,
> *Multi & magni* Men before us
> > Did stamp and swagger,
> *Probatum est, exemplum* Horace,
> > Was a bauld Bragger.
>
> Then let the doofarts fash'd wi' spleen,
> Cast up the wrang side of their een,
> Pegh, fry and girn wi' spite and teen
> > And fa a flyting,
> Laugh, for the lively lads will screen
> > Us frae back-biting.[14]

In 'The Monk and the Miller's Tale' the broad fun is distinctively Scots. James and Bessy's exchanges through the window and the confrontation scene with Hab the Miller yield nothing to English tastes.

> "Hout I", quoth she, "ye may well ken,
> 'Tis ill brought butt that's no there ben;
> When but last owk, nae farder gane,
> The laird got a' to pay his kain."[15]

is the wife's rejoinder to Hab when he demands that she cook a fine meal for their 'distinguished' guest. Such a speech must send us nowadays to the dictionary but is wholly of a piece, without unmatched materials, completely and easily self-consistent. It does not illustrate, like so much of Ramsay's verse, the uneasy interaction between literary English and printed/oral Scots as written down by seventeenth-century Scots versifiers like Robert Sempill of Beltrees and the nameless composers of the old songs. The tension between the two caused educated Scotsmen to discriminate in their use of the vocabulary to which they had been born. They aimed at standard English but actually achieved a hybrid, the Anglo-Scots spoken by preachers, professors and judges; a language which might suffice for the expository purposes of the *literati*, of such a man as David Hume (who outside his writing retained the plain speech of his childhood[16]) but could not express so much else in the thought and feeling of the Scots community.

Considering the handicap of inheriting a divided culture, a bilingual tradition – Ramsay was early familiar with the more popular Scots classics, luckily accommodated by the printers to the speech of their day, such as Barbour's *Bruce*, Hary's *Wallace*, Sir David Lindsay's anti-clerical poems and play, *A Satire Of The Three Estates* (which had its influence on the comic elegies), and, of course, the ballads and songs, at the same time that he was exposed to the English ascendancy exemplified by Pope, Prior and Gay[17] – it is remarkable that Ramsay succeeded as often as he did with his new Scots poetry. The failures are, of course, notorious, as in his verses to the tune of 'Auld Lang Syne', where the incongruities of style and diction compound an absurdity –

> Should auld Acquaintance be forgot,
>   Tho they return with Scars?
> These are the noble Heroe's lot,
>   Obtain'd in glorious Wars;
> Welcome my *Varo* to my Breast,
>   Thy Arms about me twine,
> And make me once again as blest,
>   As I was lang syne.[18]

The same incongruities show at places in 'The Gentle Shepherd', as in the unequal speeches of Sir William Worthy in his guise of a 'spaeman'. And one notes that the rustic swains Patie and Roger, together with Peggy the milkmaid, all of whom turn out in the end to be of higher caste than they know, lose much of their racy Scots as they gain in social status. Ramsay is more fully successful with uncomplicated country characters like Jenny, Bauldy and Mause, who are given a heightened but genuine and consistent Scots expression. These are not the ideally distanced and romanticised peasants of Gray and

Goldsmith, but convincing stage versions of the earthy practical people whom Ramsay knew from boyhood. A real country voice speaks in this criticism of Roger by Jenny:

> I dinna like him, Peggy, there's an end;
> A herd mair sheepish yet I never kend.
> He kaims his Hair indeed, and gaes right snug,
> With ribbon-knots at his blew bonnet-lug;
> Whilk pensily he wears a thought a-jee,
> And spreads his garters dic'd beneath his knee.
> He falds his ourlay down his breast with care
> And few gang trigger to the kirk or fair.
> For a' that, he can neither sing nor say,
> Except, "How d'ye" – or "There's a bonny day."[19]

It will be apparent that though the speech is sufficiently that of a Scots country lass it has been modified to suit the ear and understanding of those accustomed to reading English poetry. Ramsay did not coin vocabulary. He converted a number of Scots words and expressions into a phonetic approximation that an urban audience could follow; but he was not consistent in his reproduction of a given word in phonetic convention (e.g. *bain/bane*; *curtchea/kurchie*; *unco/unko/uncko*). His orthography in a very general fashion accommodated itself to English usage (e.g. *laigh* for *laich*; *sleigh* for *sleich*) but in other cases introduced peculiarly Scottish conventions (*pouer*, *shaw*, *snaw*). In *Poems* 1721 such Scottish appearances were exemplified in a simply classified list of 126 words. The unpublished verses in MS. Egerton 2023, reproduced in STS III, are rawer.

What should strike the reader is the very colloquial bias of Ramsay's (as of Fergusson's) literary Scots. Made up of borrowings from various dialects and arbitrarily spelled, it was most freely used in rustic or convivial scenes, and so invited the charge of being limited in its range of expression. Nevertheless, it is clear that Ramsay was the first to demonstrate the potentialities of modern Scots, particularly by its use in one of the major forms. 'The Gentle Shepherd' is dramatically slight but the best of its country scenes have authenticity and charm, enough to explain the popularity that made it so influential in later Scots poetry. It was therefore unfortunate that the play's distinguishing of peasant life from 'gentle' life high-lighted the special association of Scots with the former. Yet, while this treatment represented a social and political fact, the provincialisation of Scotland by its surrender of national status and dignity, it was not Ramsay's whole reading of the situation. Sir William and his son do have the use of *both* English and Scots, even if they expect peasants to know only the second.

The public face of criticism, however, turned away from Scots during the second half of the century,[20] though private correspondence occasionally reveals opinions milder than the anti-national ones expressed in print. In the 1770s, this issue came alive in the correspondence published in the Edinburgh *Weekly Magazine* over pretentious pseudonyms like Anthropos, Philo-Orthologiae, Hermes and Scoto-Britannicus.[21] But the fact was that the use of Scots, however selective, by Ramsay or Fergusson or Burns, spoke to the experience of their fellow-countrymen, reminding them of who and what they were at a time when they stood in danger of abandoning a rich cultural inheritance in favour of a foreign tradition known only by reading and report. Though the nature of this inheritance was not properly understood by Ramsay, much less by the provincialised pseudonymous contributors to *The Weekly Magazine* who sought to discriminate sharply between English and Scots, to the disadvantage of the latter, its effects in poetry, and even occasionally in prose, could not be denied. As we observed at the conclusion of our critical biography of Ramsay:

> . . . when he wrote to please English and English-minded audiences, he was no more than competent; there were dozens of poets in England (and not a few in Scotland) who could have imitated Miltonic styles with equally pleasing results, but when he tried out his Scots, Ramsay had no peer in his own time. Fergusson and Burns excepted, no Scots poet has been more deserving of the title.[22]

In this edition we have borne Ramsay's argument concerning orthography in mind and printed his spellings of both English and Scots words as they appeared in his original editions or MS. sources, on the ground that to tamper with his orthography might mislead as to sound and phrasing or even destroy the rhyme and metre originally intended. The MS. sources indicated a mainly phonetic orthography; because Scots was then a spoken more than a printed language, it fell to the poet and his printer to spell the words in their texts as it suited them. An odd consequence of this procedure was that only what was peculiarly Scots, or was indicated as such, was so considered. Needless to say, the greater part of an 'English' vocabulary had always been native to Scotsmen, but Scots forms and sounds had become disguised by an English spelling.

Our own editorial conclusion was, that the personality of Ramsay should be left to speak for itself, even to the extent of maintaining the mis-spelling of words. None of his aberrations are incomprehensible however, though they may seem quaint to a modern reader (e.g. *feavers*, *hurrycane*, *kanny*, *kow* and the doubling of consonants in *ballance*, *carrols*, *linnen*, *legg*); the mis-spelling of proper names sometimes indicates pronunciation as in *Castalius*, *Louthian*, *Rosycrucian*, and has therefore been kept. Forms like *bussy* and *currious* may well be indicators of Ramsay's own way of speaking. One oddity of Scots spelling should be noted: in the group 'lz' 'z' represents sounded 'y' (*spulzie*), and in 'nz' the sound is as in 'sing' (*menzie*, *fenzie*, *Mackenzie*).

As regards punctuation we have presented the text as in the STS volumes, but with a very few exceptions have rejected the internal capital letters and italic print common in Ramsay's day; also punctuation has had to be supplied for the three short poems reproduced from MSS. in STS Vol. III (the imitations of Horace *Odes* I, V; *Odes* I, VI; and 'The Marrow Ballad').

★   ★   ★

Robert Fergusson[23] came of Aberdeenshire stock. Born on 5th September, 1750, in Cap-and-Feather Close, Edinburgh, soon to be demolished to facilitate construction of the North Bridge, he was the second son of William Fergusson, clerk, and Elizabeth Forbes. After elementary education at a private school in the nearby Niddry's Wynd run by a Mr Philp, he entered the Edinburgh High School in 1758, the year of Ramsay's death.

At the age of 11 he was elected to the Fergusson of Strathmartine Bursary tenable at the Dundee High School and later at St Andrews University, where he remained until 1768. The young man was said to have excelled at mathematics but of his other studies it appears that only Virgil and Horace really attracted him. At the University he first showed his gifts for satirising the learned professors, and his fellow-students accounted him a fine singer.

Politically Fergusson, like Ramsay, seems to have been a sentimental Jacobite, a position that expressed the more meaningful fact of his disgust with the union of parliaments, for him as for Ramsay no necessary consequence of a British patriotism. In 'The Ghaists', ll.57, 58, Herriot is made to exclaim –

> Black be the day that e'er to England's ground
> Scotland was eikit by the UNION's bond.

The significance of this view being held in turn by the authors of all that is most valuable in modern Scots poetry challenges our attention.

As was usual in those days, Fergusson left his university without taking a degree. While he was still a student, his father died, leaving the family in straitened circumstances; he went to his uncle's home near Oldmeldrum in Aberdeenshire, presumably seeking assistance, but after six months left suddenly and on bad terms with his relative. Back in Edinburgh, he took the only job he could find, a position in the Commissary Office dealing with wills and matrimonial cases, which, his biographers agree, was monotonous, ill paid, unworthy of his abilities, but was perhaps the not too demanding job that his temperament and need to write required.

Reliable information concerning his life outside these duties is scanty, but it is clear that Fergusson spent much of his free time in the tavern society of the town, where he made many friends connected with the arts and professions. Lucky Middlemass's in the Cowgate and James Mann's in Craig's Close were two of the better-known 'locals'; in the latter The Knights Companions of the Cape, a body founded in 1764, met regularly. The Cape's objects included the promotion of good fellowship in an atmosphere of stimulating talk, light verse, story and song, similar to that of many old Edinburgh clubs but with a more distinctly Bohemian inclination. As in the Easy Club, members were known by pseudonyms. David Herd, the ballad editor, for example, adopted that of 'Sir Scrape Graysteil', the poet Thomas Mercer was 'Sir Forgetful', and the roll included a Sir Boot, Sir Brown Stout, Sir Watch, Sir Speak, Sir Sobersides, Sir Fender and many others, some of them well-known personalities in the realm of the fine arts. Fergusson became the 159th member of the Cape on 10th October, 1772, and recalling his own musical accomplishments called himself 'Sir Precenter'. His convivial gifts were appreciated and his poetic abilities warmly encouraged in the friendly atmosphere of this club.

Like Ramsay, Fergusson started by publishing derivative English verses, which appeared in Walter and Thomas Ruddiman's *Weekly Magazine, or Edinburgh Amusement*, from February, 1771. Of the fifty pieces he composed in English only a handful are more than competent exercises. His rapidly-acquired reputation as a poet was made and maintained by experiments in Scots, the earliest example of which was 'The Daft-Days', published in the magazine on 2nd January, 1772.[24] Early in 1773 a collected volume of nine Scots and twenty-seven English poems was issued by the Ruddimans, the poet's only effective patrons, a family whose interests were traditionally literary and patriotic and who had founded the *Weekly* (in 1768) with the express purpose of encouraging native genius. Soon afterwards Fergusson had 'Auld Reikie' printed independently and continued to publish Scots poems in *The Weekly Magazine* throughout the same year at the rate of about one every three weeks.

The last poem to be printed during his lifetime, 'Codicile to Rob. Fergusson's Last Will', composed in English, appeared in *The Weekly Magazine* of 23rd December, 1773. The young man's recorded poetic career lasted less than three years. The *Caledonian Mercury* of February, 1774, noted that Fergusson had "had a very dangerous sickness" and the Cape Club records mention his absence and illness and refer to a contribution which had been raised for him. Unable to work even for the meagre wage paid him in the Commissary Office, Fergusson was destitute and his family depended on aid from friends. He stopped writing poetry and accepted no more social invitations, confined his reading to the Bible and religious tracts and penned melancholy letters about his ill-health.[25]

It is not known precisely what was wrong with him. An early biographer, Alexander Peterkin,[26] ascribed his condition to syphilis, basing his information on a discussion with an anonymous informant who had known Fergusson personally. Signs of this black mood, alien to his normally mercurial poetic personality, show in the depressive power of his paraphrase of the third chapter of the Book of Job, printed in 1779 but presumably composed early in 1774. The beginning will illustrate this –

> Perish the fatal day when I was born,
> The night with dreary darkness be forlorn;
> The loathed, hateful and lamented night
> When Job, 'twas told, had first perceiv'd the light;
> Let it be dark, nor let the God on high
> Regard it with the favour of his eye;
> Let blackest darkness and death's awful shade
> Stain it, and make the trembling earth afraid;

Be it not join'd unto the varying year,
Nor to the fleeting months in swift career . . .

and the terrible conclusion –

For though nor rest nor safety blest my soul
New trouble came, new darkness, new controul.

In the known circumstances it is difficult to read these lines and think them only an uncharacteristic indulgence in the contemporary fashion of pietistic and melancholic literature.

The remaining few months of Fergusson's life were indeed without cheer. By June, 1774, he had partially recovered from his ailment, and was able to attend his sister's wedding in July – the month of the Cape Club's collection of funds on his behalf – but before the end of that same month the poet had an accident. He fell down a flight of steps, struck his head and had to be carried to his mother's house in a state of delirium. There he was looked after for a fortnight by a medical friend, Andrew Duncan,[27] who recorded the squalid conditions under which the poet lingered, subject to spells of insanity. His mother had been incapable of looking after him and had no comforts to offer, so that in spite of Duncan's efforts to prevent it, Fergusson was removed as a 'pauper lunatic' to the Edinburgh Bedlam, where the physical conditions were frightful.[28] On 17th October, 1774, he died, aged twenty-four years and one month.

Robert Burns felt an emotional kinship with his namesake, whose works he first encountered in 1782, and wrote:

O thou, my elder brother in Misfortune,
By far my elder Brother in the muse,
With tears I pity thy unhappy fate!
Why is the Bard unfitted for the world,
Yet has so keen a relish of its pleasures?[29]

and in his autobiographical letter to Dr John Moore claimed that Fergusson had caused him to come alive as a poet – "meeting with Fergusson's Scotch Poems, I strung anew my wildly-sounding, rustic lyre with emulating vigour".[30] He marked Fergusson's pauper's grave in the Canongate Churchyard with a memorial stone, and in the Preface to the 1786 Kilmarnock edition referred to him as "the poor unfortunate Fergusson".[31]

This was an accurate description, in view both of the poet's unhappy final year of life and the likelihood that with proper treatment he would have survived. If his friends did not provide this, it was, we must believe, because they did not have the means. The *Weekly Magazine* for 11th April, 1776, informs its readers that a Mr Burnet, ignorant of the poet's death, had written to offer him "a handsome settlement" in India, fare and expenses paid.[32] There is no evidence that the "Enbrugh Gentry" against whom Burns inveighed felt any such generous impulse.

Five supposed likenesses of Fergusson are known to exist. The most authentic is an oil possibly by, or after, his fellow-Knight of the Cape, Alexander Runciman, for whom the poet is thought to have sat in 1772. Only in 1960 was the subject of this painting identified as Fergusson from an inscription on the back.[33] Near-contemporary descriptions[34] make him out as of medium height and slender build, with a pale complexion, fair brown hair, a long nose and large black eyes. His forehead was high and his appearance suggested poor health.

Fergusson did not live long enough to attract attention outside his immediate circle, which was unlucky, since it is unlikely that he would have long remained without wider recognition at a time when all but the most conventional Scottish tastes were veering towards the home-bred, and when there was a dearth of significant poets. His premature departure from the scene left the role of upholder of the native tradition to Burns, whose Kilmarnock preface made tactful overtures to the *literati*, while not neglecting to mention the names of Ramsay and Fergusson, "these two justly admired Scotch poets", as his particular inspiration.

In his attitude to Scots as a poetic medium, limiting it to informal styles and the matter that best suited these, Burns is more like Ramsay than he is like Fergusson. Yet, though it was Ramsay that the critics held up to him as an example, mainly as the author of 'The Gentle Shepherd', it was Fergusson whom Burns, understandably, preferred to imitate. In his First Commonplace Book, mentioning "The excellent Ramsay and the still more excellent Fergusson",[35] he regrets that so little has been written about his own west country, and this suggestion of a regional poetry has plainly come from Fergusson's Edinburgh poems. Burns's larger purpose of being a patriot poet had the same source. It is evident that he appreciated how much more original a creator was Fergusson "the bauld and slee" than "honest Allan"; the resemblance in title, or theme and conception, between Fergusson's and Burns's better-known poems can hardly be missed.[36]

Fergusson's innovations show genius.[37] Ramsay transmitted to him the fifteenth-century comic tradition of *Christ's Kirk on the Green* but the younger poet rejected the mere farce of its narrative and altered its jingling rhyme scheme to allow a more varied and poetic comedy. His experiments with 'standart Habbie' which Ramsay had employed for humorous poetry only, show the same impatience with limiting convention; thus the serious, imaginative uses that he found for the stanza in the 'Elegy on the Death of Scots Music', 'To the Tron-kirk Bell', and within the mainly comic 'Hallow-Fair', 'Leith Races', 'The Election', discovered a range of effects that Burns was to emulate. Even in the pastoral *genre*, where Ramsay had been so effective, his originality appears: 'An Eclogue' represents a considerable advance on the older poet's less decided realism. Of this poem Matthew McDiarmid observes that it is "unique in the whole range of pastoral or rural poetry . . . One can only compare its admirable keeping of decorum with *The Twa Dogs*."[38] Fergusson's innovating artistry is most remarkable, however, in the form of the Spenserian stanza that he invented to convey the sensitive but objective scenes of his masterpiece, *The Farmer's Ingle*. Burns in his less convincing imitation, *The Cotter's Saturday Night*, injudiciously reverts to the original stanza, too leisurely and above all too literary for such a subject.

All Fergusson's variations on satirical themes – legal, political or religious, as suited him – were either freshly conceived or represented transformations of familiar material. From the publication of 'The Daft-Days' he struck sparks from his audience but because he supplied Burns with so many precedents, and because his poetic life was so short, he has been regarded as a torch-bearer, a transition-figure. He is thus too often measured by the Burns yardstick, as an influence or even as a premature explosion of Burnsian talent, perhaps a talent that, if it had been allowed, would have won to the heights of the Scots Parnassus.

For this last speculative opinion something may be said. Assuredly Burns had a more powerful and matured imagination than his "elder Brother", and his range was far wider. But, without Fergusson, more fertile in original conceptions, Burns would not have found the forms that expressed him and made him Scotland's national poet. Mr Allan MacLaine argues

Though small in bulk and relatively narrow in scope his (Fergusson's) work is unquestionably the finest body of poetry produced in Scotland during the eighteenth century before Burns.[39]

There was in fact little competition apart from that of Ramsay's work. It might be more to the point to suggest that if English poets too were considered, Fergusson, as a portrayer of town life, would then find rivals only in Pope and the more comparable Gay, whose *Trivia*[40] did for London something of what Fergusson's *Auld Reikie* did for Edinburgh – though *Trivia* is an objective description of street activity, without those personal, picturesque insights which distinguish the Scotsman's poem. But in general the 'genteel', refining tendencies of the English masters make such comparisons unprofitable. Of Fergusson's English contemporaries, Gray, Shenstone and Collins, it may be said that they seem to wish to contribute more to literature than to life.

Moreover, discussion of English and Scots poetry in the same terms and according to a defined set of criteria is bound to fall short of the fair or adequate in literary criticism. To take but one example from Fergusson, his lashing of Johnson in 'To the Principal and Professors of the University of St Andrews, on their superb treat to Dr Samuel Johnson' is animated by a fiery wit quite alien to Johnson's own devastating common-room ironies. Fergusson says that had he himself been put in charge of the culinary arrangements, he would have seen to it that this Scotophobe, this inveterate critic of his host country, was fed on "gude hamel gear" and not treated as though he were royalty –

> For ne'er sic surly wight as he
> Had met wi' sic respect frae me.

This is the old Scots flyting tradition, which in style and character is quite different from any convention that Johnson could have recognised.

The same kind of distinction applies to all Scottish writing for the late eighteenth-century English market, for the Northern temperament had to be sicklied over if it were to have any real appeal in London. Fergusson made no concession to Augustanism as a man like Goldsmith understood the term;[41] he betrayed no interest in seeking fame 'furth of Scotland'. He wrote for his friends, not for established critics or for a foreign audience, and in his day there was no accepted standard of criticism upon which contemporary Scots vernacular verse might be evaluated, other than the sentimentalist assessments for which Fergusson had no respect.

In this volume only two English poems are included, the ten-line vignette, 'The Author's Life', and the fourteen-line impression, 'On Night', illustrating Fergusson at his best in a southern style, in the second case not unlike that of Collins. They display something of the feeling for form and the significant word that is more evident in the Scots poems. To mention his other English poems, however, is only to cite echoes, borrowed felicities. Naturally the want of an individual style in English versifying is felt even more in his comic work. Dr Johnson shivering in a kilt is a splendid conception ('To Dr. Samuel Johnson: Food for a new Edition of his Dictionary', ll. 61–67), and a 'Sow of Feeling' that laments husband and children sent to the *abattoir* is an admirable response to Henry Mackenzie's lachrymose novel *The Man of Feeling*, but the inflated English of these burlesques is only mildly amusing. A much more comic effect would have been given by the reductive Scots idiom.

All the significant verse of Fergusson is developed from a base of local vernacular. The latter enables him to give his Horace a convincingly homespun character. It was an appropriate use of Scots that he had learned from Ramsay; thus one notes the similarity of colloquial phrasing and economical expression in Fergusson's version of Horace, Book I, Ode XI, and Ramsay's spirited Ode, 'To the Phiz', stanzas 1 to 8. The genius of Scots for burlesque, the ridiculous, as in the comic elegy, Fergusson seems to have appreciated early; if the subject is an index to the date his 'Elegy on the Death of Mr. David Gregory' was composed in his fourteenth year. Here the passing of a famous mathematician is made amusing – "He'll till the resurrection sleep/As sound's a tap". Each of the Professor's ludicrously detailed accomplishments gets the very final comment, "But now he's dead".

Like Douglas, the Renaissance translators, Thomas Ruddiman, Ramsay and his circle, Fergusson had patriotic motives in seeking to revivify the Scots literary language. Eighteenth-century Scots poets, however, seeing the shadow of England lengthen over the national destiny, felt compelled to take up a defensive posture that the late-mediaeval *makars*, with no sense of nation and tradition under attack, did not have to adopt. Ramsay was inclined to limit his Scots, Fergusson to make the most of his mother-tongue, which he used stridently, even aggressively, though never carelessly or uneasily. With Dunbar he is now acknowledged as a model for modern Scots-writing poets.[42] The linguistic verve exhibited by both men is largely traceable to the fact that their vocabularies were grounded in living speech and owned a wealth of communal and conventional expression. Fergusson's language is fundamentally the Scots of Edinburgh Old Town, which he enriched by importing words from other dialects, notably that of his Aberdeenshire parents, and also by creating new words upon the analogy of older ones. His idiom mingled urban with rural strains and reflected the persisting mediaeval identity of the crowded city and its hinterland.

Fergusson's genius not only appropriates 'language at large' as did the *makars* but also displays some of their architectonic qualities. His method is mainly narrative, a personal account related in a series of independent images, each one bold and standing out against a diffuse, crowded backdrop. The panoramic *Auld Reikie* is an excellent instance of this technique. Built up in brisk tetrameter couplets, the poem contrasts light and shade and mingles impressions of sight, sound, memory and even smell. The sketch of the 'bruiser' or pugilist emerging from the tavern

> . . . reeling drunk,
> Wi' fiery phizz, and ein half sunk

is made to follow hard upon the night-scene of the ex-harlot singing in the street near a lamp-post, too old to ply her former trade, while the glimpse of convivial gatherings that, like Fergusson's own Cape Club,

> . . . jocose and free,
> Gie a' to merriment and glee,
> Wi' sang and glass

marks the gradual decline of street activity as the town settles down for yet another night.

Fergusson did not idealise the denizens of the wynds and closes. 'Embro' has blemishes to match its beauties, but, as he states, "without souring nocht is sweet"; having previously shown how the delights of the morning landscape over St Giles are quickly banished by the bickerings of barefooted maidservants and the stink from their emptied chamber-pots, whereby

> They kindly shower Edina's roses,
> To quicken and regale our noses.

The absence of holograph MSS. makes it difficult to decide how the poet worked. It is tempting to discern in his verse the brilliance of insobriety, but whatever the source of his inspiration the product is plainly no careless screed.

In celebration, as of the Firth of Forth, than which

> There's nane sae spacious and sae noble[43]

or ironic commendation

> Braid Claith lends fock an unco heese,
> Makes mony kail-worms butter-flies,
> Gies mony a doctor his degrees
> > For little skaith[44]

or recollection of country peace

> Beneath the caller shady trees,
> Far frae the din o' Borrowstoun,
> Whar water plays the haughs bedoun[45]

or commiseration with his Auld Breeks, like himself heirs to the human condition –

> Still making tight wi' tither steek,
> The tither hole, the tither eik,[46]

or in so many other attitudes, Fergusson is always the craftsman, the 'maker'.

Like the English poets he imitated or prefigured, Fergusson put most of the stock classical forms to work as frames for contemporary modes, but his ability to associate language and locale in unexpected ways gave his eclogues, elegies, epistles, odes and epodes an individual quality which a stereotype lacks. A clear instance of this originality is the 'Elegy on the Death of Scots Music'. This beautifully modulated Scots poem exploits English formulae; superficially it invites comparison with certain of Ramsay's works, but the alliance here of Augustan formalism with a familiar Scottish terrain is not derived from Ramsay's prescription of native images and domestic landscapes. Fergusson is making the point that the vogue for Italianate musical settings, embellished with trills and other inessential ornaments, threatened to spoil a taste for the simpler excellence of Scots song, and merely provided instrumentalists with opportunities to show off technique. His 'Elegy' draws attention to the incongruities produced by juxtaposing foreign and home-bred elements in poetry, and invites the reader to arrive at similar conclusions in the case of music. The poem has ironic tones.

This ability to blend the lyrical with the satirical is Fergusson's most consistently perceptible poetic talent. It was also possessed in great strength by Dunbar. Both poets devoted much time to recording what purported to be solitary musings on life as it was being lived before their eyes. Thus, when Fergusson contemplates Auld Reikie he peers at his city in various perspectives, weighing, as we have noted, her good and bad points. Again, in 'The Farmer's Ingle' the grandmother's fondness for tales of superstitious terror occasions the comment –

> O mock na this, my friends! but rather mourn,
> Ye in life's brawest spring wi' reason clear,
> Wi' eild our idle fancies a' return,
> And dim our dolefu' days wi' bairnly fear;
> The mind's ay cradled when the grave is near.

in the manner of Horace dwelling on the bitter-sweet quality of all human existence. The *pallida mors* of the Roman poet is never far away, though in Scots garb Death and the De'il are intimates. There is a vast difference between the image of

> . . . Death, grim Death! with all his ghastly train[47]

and the nuisance-figure, almost practical joker (for life itself can seem a joke) addressed here –

> Death, what's ado? the de'il be licket,
> Or wi' your stang, you ne'er had pricket,
> Or our Auld Alma Mater tricket
> O' poor John Hogg.[48]

This attitude, at once sardonic and reflective, grasps contrasting aspects of the same entity, each as tangible as its co-existing opposite. When Fergusson concludes 'The Election' by predicting the early demise of the hard-drinking deacons, who will soon be

> . . . in a truff,
> Inrow'd in the lang leet
> O' death yon night[49]

what affects us is the satirical insight into the ephemeral character of mortal concerns, the ultimate unimportance of what the deacons are met to discuss, their insensitivity to the consequences of that festive night, which will be to create further vacancies in the Town Council, making necessary a further succession of elections, thus completing the ridiculous circle. Something more has been provided than the naïve Horatian epicureanism promised by the introductory tag, *nunc est bibendum*.[50]

Fergusson shared with Ramsay and Burns that quality of intimacy which, as we have noted, linked the first-named with his early audiences. But he is more clinical in his observations than the other poets, and his named characters, though they are presented in greater detail than familiars like Lucky Wood and Lucky Spence, are much less 'cosy'. Capable of a deeper interpretation of life than Ramsay, he is also capable of seeing it at a greater remove. A Dunbar-like detachment touches his art at times, as in the fantasy of *Plainstanes and Causey* which serves to convey only the factual and functional. Here the sun

> taks his leave of Thetis,
> And comes to wauken honest fock,
> That gang to wark at sax o'clock.

This slight aloofness shows also in his poetic *persona*, which rarely offers real information about himself, grave or gay. We learn little about his own despair, though in 'Ode to the Gowdspink' he comes close. In the 'Job' version, of course, the revelation is in the overtones. We know that he had his 'Stella'[51] as Burns had his Clarinda, but he kept her out of his published verse. He left only one serious love-song, 'The Lee Rigg' (which Burns admitted he could not better),[52] and his complaints about the harshness of reality are general. Unlike 'canty Allan', who is almost a period-piece, Fergusson, though never a poetical wraith, lacks physical presence. He is to be seen as a face in the old Embro crowd through whose "real livan words" we are given glimpses of the pulsating life about him.

Our presentation of Fergusson offered fewer editorial problems than did that of Ramsay. In the first place, of the poems printed here all original sources are printed ones. Furthermore, Fergusson's spelling was careful and can be significant, much more so than Ramsay's. Even when he uses English spelling his pronunciation is nearly always Scots (*dead* rhymes with *need* and not with *redd*), often identifiably of a particular dialect, Lothian (*lose* rhymes with *gloss*) or less frequently Buchan (*guid* rhymes with *need*), and by altering consonants (*pring* for *bring*, *hafe* for *have*, *marsh* for *march*) he conveys the Gaelic accents of the City Guard.[53] However, exceptions are not hard to find and Fergusson occasionally relies upon an English pronunciation should rhyme demand it (*out* rhymes with *nowt* and not with *toot*). Like Ramsay, he was inconsistent in spelling words containing the diphthongs *ou* and *ow* (*cowp* rhymes with *loup*); also, unsounded 'g' in '-ing' may or may not be retained – *faintin* and *wanton* are found in a rhyming sequence, but a few lines farther on in another sequence, *burning* with *mourning*.

Fergusson's Scots poems, like Ramsay's, were meant to be read aloud, but they ask more of the reader. The Old Town was a gathering-place for many regional habits of speech and he drew on whatever resources of vocabulary and pronunciation he could find – living speech, literary usage past and present, thieves' slang, Gaelic borrowings. An adequate glossary to his Scots poems would contain more than 1600 words, of which only about one third were used by Ramsay.

The present editors have kept the spelling and punctuation of Fergusson's poems as published, but have omitted capitals and italics where they could do so without loss of significance. As with Ramsay's texts printers may have been tempted to give their own phonetic interpretation, and common words or those with a literary precedent would be made to conform to whatever conventional usage had evolved. It would be dangerous, however, to assume that they interfered significantly with the author's scripts, though they would doubtless advise him which spellings would be most easily comprehended.

NOTES

1. For fuller biographical information on Ramsay and Fergusson, see the Scottish Text Society's editions (cited here as STS *Ramsay* and STS *Fergusson*).
2. The best account of his career is given in Alastair Smart, *The Life and Art of Allan Ramsay* (London 1952) and there are many references to him in John Fleming, *Robert Adam and His Circle in Edinburgh and Rome* (London, 1966).
3. On the Easy Club see Andrew Gibson, *New Light on Allan Ramsay* (Edinburgh, 1927), 35–63, and the transcript of the Club's MS. *Journal* in STS *Ramsay*, V.
4. It is likely that Gay and Ramsay met there in 1729. See STS *Ramsay*, IV, 70, note 148.
5. The subscription list to his 1721 volume of *Poems* contained 476 names and was incomplete: it included Alexander Pope and Sir Richard Steele.
6. The pupils of Haddington Grammar School asked Ramsay to make a 'ballad-opera' out of *The Gentle Shepherd* after attending a performance of John Gay's *Beggar's Opera* in October, 1728. The poet was said to have regretted the conversion, though the work was enthusiastically received from the start. It is possible that *The Gentle Shepherd* was written in the first place for production as a school play. The early drafts, which are in Edinburgh University Library, are dated 1724 and contain a reference to John Lesley, Rector of Haddington Grammar School. *The Gentle Shepherd* may have been performed in 1725, when it was published.

7. STS *Ramsay* III and IV contain all known miscellaneous and uncollected poems, together with attributed verses, with one exception, 'A Poem to the Memory of the Famous Archibald Pitcairn, M.D.' (1713), no copy of which has been found.

8. See STS *Ramsay*, IV, 33–40; 67, note 99.

9. *e.g.* 'The Marrow Ballad' and Ramsay's letter to Lord Dalhousie dated April 7th, 1739 (STS *Ramsay*, IV, 213–14).

10. *ibid.*, STS *Ramsay*, IV, 68, notes 115 and 122.

11. *ibid.*, 69, note 138.

12. edn. of 1800, lxxxii.

13. STS *Ramsay*, I, xx.

14. 'Familiar Epistles' (Answer II), 55–6.

15. *op. cit.*, 43–6.

16. Ernest C. Mossner, *The Life of David Hume* (Edinburgh and London, 1954), 370–1.

17. 'The Quadruple Alliance,' STS *Ramsay*, III, 49, 1–2: "Swift, Sandy [Pope], Young, and Gay,/Are still my heart's delight."

18. 'The Kind Reception. To the Tune of Auld Lang Syne', STS *Ramsay*, I, 45.

19. 'The Gentle Shepherd', Act I, Scene II, 35–44.

20. See these criticisms of 'The Gentle Shepherd' – Hugh Blair, *Lectures on Rhetoric and Belles-Lettres* (London: 1783, 3 vols), II, 352 (lecture xxxix); James Beattie, *Essays on Poetry and Music as They Affect the Mind; on Laughter and Ludicrous Composition* (London, 1776; 3rd edn. 1779), 383; Henry Mackenzie's review of Burns's Kilmarnock edition in *The Lounger* 97, Sat., 9th December, 1786.

21. Horst Drescher (ed.), *Henry Mackenzie Letters to Mrs Elizabeth Rose of Kilravock 1768–1815* (Edinburgh and London, 1967), 176 (letter 73, written 1775). Beattie's anonymous address to Alexander Ross (cf. note 27a) also suggests that even his attitude to Scots was ambivalent. Beattie's later remarks in the *Essay on Laughter* are, however, extremely hostile to the use of Scots. On the correspondents in the *Magazine* see STS *Fergusson*, I, 140.

22. STS *Ramsay*, IV, 169.

23. See note 1. M. P. McDiarmid's 'The Poet's Life' in STS *Fergusson*, I, 1–117 is the basis of our short biographical account.

24. Other Scots contributions to the *Weekly* were James Beattie's anonymous verse-epistle to Alexander Ross, reprinted from the *Aberdeen Journal* of 6th June, 1768, appearing in Ruddiman's journal on September, preceding 'The Daft-Days' by 3½ years; the excellent imitation of Horace, *Odes*, I, ix, signed by the unidentified 'Vanlu' of Aberdeen (printed in STS *Fergusson*, II, 246–7); William Skinner's convivial song 'Tullochgorum' in two versions and the anonymous 'Luve Sang'. See Ian C. Walker, 'Scottish Verse in *The Weekly Magazine*' (*Studies in Scottish Literature*, Vol. V, No. 1, July, 1967), 3–13.

25. See STS *Fergusson*, I, 73–4. One fashionable work which he read at this time

was James Hervey's *Meditations Among the Tombs* (London, 1745–7). Burns included the book in his list of formative reading-matter given in the auto-biographical letter to Moore (2nd August, 1787). Cf. note 30 *infra*.

26. See STS *Fergusson*, I, 69. Peterkin's account was prefixed to an edition of the poet's works published in 1807; the diagnosis is conceivable in the light of Hunter's contemporary researches though the venereal diseases were not fully understood until over a century later. The following is part of a note contributed by the late Stuart McGregor, MB ChB (Edin.), DPH (Lond.), Lecturer in Social and Preventive Medicine at the University of the West Indies and a well-known Scottish poet and novelist: From the evidence on record it would be unwise to diagnose syphilis, although the possibility of congenital syphilis cannot be entirely excluded. The injury from which Fergusson suffered is unlikely to have been a major aetiological factor, although his fall may have helped to precipitate a psychotic crisis; a history involving trauma of the skull is frequently found in mental illness, but is rarely significant. The likeliest diagnosis is that of a depressive illness approaching psychotic dimensions. Such a type of malady is the great psychological affliction of the creative writer.

27. See Robert Chambers, *A Biographical Dictionary of Eminent Scotsmen* (Glasgow, 1835, 4 vols) for a full account of Duncan's life. Duncan was to become the pioneer of mental therapy in Scotland and stated that Fergusson's case had directed his career. See STS *Fergusson*, I, 75–7.

28. Sydney Goodsir Smith (ed.), *Robert Fergusson 1750–74* (Edinburgh and London, 1952), Appendix I, 197–9 ('The Edinburgh Bedlam').

29. Inscribed in a copy of the second edition of Fergusson's *Poems*. For a reproduction, see Smith *op. cit.*, facing 35.

30. *The Letters of Robert Burns*, ed. J. De Lancey Ferguson (Oxford, 1931), I, 113.

31. See *Letters, ed. cit.*, I, 72, 78, 358, II, 109 for reference to the memorial stone, erected in 1789.

32. See STS *Fergusson*, I, 78–9.

33. See William Gillis, 'An Authentic Fergusson Portrait' (*Studies in Scottish Literature*, Vol. I, No. 4, April, 1964), 21–2, with a reproduction of the picture itself, which now hangs in the Scottish National Portrait Gallery.

34. See STS *Fergusson*, I, 112.

35. *Robert Burns's First Commonplace Book 1783–85*, ed. J. C. Ewing and D. Cook (Glasgow, 1938).

36. *e.g.* 'The Farmer's Ingle' and 'The Cotter's Saturday Night'; 'Hallow Fair' and 'Holy Fair'; 'The Election' and 'The Ordination'; 'The Mutual Complaint of Plainstanes and Causey' and 'The Twa Dogs'; 'Ode to the Gowdspink' and 'To a Mountain Daisy'; 'To my Auld Breeks' and 'The Auld Farmer's New-Year-Morning Salutation to His Auld Mare, Maggie' are some of the more obvious parallels. Others are suggested in the notes to individual poems.

37. See *Fergusson*, I, 168–73, also Allan H. MacLaine, *Robert Fergusson* (New York, 1965), *passim*.
38. *Fergusson*, II, 269.
39. *op. cit.*, 162–3.
40. Allan H. MacLaine, 'Robert Fergusson's *Auld Reikie* and the Poetry of City Life' (*Studies in Scottish Literature*, Vol. I, No. 2, October, 1963), 99–110.
41. cf. Goldsmith's 'An Account of the Augustan Age in England', published in *The Bee*, No. VIII, Sat., 25th November, 1759 (Arthur Friedman (ed.), *Collected Works of Oliver Goldsmith* (Oxford, 1966, 4 vols), I, 498–505.
42. Apart from Burns, Stevenson and imitators like Charles Keith and John Mayne, the most forthright disciple of Fergusson has been 'Robert Garioch' (Robert Sutherland). In an address composed for his master's 200th anniversary in 1950, Garioch struck out the authentic note of Scots lyricism in his own praise of Fergusson's achievement with "real livan words". See S. G. Smith, *ed. cit.*, 1–10 ('To Robert Fergusson').
43. 'Caller Oysters', 5.
44. 'Braid Claith', 43–6.
45. 'Hame Content. A Satire', 20–2.
46. 'To my Auld Breeks', 7–8.
47. 'The Town and Country Contrasted', 32.
48. 'Elegy on John Hogg, late Porter to the University of St Andrews', 1–4. For another example see 'Auld Reikie', 165–6.
49. *op. cit.*, 134–5.
50. Horace, *Odes*, I, xxxvii.
51. On Fergusson's unrequited love for 'Stella', a married woman and poetess, see the STS edition, I, 30–1, 102–6.
52. *Letters, ed. cit.*, II, 126 (letter 511, to James Thomson).
53. For further examples see Albert D. Mackie, 'Fergusson's Language; Braid Scots Then and Now' in S. G. Smith's collection of essays, 123–47.

SELECT BIBLIOGRAPHY

ALLAN RAMSAY

John Burns Martin, 'A Bibliography of the Writings of Allan Ramsay' in *Records of the Glasgow Bibliographical Society*, Vol. X, 1931; reprinted with additions and modifications in Ramsay's *Works*, Vol. VI (Scottish Text Society), for which see below. John Burns Martin, *Allan Ramsay: a Study of His Life and Works*, Cambridge: Harvard University Press, 1931, also has a bibliography which includes secondary sources.

The authoritative edition is now *The Works of Allan Ramsay*, in six volumes, printed for the Scottish Text Society by William Blackwood & Sons Ltd., Edinburgh and London, the first two volumes being edited by the late John Burns Martin and John Walter Oliver, the remaining four by Alexander Manson Kinghorn and Alexander Law. The whole consists of the following – Vol. I: *Poems*, 1721; Third Series 19. Vol. II: *Poems*, 1728; Third Series 20; 1953. Vol. III: Poems, Miscellaneous And Uncollected; Third Series 29; 1961. Vol. IV: A Biographical and Critical Introduction, Letters, Prose, Poems Not Hitherto Collected, Poems Attributed to Ramsay, Poems About Ramsay; Fourth Series 6; 1970. Vol. V: Journal Of The Easy Club, A Collection Of Scots Proverbs, The Early Drafts Of *The Gentle Shepherd*; Fourth Series, 8; 1972. Vol. VI: Commentary, Notes and Critical Apparatus, Select Bibliography, Index; Fourth Series – yet to appear. A notable appreciation is that of J. W. Mackail, 'Allan Ramsay and the Romantic Revival', in *Essays and Studies*, Vol. X, 1924.

ROBERT FERGUSSON

The Poems Of Robert Fergusson (Scottish Text Society), ed. Matthew P. McDiarmid. This comprises – Vol. I: Introduction (The Poet's Life, A Study of the Poetry of Robert Fergusson); Third Series 21; 1954. Vol. II: Bibliography, The Poems, Appendices, Notes, Glossary and Indices; Third Series 24; 1956. In the above volume has been incorporated the contents of John A. Fairley's *A Bibliography of Robert Fergusson* (Glasgow, 1915) and *The Unpublished Poems Of Robert Fergusson* (Edinburgh, 1955) by William Gillis.

With the historical and critical commentary in Vol. I of the Scottish Text Society edition may be read *Robert Fergusson 1750–74: Essays by Various Hands to Commemorate the Bicentenary of his Birth*, ed. Sydney Goodsir Smith (Edinburgh, 1952). The 'Hands' here are Hugh MacDiarmid, Douglas Young, John W. Oliver, John Spiers, James B. Caird, Albert D. Mackie, Alexander Law, William Montgomerie, and the editor. A recent study much to be recommended is *Robert Fergusson* (New York, 1965), by Allan H. MacLaine.

POEMS BY ALLAN RAMSAY

ELEGY ON MAGGY JOHNSTON,
who died Anno 1711

Auld Reeky! Mourn in sable hue,
Let fouth of tears dreep like May dew.
To braw Tippony bid adieu,
      Which we, with greed,
Bended as fast as she cou'd brew.   5
      But ah! she's dead.

To tell the truth now Maggy dang,
Of customers she had a bang;
For lairds and souters a' did gang
      To drink bedeen,   10
The barn and yard was aft sae thrang,
      We took the green.

And there by dizens we lay down,
Syne sweetly ca'd the healths arown,
To bonny lasses black or brown,   15
      As we loo'd best;
In bumpers we dull cares did drown,
      And took our rest.

Maggy Johnston lived about a mile southward of Edinburgh, kept a little farm, and had a particular art of brewing a small sort of ale agreeable to the taste, very white, clear and intoxicating, which made people who loved to have a good pennyworth for their money be her frequent customers. And many others of every station, sometimes for diversion, thought it no affront to be seen in her barn or yard.

l.1 *Auld Reeky.* A name the country people give Edinburgh from the cloud of smoak or reek that is always impending over it.

l.3 *To braw Tippony.* She sold the Scots pint, which is near to two quarts English, for twopence.

l.7 *Maggy dang.* He *dings,* or *dang,* is a phrase which means *to excel or get the better.*

3

When in our poutch we fand some clinks,
And took a turn o'er Bruntsfield-Links,   20
Aften in Maggy's at Hy-jinks,
                    We guzl'd scuds,
Till we could scarce wi' hale out drinks
                    Cast aff our duds.

We drank and drew, and fill'd again,   25
O wow but we were blyth and fain!
When ony had their count mistain,
                    O it was nice
To hear us a' cry, Pike ye'r bain
                    And spell ye'r dice.   30

Fou closs we us'd to drink and rant,
Until we did baith glowre and gaunt,
And pish and spew, and yesk and maunt,
                    Right swash I true;
Then of auld stories we did cant   35
                    Whan we were fou.

l.20 *Bruntsfield Links.* Fields between Edinburgh and Maggy's, where the citizens
   commonly play at the gowff.
l.21 *Hy-jinks.* A drunken game, or new project to drink and be rich: thus, the
   quaff or cup is filled to the brim, then one of the company takes a pair of dice,
   and after crying "Hy-jinks!", he throws them out.
      The number he casts up points out the person must drink, he who threw beginning
   at himself, Number One, and so round till the number of the person agree with
   that of the dice (which may fall upon himself if the number be within twelve);
   then he sets the dice to him, or bids him take them: he on whom they fall is
   obliged to drink, or pay a small forfeiture in money, then throws, and so on. But
   if he forget to cry "Hy-jinks!" he pays a forfeiture into the bank. Now he on whom
   it falls to drink, if there be any thing in bank worth drawing, gets it all if he drinks.
   Then with a great deal of caution he empties his cup, sweeps up the money, and
   orders the cup to be filled again, and then throws; for if he err in the articles, he
   loses the privilege of drawing the money. The articles are: (1) drink, (2) draw,
   (3) fill, (4) cry "Hy-jinks!", (5) count just, (6) chuse your doublet man, *viz.* when
   two equal numbers of the dice is thrown, the person whom you chuse must pay a
   double of the common forfeiture, and so must you when the dice is in his hand. A
   rare project this, and no Bubble I can assure you, for a covetous fellow may save
   money, and get himself as drunk as he can desire in less than an hour's time.
l.29 *Pike ye'r bain.* Is a cant phrase: when one leaves a little in the cup he is advised
   to pike his bone, *i.e.* drink it clean out.

Whan we were weary'd at the gowff,
Then Maggy Johnston's was our howff;
Now a' our gamesters may sit dowff,
                    Wi' hearts like lead,   40
Death wi' his rung rax'd her a yowff,
                    And sae she died.

Maun we be forc'd thy skill to tine?
For which we will right sair repine;
Or hast thou left to bairns of thine   45
                    The pauky knack
Of brewing ale amaist like wine?
                    That gar'd us crack.

Sae brawly did a pease-scon toast
Biz i' the queff and flie the frost;   50
There we gat fou wi' little cost,
                    And muckle speed,
Now wae worth death, our sport's a' lost,
                    Since Maggy's dead.

Ae simmer night I was sae fou,   55
Amang the riggs I geed to spew;
Syne down on a green bawk, I trow
                    I took a nap,
And soucht a' night balillilow
                    As sound's a tap.   60

And whan the dawn begoud to glow,
I hirsled up my dizzy pow,
Frae 'mang the corn like wirricow,
                    Wi' bains sae sair,
And ken' nae mair than if a ew   65
                    How I came there.

l.41 *Rax'd her a youff.* Reached her a blow.
l.50 *Flie the frost.* Or fright the frost or coldness out of it.
l.55 *Ae simmer night,* &c. The two following stanzas are a true narrative:
        On that slid place where I 'maist brake my bains,
        To be a warning I set up twa stains,
        That nane may venture there as I have done,
        Unless wi' frosted nails he clink his shoon.

Some said it was the pith of broom
That she stow'd in her masking-loom,
Which in our heads rais'd sic a foom,
                    Or some wild seed,   70
Which aft the chaping stoup did toom,
                    But fill'd our head.

But now since 'tis sae that we must
Not in the best ale put our trust,
But whan we're auld return to dust,   75
                    Without remead,
Why shou'd we tak it in disgust
                    That Maggy's dead.

Of warldly comforts she was rife,
And liv'd a lang and hearty life,   80
Right free of care, or toil, or strife
                    Till she was stale,
And ken'd to be a kanny wife
                    At brewing ale.

Then farewell Maggy douce and fell,   85
Of brewers a' thou boor the bell;
Let a' thy gossies yelp and yell,
                    And without feed,
Guess whether ye're in heaven or hell,
                    They're sure ye're dead.   90

Epitaph
O rare Maggy Johnston

ELEGY ON JOHN COWPER,
KIRK-TREASURER'S MAN
Anno 1714

I wairn ye a' to greet and drone,
John Cowper's dead. Ohon! Ohon!
To fill his post, alake there's none,
        That with sic speed
Cou'd sa'r sculdudry out like John,   5
        But now he's dead.

He was right nacky in his way,
And eydent baith be night and day,
He wi' the lads his part cou'd play,
        When right sair fleed,   10
He gart them good bill-siller pay,
        But now he's dead.

Of whore-hunting he gat his fill,
And made be't mony pint and gill:

'Tis necessary for the illustration of this Elegy to strangers to let them a little into the history of the Kirk-Treasurer and his man. The Treasurer is chosen every year, a citizen respected for riches and honesty. He is vested with an absolute power to seize and imprison the girls that are too impatient to have on their green gown before it be hem'd; them he strictly examines, but no liberty to be granted till a fair account be given of these persons they have obliged. It must be so: a list is frequently given sometimes of a dozen or thereby of married or unmarried unfair traders whom they secretly assisted in running their goods, these his Lordship makes pay to some purpose according to their ability, for the use of the poor: If the lads be obstreperous, the Kirk-sessions, and worst of all, the Stool of Repentance is threatned, a punishment which few of any spirit can bear.

The Treasurer being changed every year, never comes to be perfectly acquainted with the affair; but their general servant continuing for a long time is more expert at discovering such persons, and the places of their resort, which makes him capable to do himself and customers both a good or an ill turn. John Cowper maintained this post with activity and good success for several years.

l.5 *Sa'r sculdudry.* In allusion to a scent dog, *sa'r* from *savour* or *smell, sculdudry* a name commonly given to whoring.
l.11 *Bill-siller.* Bull-silver.
       "She saw the cow well served, and took a groat." Gay.

Of his braw post he thought nae ill,   15
         Nor did nae need,
Now they may mak a kirk and mill
         O't, since he's dead.

Altho he was nae man of weir,
Yet mony a ane, wi' quaking fear,   20
Durst scarce afore his face appear,
         But hide their head;
The wylie carl he gather'd gear,
         And yet he's dead.

Ay now to some part far awa,   25
Alas, he's gane and left it a'!
Maybe to some sad whilliwhaw
         O' fremit blood,
'Tis an ill wind that dis na blaw
         Some body good.   30

Fy upon Death, he was to blame
To whirle poor John to his lang hame:
But though his arse be cauld, yet fame,
         Wi' tout of trumpet,
Shall tell how Cowper's awfou name   35
         Cou'd flie a strumpet.

He kend the bawds and louns fou well,
And where they us'd to rant and reel
He paukily on them cou'd steal,
         And spoil their sport;   40
Aft did they wish the muckle De'il
         Might tak him for't.

But ne'er a ane of them he spar'd,
E'en tho there was a drunken laird
To draw his sword, and make a faird   45
         In their defence,

1.27 *Whilliwha of fremit blood*. *Whilliwha* is a kind of insinuating deceitful fellow;
   fremit blood, not a kin, because he had then no legitimate heirs of his own body.
1.45 *Make a faird*. A bustle like a bully.

8

John quietly put them in the Guard
                    To learn mair sense.

There maun they ly till sober grown,
The lad neist day his fault maun own;   50
And to keep a' things hush and low'n,
                    He minds the poor,
Syne, after a' his ready's flown,
                    He damns the whore.

And she, poor jade, withoutten din,   55
Is sent to Leith-wynd Fit to spin,
With heavy heart and cleathing thin,
                    And hungry wame,
And ilky month a well-paid skin,
                    To mak her tame.   60

But now they may scoure up and down,
And safely gang their wakes arown,
Spreading the clap throw a' the town,
                    But fear or dread;
For that great kow to bawd and lown,   65
                    John Cowper's dead.

Shame faw ye'r chandler chafts, O Death;
For stapping of John Cowper's breath;
The loss of him is publick skaith:
                    I dare well say,   70
To quat the grip he was right laith
                    This mony a day.

Postscript

Of umquhile John to lie or bann,
Shaws but ill will, and looks right shan,
But some tell odd tales of the man,   75
                    For fifty head

l.52 *He minds the poor.* Pays hush money to the Treasurer.
l.56 *Leith-wynd Fit.* The House of Correction at the Foot of Leith-wynd, such as Bridewell in London.
l.67 *Chandler chafts.* Lean or meager-cheeked, when the bones appear like the sides or corners of a candlestick, which in Scots we call a chandler.

9

Can gi'e their aith they've seen him gawn
                    Since he was dead.

Keek but up throw the Stinking Stile,
On Sunday morning a wee while,   80
At the kirk door out frae an isle,
                    It will appear;
But tak good tent ye dinna file
                    Ye'r breeks for fear.

For well we wat it is his ghaist.   85
Wow, wad some fouk that can do't best
Speak till't, and hear what it confest;
                    'Tis a good deed
To send a wand'ring saul to rest
                    Amang the dead.   90

l.77 *Seen him gawn*. The common people when they tell their tales of ghosts appearing, they say he has been seen *gawn* or stalking.

l.79 *Stinking stile*. Opposite to this place is the door of the church which he attends, being a beadle.

l.86 *Wow . . . do't best*. 'Tis another vulgar notion that a ghost will not be laid to rest till some priest speak to it, and get account what disturbs it.

ELEGY ON LUCKY WOOD IN
THE CANONGATE, May 1717

O Cannigate! Poor elritch hole!
What loss, what crosses does thou thole!
London and Death gars thee look drole,
                    And hing thy head;

Lucky Wood kept an ale-house in the Canongate, was much respected for hospitality, honesty, and the neatness both of her person and house.

l.3 *London and Death*. The place of her residence being the greatest sufferer, by the loss of our Members of Parliament, which London now enjoys, many of them having their houses there, being the suburb of Edinburgh nearest the King's palace: this with the death of Lucky Wood are sufficient to make the place ruinous.

Wow, but thou has e'en a cauld coal   5
              To blaw indeed.

Hear me ye hills and every glen,
Ilk craig, ilk cleugh and hollow den,
And echo shrill, that a' may ken
              The waefou thud,   10
Be rackless Death, wha came unsenn
              To Lucky Wood.

She's dead o'er true, she's dead and gane,
Left us and Willie burd alane,
To bleer and greet, to sob and mane,   15
              And rugg our hair,
Because we'll ne'r see her again
              For evermair.

She gae'd as fait as a new prin,
And kept her housie snod and been;   20
Her peuther glanc'd upo' your een
              Like siller plate;
She was a donsie wife and clean,
              Without debate.

It did ane good to see her stools,   25
Her boord, fire-side and facing tools;
Rax, chandlers, tangs, and fire-shools,
              Basket wi' bread.
Poor facers now may chew pea-hools,
              Since Lucky's dead.   30

l.11 *Came unsenn*: or unsent for. There's nothing extraordinary in this, it being his common custom, except in some few instances of late since the falling of the Bubbles.

l.14 *Willie*. Her husband William Wood.

l.26 *Facing tools*. Stoups (or pots) and cups, so called from the *facers*. See l.29.

l.29 *Poor facers*. The facers were a club of fair drinkers who inclined rather to spend a shilling on ale than twopence for meat. They had their name from a rule they observed of obliging themselves to throw all they left in the cup in their own faces; wherefore to save their face and cloaths they prudently sucked the liquor clean out.

She ne'er gae in a lawin fause,
Nor stoups a froath aboon the hause,
Nor kept dow'd tip within her waw's,
        But reaming swats;
She never ran sour jute, because   35
        It gee's the batts.

She had the gate sae well to please,
With *gratis* beef, dry fish, or cheese;
Which kept our purses ay at ease,
        And health in tift,   40
And lent her fresh nine gallon trees
        A hearty lift.

She ga'e us aft hail legs o' lamb,
And did nae hain her mutton ham;
Then ay at Yule, when e'er we came,   45
        A bra' goose pye,
And was na that good belly baum?
        Nane dare deny.

The Writer lads fow well may mind her,
Furthy was she, her luck design'd her   50
Their common mither, sure nane kinder
        Ever brake bread;
She has na left her make behind her,
        But now she's dead.

To the sma' hours we aft sat still,   55
Nick'd round our toasts and snishing mill;
Good cakes we wanted ne'r at will,
        The best of bread,
Which often cost us mony a gill,
        To Aikenhead.   60

l.31 *She ne'er gae in,* &c. All this verse is a fine picture of an honest ale-seller; a rarity.

l.60 *To Aikenhead's.* The Nether-Bow porter, to whom Lucky's customers were often obliged for opening the port for them, when they staid out till the small hours after midnight.

Cou'd our saut tears like Clyde down rin,
And had we cheeks like Corra's Lin,
That a' the warld might hear the din
                    Rair frae ilk head;
She was the wale of a' her kin,   65
                    But now she's dead.

O Lucky Wood, 'tis hard to bear
The loss; but Oh! we maun forbear:
Yet sall thy memory be dear
                    While blooms a tree,   70
And after ages bairns will spear
                    'Bout thee and me.

Epitaph

Beneath this sod
Lies Lucky Wood,
Whom a' men might put faith in;   75
Wha was na sweer,
While she winn'd here,
To cramm our wames for naithing.

1.62 *Like Corra's Lin.* A very high precipice nigh Lanerk, over which the River
of Clyde falls, making a great noise which is heard some miles off.

LUCKY SPENCE'S LAST ADVICE

Three times the carline grain'd and rifted,
Then frae the cod her pow she lifted,
In bawdy policy well gifted,
                    When she now faun,
That Death na langer wad be shifted,   5
                    She thus began:

Lucky Spence, a famous bawd who flourished for several years about the
beginning of the eighteenth century; she had her lodgings near Holyrood-house.
She made many a benefit night to herself by putting a trade in the hands of young
lasses that had a little pertness, strong passions, abundance of laziness, and no
fore-thought.

My loving lasses, I maun leave ye,
But dinna wi' ye'r greeting grieve me,
Nor wi' your draunts and droning deave me,
        But bring's a gill;   10
For faith, my bairns, ye may believe me,
        'Tis 'gainst my will.

O black-ey'd Bess and mim-mou'd Meg,
O'er good to work or yet to beg;
Lay sunkots up for a sair leg,   15
        For whan ye fail,
Ye'r face will not be worth a feg,
        Nor yet ye'r tail.

When e'er ye meet a fool that's fow,
That ye're a maiden gar him trow,   20
Seem nice, but stick to him like glew;
        And whan set down,
Drive at the jango till he spew,
        Syne he'll sleep soun.

Whan he's asleep, then dive and catch   25
His ready cash, his rings or watch;
And gin he likes to light his match
        At your spunk-box,
Ne'er stand to let the fumbling wretch
        E'en take the pox.   30

Cleek a' ye can be hook or crook,
Ryp ilky poutch frae nook to nook;
Be sure to truff his pocket-book,
        Saxty pounds Scots
Is nae deaf nits: In little bouk   35
        Lie great bank-notes.

l.13 *Mim-mou'd.* Expresses an affected modesty by a preciseness about the mouth.
l.27 *Light his match.* I could give a large annotation on this sentence, but do not
    incline to explain every thing, lest I disoblige future criticks by leaving
    nothing for them to do.
l.35 *Is nae deaf nits,* or empty nuts: this is a negative manner of saying a thing is
    substantial.

To get a mends of whinging fools,
That's frighted for repenting-stools.
Wha often, whan their metal cools,
    Turn sweer to pay,   40
Gar the kirk-boxie hale the dools
    Anither day.

But dawt Red Coats, and let them scoup,
Free for the fou of cutty stoup;
To gee them up, ye need na hope   45
    E'er to do well:
They'll rive ye'r brats and kick your doup,
    And play the Deel.

There's ae sair cross attends the craft,
That curst Correction-house, where aft   50
Vild Hangy's taz ye'r riggings saft
    Makes black and blae,
Enough to pit a body daft;
    But what'll ye say.

Nane gathers gear withouten care,   55
Ilk pleasure has of pain a skare;
Suppose then they should tirl ye bare,
    And gar ye fike,
E'en learn to thole; 'tis very fair
    Ye're nibour like.   60

Forby, my looves, count upo' losses,
Ye'r milk-white teeth and cheeks like roses,

---

l.37 *To get a mends.* To be revenged of *whindging fools*, fellows who wear the wrong side of their faces outmost, pretenders to sanctity, who love to be smugling in a corner.

l.41 *Gar the kirk-boxie . . . dools.* Delate them to the Kirk-Treasurer. *Hale the dools* is a phrase used at foot-ball, where the party that gains the goal or dool is said to hail it or win the game, and so draws the stake.

l.44 *Cutty stoup.* Little pot, *i.e.* a gill of brandy.

l.51 *Hangy's taz.* If they perform not the task assigned them, they are whipt by the hangman.

l.54 *But what'll ye say.* The emphasis of this phrase, like many others, cannot be understood but by a native.

Whan jet-black hair and brigs of noses,
        Faw down wi' dads
To keep your hearts up 'neath sic crosses,   65
        Set up for bawds.

Wi' well-crish'd loofs I hae been canty,
Whan e'er the lads wad fain ha'e faun t'ye;
To try the auld game Taunty Raunty,
        Like coofers keen,   70
They took advice of me your aunty,
        If ye were clean.

Then up I took my siller ca'
And whistl'd benn whiles ane, whiles twa;
Roun'd in his lug, that there was a   75
        Poor country Kate,
As halesom as the well of Spaw,
        But unka blate.

Sae whan e'er company came in,
And were upo' a merry pin,   80
I slade away wi' little din
        And muckle mense,
Left conscience judge, it was a' ane
        To Lucky Spence.

My bennison come on good doers,   85
Who spend their cash on bawds and whores;
May they ne'er want the wale of cures
        For a sair snout:
Foul fa' the quacks wha that fire smoors,
        And puts nae out.   90

l.74 *And whistled ben.* *But* and *ben* signify different ends or rooms of a house; to gang *but* and *ben* is to go from one end of the house to the other.

l.75 *Roun'd in his lug.* Whispered in his ear.

l.83 *Left conscience judge.* It was her usual way of vindicating herself to tell ye, when company came to her house could she be so uncivil as to turn them out? If they did any bad thing, said she, between God and their conscience be't.

l.89 *Fire smoors.* Such quacks as bind up the external symptoms of the pox, and drive it inward to the strong holds, whence it is not so easily expelled.

My malison light ilka day
On them that drink, and dinna pay,
But tak a snack and rin away;
                May't be their hap
Never to want a gonorrhœa,   95
                Or rotten clap.

Lass gi'e us in anither gill,
A mutchken, Jo, let's tak our fill;
Let Death syne registrate his bill
                Whan I want sense,   100
I'll slip away with better will,
                Quo' Lucky Spence.

FAMILIAR EPISTLES BETWEEN LIEUTENANT WILLIAM HAMILTON AND ALLAN RAMSAY

EPISTLE I
Gilbertfield, June 26th, 1719

O fam'd and celebrated Allan!
Renownéd Ramsay, canty callan,
There's nowther Highlandman nor Lawlan,
                In poetrie,
But may as soon ding down Tamtallan   5
                As match wi' thee.

For ten times ten, and that's a hunder,
I ha'e been made to gaze and wonder,
When frae Parnassus thou didst thunder,
                Wi' wit and skill,   10
Wherefore I'll soberly knock under,
                And quat my quill.

Of poetry the hail quintessence
Thou hast sucked up, left nae excrescence

l.5 *Tamtallon.* An old fortification upon the Firth of Forth in East Lothian.

17

To petty poets, or sic messens,   15
            Tho round thy stool,
They may pick crumbs, and lear some lessons
            At Ramsay's school.

Tho Ben and Dryden of renown
Were yet alive in London Town,
Like kings contending for a crown;   20
            'Twad be a pingle,
Whilk o' you three wad gar words sound
            And best to gingle.

Transform'd may I be to a rat,   25
Wer't in my pow'r but I'd create
Thee upo' sight the Laureat
            Of this our age,
Since thou may'st fairly claim to that
            As thy just wage.   30

Let modern poets bear the blame
Gin they respect not Ramsay's name,
Wha soon can gar them greet for shame,
            To their great loss;
And send them a' right sneaking hame   35
            Be Weeping-Cross.

Wha bourds wi' thee had need be warry,
And lear wi' skill thy thrust to parry,
When thou consults thy dictionary
            Of ancient words,   40
Which come from thy poetick quarry,
            As sharp as swords.

l.19 *Tho Ben.* The celebrated Ben Johnston (*sic*).
l.27 *The Laureat.*
            Scots Ramsay pressed hard, and sturdily vaunted,
            He'd fight for the laurel before he would want it:
            But risit Apollo, and cry'd, "Peace there old Stile,
            Your wit is obscure to one half of the isle!"
                                B. Sess. of Poets.

18

Now tho I should baith reel and rottle,
And be as light as Aristotle,
At Ed'nburgh we sall ha'e a bottle   45
          Of reaming claret,
Gin that my haff-pay siller shottle
          Can safely spare it.

At crambo then we'll rack our brain,
Drown ilk dull care and aiking pain,   50
Whilk aften does our spirits drain
          Of true content;
Wow, Wow! But we's be wonder fain,
          When thus acquaint.

Wi' wine we'll gargarize our craig,   55
Then enter in a lasting league,
Free of ill aspect or intrigue,
          And gin you please it,
Like princes when met at the Hague,
          We'll solemnize it.   60

Accept of this and look upon it
With favour, though poor I have done it;
Sae I conclude and end my sonnet,
          Who am most fully,
While I do wear a hat or bonnet,   65
          Yours – wanton Willy.

Postscript

By this my postscript I incline
To let you ken my hail design
Of sic a lang imperfect line,
          Lyes in this sentence,   70
To cultivate my dull ingine
          By your acquaintance.

l.47 *Haff-pay*. He held his commission honourably in my Lord Hyndford's regiment.

And may the stars wha shine aboon
With honour notice real merit,
Be to my friend auspicious soon,
And cherish ay sae fine a spirit.

Your answer therefore I expect,
And to your friend you may direct
At Gilbertfield do not neglect   75
            When ye have leisure,
Which I'll embrace with great respect
            And perfect pleasure.

75 *Gilbertfield*. Nigh Glasgow.

ANSWER I
Edinburgh, July 10th, 1719

Sonse fa me, witty, wanton Willy,
Gin blyth I was na as a filly;
Not a fow pint, nor short hought gilly,
            Or wine that's better,
Cou'd please sae meikle, my dear billy,   5
            As thy kind letter.

Before a lord and eik a knight
In Gossy Don's be candle light,
There first I saw't and ca'd it right,
            And the maist feck   10
Wha's seen't sinsyne, they ca'd as tight
            As that on Heck.

Ha, heh! thought I, I canna say,
But I may cock my nose the day,
When Hamilton the bauld and gay   15
            Lends me a heezy,
In verse that slides sae smooth away,
            Well tell'd and easy.

Sae roos'd by ane of well kend mettle,
Nae sma did my ambition pettle;   20
My canker'd criticks it will nettle,
            And e'en sae be't:
This month I'm sure I winna fettle,
            Sae proud I'm wi't.

20

When I begoud first to cun verse,   25
And could your *Ardry Whins* rehearse,
Where Bonny Heck ran fast and fierce,
          It warm'd my breast;
Then emulation did me pierce,
          Whilk since ne'er ceast.   30

May I be licket wi' a bittle,
Gin of your numbers I think little;
Ye're never rugget, shan, nor kittle,
          But blyth and gabby,
And hit the spirit to a tittle,   35
          Of Standart *Habby*.

Ye'll quat your quill! That were ill-willy,
Ye's sing some mair yet, nill ye will ye;
O'er meikle haining wad but spill ye,
          And gar ye sour,   40
Then up and war them a' yet, Willy,
          'Tis in your power.

To knit up dollers in a clout,
And then to eard them round about,
Syne to tell up, they downa lout
          To lift the gear;   45
The malison lights on that rout,
          Is plain and clear.

The chiels of London, Cam, and Ox,
Ha'e raised up great poetick stocks   50
Of Rapes, of Buckets, Sarks and Locks,
          While we neglect
To shaw their betters. This provokes
          Me to reflect

---

l.26 *Ardry Whins.* The last words of *Bonny Heck,* of which he was author.

l.36 *Standart Habby.* The Elegy on Habby Simpson, Piper of Kilbarchan, a finished
    piece of its kind.

On the lear'd days of Gawn Dunkell.   55
Our country then a tale cou'd tell,
Europe had nane mair snack and snell
        At verse or prose;
Our kings were poets too themsell,
        Bauld and jocose.   60

To Ed'nburgh, Sir, when e'er ye come,
I'll wait upon ye, there's my thumb,
Were't frae the gill-bells to the drum,
        And take a bout,
And faith, I hope we'll no sit dumb,   65
        Nor yet cast out.

l.55 *Gawn Dunkell.* Gawn Douglas, brother to the Earl of Angus, Bishop of
Dunkell, who besides several original poems hath left a most exact translation
of Virgil's *Æneis.*
l.59 *Our kings.* James the First and Fifth.
l.63 *Frae . . . bells.* From half-an-hour before twelve at noon, when the musick
bells begin to play, frequently called the gill-bells from peoples taking a
wheting dram at that time. *To the drum,* ten-a-clock at night, when the drum
goes round to warn sober folks to call for a bill.

EPISTLE II
Gilbertfield, July 24th, 1719

Dear Ramsay,

When I receiv'd thy kind epistle,
It made me dance, and sing, and whistle;
O sic a fyke, and sic a fistle
        I had about it!
That e'er was Knight of the Scots Thistle   5
        Sae fain, I doubted.

l.5 *Knight . . . Thistle.* The antient and most noble Order of Knighthood, erected
by King Achaius. The ordinary ensign worn by the Knights of the Order was
a green ribband, to which was appended a thistle of gold crowned with an
imperial crown within a circle of gold, with this motto, *Nemo me impune
lacesset. (sic).*

The bonny lines therein thou sent me,
How to the nines they did content me;
Tho', Sir, sae high to compliment me,
                    Ye might defer'd,   10
For had ye but haff well a kent me,
                    Some less wad ser'd.

With joyfou heart beyond expression,
They're safely now in my possession:
O gin I were a winter-session   15
                    Near by thy lodging,
I'd closs attend thy new profession,
                    Without e'er budging.

In even down earnest, there's but few
To vie with Ramsay dare avow,   20
In verse, for to gi'e thee thy due,
                    And without fleetching,
Thou's better at that trade, I trow,
                    Than some's at preaching.

For my part, till I'm better leart,   25
To troke with thee I'd best forbear't;
For an' the fouk of Edn'burgh hear't,
                    They'll ca' me daft,
I'm unco' irie and dirt-feart
                    I make wrang waft.   30

Thy verses, nice as ever nicket,
Made me as canty as a cricket;
I ergh to reply, lest I stick it,
                    Syne like a coof
I look, or ane whose poutch is picket   35
                    As bare's my loof.

Heh winsom! How thy saft sweet stile,
And bonny auld words gar me smile;
Thou's travel'd sure mony a mile
                    Wi' charge and cost,   40

l.24 *Than . . . preaching.* This compliment is intirely free of the fulsome hyperbole

To learn them thus keep rank and file,
                    And ken their post.

For I maun tell thee, honest Allie,
I use the freedom so to call thee,
I think them a' sae bra and walie,   45
                    And in sic order
I wad nae care to be thy vallie,
                    Or thy recorder.

Has thou with Rosycrucians wandert?
Or thro' some doncie desart danert?   50
That with thy magick, town and landart,
                    For ought I see,
Maun a' come truckle to thy standart
                    Of poetrie.

Do not mistake me, dearest heart,   55
As if I charg'd thee with black art;
'Tis thy good genius still alart,
                    That does inspire
Thee with ilk thing that's quick and smart,
                    To thy desire.   60

E'en mony a bonny knacky tale,
Bra to set o'er a pint of ale:
For fifty guineas I'll find bail,
                    Against a bodle,
That I wad quat ilk day a mail,   65
                    For sic a nodle.

And on condition I were as gabby,
As either thee, or honest *Habby*,
That I lined a' thy claes wi' tabby,
                    Or velvet plush,   70
And then thou'd be sae far frae shabby,
                    Thou'd look right sprush.

---

l.49 *Rosycrucians*. A people deeply learned in the occult sciences, who conversed
    with aerial beings. Gentlemanny (*sic*) kind of necromancers, or so.

What tho young empty airy sparks
May have their critical remarks
On thir my blyth diverting warks;   75
          'Tis sma presumption
To say they're but unlearned clarks,
          And want the gumption.

Let coxcomb criticks get a tether
To ty up a' their lang loose lether;   80
If they and I chance to forgether,
          The tane may rue it,
For an' they winna had their blether,
          They's get a flewet.

To learn them for to peep and pry   85
In secret drolls 'twixt thee and I;
Pray dip thy pen in wrath, and cry,
          And ca' them skellums,
I'm sure thou needs set little by
          To bide their bellums.   90

Wi' writing I'm so bleirt and doited,
That when I raise, in troth I stoited;
I thought I should turn capernoited,
          For wi' a gird,
Upon my bum I fairly cloited   95
          On the cald eard.

Which did oblige a little dumple
Upon my doup, close by my rumple:
But had ye seen how I did trumple,
          Ye'd split your side,   100
Wi' mony a long and weary wimple,
          Like Trough of Clyde.

ANSWER II
Edinburgh, August 4th, 1719

Dear Hamilton, ye'll turn me dyver,
My muse sae bonny ye descrive her,
Ye blaw her sae, I'm fear'd ye rive her,
    For wi' a whid,
Gin ony higher up ye drive her,   5
    She'll rin red-wood.

Said I, – "Whisht", quoth the vougy jade,
"William's a wise judicious lad,
Has havins mair than e'er ye had,
    Ill-bred bog-staker;   10
But me ye ne'er sae crouse had craw'd,
    Ye poor scull-thacker.

It sets you well indeed to gadge!
E'er I t' Appollo did ye cadge,
And got ye on his honour's badge,   15
    Ungratefou beast,
A Glasgow capon and a fadge
    Ye thought a feast.

Swith to Castalius' fountain-brink,
Dad down a-grouf, and take a drink,   20
Syne whisk out paper, pen and ink,
    And do my bidding;
Be thankfou, else I'se gar ye stink
    Yet on a midding."

l.6 *Rin red-wood.* Run distracted.
l.10 *Ill . . . me,* &c. The Muse, not unreasonably angry, puts me here in mind of the favours she has done by bringing me from stalking over bogs or wild marishes, to lift my head a little brisker among the polite world, which could never been acquired by the low movements of a mechanick.
l.12 *Scull-thacker, i.e.* thatcher of sculls.
l.13 *It . . . gadge.* Ironically she says, "It becomes me mighty well to talk haughtily and afront my benefactoress, by alledging so meanly that it were possible to praise her out of her solidity."
l.17 *A Glasgow capon,* &c. A herring. *A fadge.* A course (*sic*) kind of leavened bread, used by the common people.
l.20 *Dad down a grouf.* Fall flat on your belly.

"My mistress dear, your servant humble,"   25
Said I, "I shou'd be laith to drumble
Your passions, or e'er gar ye grumble,
                   'Tis ne'er be me
Shall scandalize, or say ye bummil
                   Ye'r poetrie.   30

Frae what I've tell'd, my friend may learn
How sadly I ha'e been forfairn,
I'd better been a yont side Kairn-
                   amount, I trow;
I've kiss'd the taz like a good bairn."   35
                   Now, Sir, to you.

Heal be your heart, gay couthy carle,
Lang may ye help to toom a barrel;
Be thy crown ay unclowr'd in quarrel,
                   When thou inclines
To knoit thrawn gabbed sumphs that snarl   40
                   At our frank lines.

Ilk good chiel says, Ye're well worth gowd,
And blythness on ye's well bestow'd,
'Mang witty Scots ye'r name's be row'd,
                   Ne'er fame to tine;   45
The crooked clinkers shall be cow'd,
                   But ye shall shine.

Set out the burnt side of your shin,
For pride in poets is nae sin,   50
Glory's the prize for which they rin,
                   And fame's their jo;
And wha blaws best the horn shall win:
                   And wharefore no?

l.33 *Karn-amount.* A noted hill in the north of Scotland.
l.35 *I've . . . taz.* Kiss'd the rod. Owned my fault like a good child.
l.47 *The crooked clinkers,* &c. The scribling rhimers, with their lame versification.
   Shall be cow'd, i.e. shorn off.
l.49 *Set out . . . shin.* As if one would say, walk stately with your toes out. An
   expression used when we would bid a person (merrily) look brisk.

Quisquis vocabit nos vain-glorious,   55
Shaw scanter skill, than *malos mores*,
Multi et magni men before us
                    Did stamp and swagger,
Probatum est, exemplum Horace,
                    Was a bauld bragger.   60

Then let the doofarts fash'd wi' spleen,
Cast up the wrang side of their een,
Pegh, fry and girn wi' spite and teen,
                    And fa a flyting,
Laugh, for the lively lads will screen   65
                    Us frae back-biting.

If that the gypsies dinna spung us,
And foreign whiskers ha'e na dung us;
Gin I can snifter thro' mundungus,
                    Wi' boots and belt on,   70
I hope to see you at St. Mungo's
                    Atween and Beltan.

l.71 *St. Mungo's.* The high church of Glasgow.

HORACE TO VIRGIL, ON HIS TAKING A VOYAGE TO ATHENS

Sic te diva potens Cypri –

O Cyprian Goddess twinkle clear,
And Helen's brithers ay appear;
Ye stars wha shed a lucky light,
Auspicious ay keep in a sight;
King Eol, grant a tydie tirl,   5
But boast the blast that rudely whirl;
Dear ship, be canny with your care,
At Athens land my Virgil fair,
Syne soon and safe, baith lith and spaul,

28

Bring hame the tae haff o' my saul.   10
   Daring and unco stout he was,
With heart hool'd in three sloughs of brass,
Wha ventur'd first on the rough sea,
With hempen branks and horse of tree:
Wha on the weak machine durst ride   15
Throu' tempests, and a rairing tide,
Nor clinty craigs, nor hurrycane,
That drives the Adriatick main
And gars the ocean gowl and quake,
Cou'd e'er a soul sae sturdy shake.   20
The man wha cou'd sic rubs win o'er,
Without a wink at Death might glow'r,
Wha unconcern'd can take his sleep
Amang the monsters of the deep.
   Jove vainly twin'd the sea and eard,   25
Since mariners are not afraid
With laws of nature to dispence,
And impiously treat Providence.
Audacious men at nought will stand
When vicious passions have command.   30
Prometheus ventur'd up and staw
A lowan coal frae Heav'ns high ha';
Unsonsy thift, which feavers brought
In bikes, which fowk like sybous hought:
Then Death erst slaw began to ling,   35
And fast as haps to dart his sting.
Neist Dedalus must contradict
Nature forsooth, and feathers stick
Upon his back, syne upward streek,
And in at Jove's high winnocks keek,   40
While Hercules, wi's timber mell,
Plays rap upo' the yates of Hell.
   What is't man winna ettle at?
E'en wi' the Gods he'll bell the cat:
Tho Jove be very laith to kill,   45
They winna let his bowt ly still.

TO THE PHIZ AN ODE

Vides ut alta stet nive candidum
Soracte . . .

Horace

Look up to Pentland's towring taps,
Buried beneath great wreaths of snaw,
O'er ilka cleugh, ilk scar and slap,
As high as ony Roman wa'.

Driving their baws frae whins or tee,   5
There's no ae gowfer to be seen,
Nor dousser fowk wysing a jee
The byas bouls on Tamson's green.

Then fling on coals, and ripe the ribs,
And beek the house baith butt and ben,   10
That mutchken stoup it hads but dribs,
Then let's get in the tappit hen.

Good claret best keeps out the cauld,
And drives away the winter soon,
It makes a man baith gash and bauld,   15
And heaves his saul beyond the moon.

Leave to the gods your ilka care,
If that they think us worth their while,
They can a rowth of blessings spare,
Which will our fashious fears beguile.   20

For what they have a mind to do,
That will they do, should we gang wood,
If they command the storms to blaw,
Then upo' sight the hailstains thud.

But soon as e'er they cry, "Be quiet,"   25
The blatt'ring winds dare nae mair move,
But cour into their caves, and wait
The high command of supreme Jove.

Let neist day come as it thinks fit,
The present minute's only ours,   30
On pleasure let's imploy our wit,
And laugh at fortune's feckless power.

Be sure ye dinna quat the grip
Of ilka joy when ye are young,
Before auld age your vitals nip,   35
And lay ye twafald o'er a rung.

Sweet youth's a blyth and heartsome time,
Then lads and lasses while it's May,
Gae pou the gowan in its prime,
Before it wither and decay.   40

Watch the saft minutes of delyte,
When Jenny speaks beneath her breath,
And kisses, laying a the wyte
On you if she kepp ony skaith.

Haith ye're ill bred, she'll smiling say,   45
Ye'll worry me ye greedy rook;
Syne frae your arms she'll rin away,
And hide her sell in some dark nook:

Her laugh will lead you to the place
Where lies the happiness ye want,   50
And plainly tells you to your face,
Nineteen nay-says are haff a grant.

Now to her heaving bosom cling,
And sweetly toolie for a kiss,
Frae her fair finger whop a ring,   55
As taiken of a future bliss.

These bennisons, I'm very sure,
Are of the gods indulgent grant;
Then surly carles, whisht, forbear
To plague us with your whining cant.   60

AN ODE TO MR. FORBES

Solvitur acris hiems . . .
                                        Horace

Now gowans sprout and lavrocks sing,
And welcome west winds warm the spring,
O'er hill and dale they saftly blaw,
And drive the winter's cauld awa.
The ships lang gyzen'd at the peer   5
Now spread their sails and smoothly steer,
The nags and nowt hate wissen'd strae,
And frisking to the fields they gae,
Nor hynds wi' elson and hemp lingle
Sit solling shoon out o'er the ingle.   10
Now bonny haughs their verdure boast,
That late were clade wi' snaw and frost,
With her gay train the Paphian queen
By moon-light dances on the green,
She leads while nymphs and graces sing,   15
And trip around the fairy ring.
Meantime poor Vulcan hard at thrift,
Gets mony a sair and heavy lift,
Whilst rinnen down, his haff-blind lads
Blaw up the fire, and thump the gads.   20
   Now leave your fitsted on the dew,
And busk ye'r sell in habit new.
Be gratefu' to the guiding powers,
And blythly spend your easy hours.
O canny Forbes! tutor time,   25
And live as lang's ye'r in your prime;
That ill-bred Death has nae regard
To king or cottar, or a laird,
As soon a castle he'll attack,
As waus of divots roof'd wi' thack.   30
Immediately we'll a' take flight
Unto the mirk realms of night,
As stories gang, with gaists to roam,
In gloumie Pluto's gousty dome;
Bid fair good-day to pleasure syne   35

Of bonny lasses and red wine.
    Then deem ilk little care a crime,
Dares waste an hour of precious time;
And since our life's sae unko short,
Enjoy it a', ye've nae mair for't.   40

HORACE: BOOK I, ODE V

Quis multa gracilis te puer in rosa
Perfusus . . .

What young raw muisted beau bred at his glass
Now wilt thou on a rose's bed carress?
Wha niest to thy white breasts wilt thow intice,
With hair unsnooded and without thy stays?
O bonny lass, wi' thy sweet landart air,   5
How will thy fikle humour gie him care.
When'er thou takes the fling-strings, like the wind
That jaws the ocean, thou'lt disturb his mind.
When thou looks smirky, kind, and claps his cheek:
To poor friends then he'l hardly look or speak.   10
The coof believes't na, but right soon he'll find
Thee light as cork and wav'ring as the wind.
On that slid place where I 'maist brake my bains,
To be a warning I set up twa stains,
That nane may venture there as I hae done,   15
Unless wi' frosted nails he clink his shoon.

33

HORACE: BOOK I, ODE VI

To His Grace John, Duke of Argyle

Scriberis Vario fortis et hostium
Victor Maeonii . . .

Harmonious Pope, wha made th'inspired Greek
In British phrase his winsome Iliad speak,
Shoud son'rous sing what bairns unborn shall read,
O great Argyle, ilk martial doughty deed
Of thine in a' thy conduct and carreer,   5
In closet schems and reeking fields of wier.
Campbell's brave chief, we mensfowly decline
To sing the heroes of King Fergus' line,
Corbredus Gald, in feght unkend to tire,
Or Caractatus shogan Rome's empire.   10
A blateness shoars me sair that I wad tine
My sell and spill a subject sae divine,
If I should mint aboon my sphere to flee
And sing the glorys of cround heads and thee.
Wha can descrive the pusiant god of war   15
In's adamantine coat and brasen car,
Drawn by fierce lyons through ten thousand faes,
Garing their heart strings crack wher e'er he gaes?
Wha can at Bannockburn bauld Bruce display,
Or thee at Mallplackae, forcing thy way?   20
Enough for me to draw a countrey dance,
And how blyth gossips drink the young wife's hans,
With ourlies clean how Tam and me fou feat
Wad rin an wrestle round the rucks wi' Kate.

THE VISION

Compylit in Latin be a most lernit Clerk★ in Tyme of our Hairship and Oppression, anno 1300, and translatit in 1524.

I

Bedoun the bents of Banquo brae
Milane I wandert waif and wae,
   Musand our main mischaunce;
How be thay faes we are undone,
That staw the sacred stane frae Scone,   5
   And leids us sic a daunce:
Quhyle Inglands Edert† taks our tours,
   And Scotland ferst obeys,
Rude ruffians ransakk ryal bours,
   And Baliol homage pays;   10
     Throch feidom our freidom
     Is blotit with this skore,
     Quhat Romans or no mans
     Pith culd eir do befoir.

[The distressed wanderer seeks shelter in a storm; grieving over his country's fate he falls asleep and dreams that he meets Scotland's Guardian Spirit, a tall, armed, commanding figure, who bids him have no fear –]

VII

"For I am of ane hie station,   85
The Warden of this auntient nation,
   And can nocht do the wrang";
I vissyt him then round about,

★ The History of the Scots Sufferings by the unworthy Condescension of Baliol to Edward I of England, till they recovered their Independence by the Conduct and Valour of the Great BRUCE, is so universally known, that any Argument to this antique Poem seems useless.

† The old Chair (now in Westminster Abbey) in which the Scots Kings were always crown'd, wherein there is a Piece of Marble with this Inscription:
    Ni fallat fatum, SCOTI, *quocunque locatum*
    Invenient lapidem, regnare tenentur ibidem.

Syne with a resolution stout,
    Speird, Quhair he had bene sae lang?   90
Quod he, "Althocht I sum forsuke,
    Becaus they did me slicht,
To hills and glens I me betuke,
    To them that luves my richt;
        Quhase mynds yet inclynds yet   95
        To damm the rappid spate,
        Devysing and prysing
        Freidom at ony rate.

VIII

Our trechour peirs thair tyranns treit,
Quha jyb them, and thair substance eit,   100
    And on thair honour stramp;
They, pure degenerate! bend thair baks,
The victor, Langshanks, proudly cracks
    He has blawn out our lamp:
Quhyle trew men, sair complainand, tell,   105
    With sobs, thair silent greif,
How Baliol thair richts did sell,
    With small howp of reliefe;
        Regretand and fretand
        Ay at his cursit plot,   110
        Quha rammed and crammed
        That bargin down thair throt.

IX

Braif gentrie sweir and burgers ban,
Revenge is muttert be ilk clan
    Thats to their nation trew;   115
The cloysters cum to cun the evil,
Mailpayers wiss it to the Devil
    With its contryving crew:
The hardy wald with hairty wills,
    Upon dyre vengance fall;   120
The feckless fret owre heuchs and hills,
    And Echo answers all,

Repetand and greitand,
With mony a sair alace,
For blasting and casting   125
Our honour in disgrace."

X

"Waes me! quod I, our case is bad,
And mony of us ar gane mad,
    Sen this disgraceful paction.
We are felld and herryt now by forse;   130
And hardly help fort, thats yit warse,
    We are sae forfairn with faction.
Then has not he gude cause to grumble,
    Thats forst to be a slaif;
Oppression dois the judgment jumble   135
    And gars a wyse man raif.
        May cheins then, and pains then
        Infernal be thair hyre
        Quha dang us, and flang us
        Into this ugsum myre."   140

[The Wanderer, continuing to lament, asks about the future –]

XIII

"Say then", said I, "at your hie sate,
Lernt ye ocht of auld Scotland's fate,   170
    Gif eir schoil be her sell?"
With smyle celest, quod he, "I can,
But its nocht fit an mortal man
    Sould ken all I can tell:
But part to the I may unfold,   175
    And thou may saifly ken,
Quhen Scottish peirs slicht Saxon gold,
    And turn trew heartit men;
        Quhen knaivry and slaivrie,
        Ar equally dispysd,   180
        And loyalte and royalte,
        Universalie are prysd.

XIV

Quhen all your trade is at a stand,
And cunzie clene forsaiks the land,
   Quhilk will be very sune, 185
Will preists without their stypands preich?
For nocht will lawyers causes streich?
   Faith thats nae easy done.
All this and mair maun cum to pass,
   To cleir your glamourit sicht; 190
And Scotland maun be made an ass
   To set her jugment richt.
     Theyil jade hir and blad hir,
     Untill scho brak hir tether,
     Thocht auld schois, yit bauld schois, 195
     And teuch lyke barkit lether.

XV

But mony a corss shall braithles ly,
And wae sall mony a widow cry,
   Or all rin richt again;
Owre Cheviot prancing proudly north, 200
The faes sall tak the feild neir Forthe,
   And think the day their ain:
But burns that day sall rin with blude
   Of them that now oppress;
Thair carcasses be corbys fude, 205
   By thousands on the gress.
     A king then sall ring then,
     Of wyse renoun and braif,
     Quhase pusians and sapiens,
     Sall richt restoir and saif." 210

[From a Council of the Guardian Spirits of other nations held in an aerial castle a messenger comes to summon the 'Warden' of Scotland.]

XXVI

Quhyle thus he talkit, methocht ther came
A wondir fair etherial dame,

38

And to our Warden sayd,
"Grit Callidon I cum in serch
Of you, frae the hych starry arch,   355
    The Counsill wants your ayd;
Frae every quarter of the sky,
    As swift as quhirl-wynd,
With spirits speid the chiftains hy,
    Sum grit thing is desygnd.   360
        Owre muntains be funtains,
        And round ilk fairy ring,
        I haif chaist ye, O haist ye,
        They talk about your king."

XXVII

With that my hand methocht he schuke,   365
And wischt I happyness micht bruke,
    To eild be nicht and day;
Syne quicker than an arrows flicht
He mountit upwarts frae my sicht,
    Straicht to the Milkie Way;   370
My mynd him followit throw the skyes,
    Untill the brynie streme
For joy ran trinckling frae myne eyes,
    And wakit me frae dreme;
        Then peiping, half sleiping,   375
        Frae furth my rural beild,
        It eisit me and pleisit me
        To see and smell the feild.

XXVIII

For Flora in hir clene array,
New washen with a showir of May,   380
    Lukit full sweit and fair;
Quhyle hir cleir husband frae aboif
Sched doun his rayis of genial luve,
    Hir sweits perfumt the air;
The winds war husht, the welkin cleird,   385
    The glumand clouds war fled,

And all as saft and gay appeird
　As ane Elysion sched;
　　Quhilk heisit and bleisit
　　My heart with sic a fyre,　　　　　　　　　390
　　As raises these praises
　　That do to heaven aspyre.

Quod AR. SCOT.

MY PEGGY IS A YOUNG THING

My Peggy is a young thing,
　Just enter'd in her teens,
Fair as the day, and sweet as May,
Fair as the day, and always gay.
　My Peggy is a young thing,　　　　　　　　5
　　And I'm not very auld,
　　Yet well I like to meet her at
　　The wawking of the fauld.

My Peggy speaks sae sweetly,
　When e'er we meet alane.　　　　　　　　　10
I wish nae mair, to lay my care,
I wish nae mair, of a' that's rare.
　My Peggy speaks sae sweetly,
　　To a' the lave I'm cauld;
　　But she gars a' my spirits glow　　　　　　15
　　At wawking of the fauld.

My Peggy smiles sae kindly,
　Whene'er I whisper love,
That I look down on a' the town,
That I look down upon a crown.　　　　　　　20
　My Peggy smiles sae kindly,
　　It makes me blyth and bauld.
　　And naithing gi'es me sic delight,
　　As wawking of the fauld.

My Peggy sings sae saftly,   25
   When on my pipe I play;
By a' the rest, it is confest,
By a' the rest, that she sings best.
   My Peggy sings sae saftly,
    And in her sangs are tald,   30
With innocence the wale of sense,
    At wawking of the fauld.

THE GENTLE SHEPHERD,
A PASTORAL COMEDY

The Persons

MEN

Sir William Worthy
Patie   The Gentle Shepherd in love with Peggy
Roger   A rich young shepherd in love with Jenny
Symon
Glaud   } Two old shepherds, tenants to Sir William
Bauldy   A hynd engaged with Neps

WOMEN

Peggy   Thought to be Glaud's niece
Jenny   Glaud's only daughter
Mause   An old woman supposed to be a witch
Elspa   Symon's wife
Madge   Glaud's sister

SCENE   A shepherd's village and fields some few
           miles from Edinburgh
Time of Action   Within twenty hours

THE GENTLE SHEPHERD

Act I, Scene I

Beneath the south side of a craigy beild,
Where crystal springs the halesome waters yield,
Twa youthful shepherds on the gowans lay,
Tenting their flocks ae bonny morn of May.
Poor Roger granes till hollow echoes ring;
But blyther Patie likes to laugh and sing.   5

Patie and Roger

Pat.   This sunny morning, Roger, chears my blood,
And puts all nature in a jovial mood.
How heartsome 'tis to see the rising plants?
To hear the birds chirm o'er their pleasing rants?   10
How halesome 'tis to snuff the cauler air,
And all the sweets it bears when void of care?
What ails thee, Roger, then? What gars thee grane?
Tell me the cause of thy ill season'd pain.

Rog.   I'm born, O Patie! to a thrawart fate;   15
I'm born to strive with hardships sad and great.
Tempest may cease to jaw the rowan flood,
Corbies and tods to grein for lambkins blood;
But I, opprest with never-ending grief,
Maun ay despair of lighting on relief.   20

Pat.   The bees shall loath the flower, and quit the hive,
The saughs on boggie-ground shall cease to thrive,
Ere scornful queans, or loss of warldly gear,
  Shall spill my rest, or ever force a tear.

Rog.   Sae might I say; but 'tis no easy done   25
By ane whase saul is sadly out of tune.

You have sae saft a voice, and slid a tongue,
You are the darling of baith auld and young.
If I but ettle at a sang, or speak,
They dit their lugs, syne up their leglens cleek;   30
And jeer me hameward frae the loan or bught,
While I'm confus'd with mony a vexing thought:
Yet I am tall, and as well-built as thee,
Nor mair unlikely to a lass's eye.
For ilka sheep ye have, I'll number ten,   35
And should, as ane may think, come farer ben.

Pat.   But ablins, nibour, ye have not a heart,
         And downa eithly wi' your cunzie part.
         If that be true, what signifies your gear?
         A mind that's scrimpit never wants some care.   40

Rog.   My byar tumbled, nine braw nowt were smoor'd,
         Three elf-shot were; yet I these ills endur'd:
         In winter last, my cares were very sma',
         Tho' scores of wathers perish'd in the snaw.

Pat.   Were your bein rooms as thinly stock'd as mine,   45
         Less you wad lose, and less you wad repine.
         He that has just enough, can soundly sleep;
         The o'ercome only fashes fowk to keep.

Rog.   May plenty flow upon thee for a cross,
         That thou mayst thole the pangs of mony a loss.   50
         O mayst thou doat on some fair paughty wench,
         That ne'er will lout thy lowan drouth to quench,
         'Till bris'd beneath the burden, thou cry dool,
         And awn that ane may fret that is nae fool.

Pat.   Sax good fat lambs I sald them ilka clute   55
         At the West-port, and bought a winsome flute,
         Of plum-tree made, with iv'ry virles round,
         A dainty whistle with a pleasant sound:
         I'll be mair canty wi't, and ne'er cry dool,
         Than you with all your cash, ye dowie fool.   60

44

Rog.   Na, Patie, na! I'm nae sic churlish beast,
              Some other thing lyes heavier at my breast:
              I dream'd a dreary dream this hinder night,
              That gars my flesh a' creep yet with the fright.

Pat.   Now to a friend how silly's this pretence,   65
              To ane wha you and a' your secrets kens:
              Daft are your dreams, as daftly wad ye hide
              Your well seen love, and dorty Jenny's pride.
              Take courage, Roger, me your sorrows tell,
              And safely think nane kens them but your sell.   70

Rog.   Indeed now, Patie, ye have guessed o'er true,
              And there is nathing I'll keep up frae you.
              Me dorty Jenny looks upon a-squint;
              To speak but till her I dare hardly mint:
              In ilka place she jeers me air and late,   75
              And gars me look bumbaz'd, and unko blate:
              But yesterday I met her 'yont a know,
              She fled as frae a shellycoat or kow.
              She Bauldy loes, Bauldy that drives the car;
              But gecks at me, and says I smell of tar.   80

Pat.   But Bauldy loes not her, right well I wat;
              He sighs for Neps – sae that may stand for that.

Rog.   I wish I cou'dna loo her – but in vain,
              I still maun doat, and thole her proud disdain.
              My Bawty is a cur I dearly like,   85
              Even while he fawn'd, she strak the poor dumb tyke:
              If I had fill'd a nook within her breast,
              She wad have shawn mair kindness to my beast.
              When I begin to tune my stock and horn,
              With a' her face she shaws a caulrife scorn.   90
              Last night I play'd, ye never heard sic spite,
              O'er Bogie was the spring, and her delyte;
              Yet tauntingly she at her cousin speer'd,
              Gif she cou'd tell what tune I play'd, and sneer'd.
              Flocks, wander where ye like, I dinna care,   95
              I'll break my reed, and never whistle mair.

Pat.	E'en do sae, Roger, wha can help misluck,
	Saebeins she be sic a thrawin-gabet chuck?
	Yonder's a craig, since ye have tint all hope,
	Gae till't your ways, and take the lover's lowp. 100

Rog.	I needna mak sic speed my blood to spill,
	I'll warrant death come soon enough a will.

Pat.	Daft gowk! Leave off that silly whindging way;
	Seem careless, there's my hand ye'll win the day.
	Hear how I serv'd my lass I love as well 105
	As ye do Jenny, and with heart as leel:
	Last morning I was gay and early out,
	Upon a dike I lean'd glowring about,
	I saw my Meg come linkan o'er the lee;
	I saw my Meg, but Meggy saw na me: 110
	For yet the sun was wading thro' the mist,
	And she was closs upon me ere she wist;
	Her coats were kiltit, and did sweetly shaw
	Her straight bare legs that whiter were than snaw;
	Her cockernony snooded up fou sleek, 115
	Her haffet-locks hang waving on her cheek;
	Her cheek sae ruddy, and her een sae clear;
	And O! Her mouth's like ony hinny pear.
	Neat, neat she was, in bustine waste-coat clean,
	As she came skiffing o'er the dewy green. 120
	Blythsome, I cry'd, my bonny Meg, come here,
	I ferly wherefore ye're sae soon asteer;
	But I can guess, ye're gawn to gather dew:
	She scoured awa, and said, "What's that to you?"
	"Then fare ye well, Meg Dorts, and e'en's ye like," 125
	I careless cry'd, and lap in o'er the dike.
	I trow, when that she saw, within a crack,
	She came with a right thievless errand back;
	Misca'd me first, – then bade me hound my dog
	To wear up three waff ews stray'd on the bog. 130
	I leugh, and sae did she; then with great haste
	I clasp'd my arms about her neck and waste,
	About her yielding waste, and took a fouth
	Of sweetest kisses frae her glowing mouth.

While hard and fast I held her in my grips,   135
My very saul came lowping to my lips.
Sair, sair she flet wi' me 'tween ilka smack;
But well I kent she meant nae as she spake.
Dear Roger, when your jo puts on her gloom,
Do ye sae too, and never fash your thumb.   140
Seem to forsake her, soon she'll change her mood;
Gae woo anither, and she'll gang clean wood.

Rog.   Kind Patie, now fair fa' your honest heart,
Ye're ay sae cadgy, and have sic an art
To hearten ane: For now as clean's a leek,   145
Ye've cherished me since ye began to speak.
Sae, for your pains, I'll make ye a propine,
My mother (rest her saul) she made it fine,
A tartan plaid, spun of good hawslock woo,
Scarlet and green the sets, the borders blew,   150
With spraings like gowd and siller, cross'd with black;
I never had it yet upon my back.
Well are ye wordy o't, wha have sae kind
Red up my revel'd doubts, and clear'd my mind.

Pat.   Well hald ye there; – and since ye've frankly made   155
A present to me of your braw new plaid,
My flute's be your's, and she too that's sae nice
Shall come a will, gif ye'll tak my advice.

Rog.   As ye advise, I'll promise to observ't;
But ye maun keep the flute, ye best deserv't.   160
Now tak it out, and gie's a bonny spring,
For I'm in tift to hear you play and sing.

Pat.   But first we'll take a turn up to the height,
And see gif all our flocks be feeding right.
Be that time bannocks, and a shave of cheese,   165
Will make a breakfast that a laird might please;
Might please the daintiest gabs, were they sae wise,
To season meat with health instead of spice.
When we have tane the grace-drink at this well,
I'll whistle fine, and sing t'ye like my sell.   170

Act I, Scene II

A flowrie howm between twa verdent braes,
Where lasses use to wash and spread their claiths,
A trotting burnie wimpling through the ground,
Its channel peebles, shining, smooth and round;
Here view twa barefoot beauties clean and clear; 5
First please your eye, next gratify your ear,
While Jenny what she wishes discommends,
And Meg with better sense true love defends.

Peggy and Jenny

Jen.   Come, Meg, let's fa' to wark upon this green,
The shining day will bleech our linen clean; 10
The water's clear, the lift unclouded blew,
Will make them like a lilly wet with dew.

Peg.   Go farer up the burn to Habby's How,
Where a' the sweets of spring and summer grow;
Between twa birks, out o'er a little lin 15
The water fa's, and makes a singand din;
A pool breast-deep beneath, as clear as glass,
Kisses with easy whirles the bordring grass:
We'll end our washing while the morning's cool,
And when the day grows het, we'll to the pool, 20
There wash our sells – 'tis healthfu' now in May,
And sweetly cauler on sae warm a day.

Jen.   Daft lassie, when we're naked, what'll ye say,
Gif our twa herds come brattling down the brae,
And see us sae? That jeering fallow Pate 25
Wad taunting say, "Haith, lasses, ye're no blate!"

Peg.   We're far frae ony road, and out of sight;
The lads they're feeding far beyont the height:
But tell me now, dear Jenny, (we're our lane)
What gars ye plague your wooer with disdain? 30
The nibours a' tent this as well as I,
That Roger loos you, yet ye carena by.

What ails ye at him? Trowth, between us twa,
He's wordy you the best day e'er ye saw.

Jen.   I dinna like him, Peggy, there's an end;   35
        A herd mair sheepish yet I never kend.
        He kaims his hair indeed, and gaes right snug,
        With ribbon-knots at his blew bonnet-lug;
        Whilk pensily he wears a thought a-jee,
        And spreads his garters diced beneath his knee.   40
        He falds his owrlay down his breast with care;
        And few gang trigger to the kirk or fair.
        For a' that, he can neither sing nor say,
        Except "How d'ye" – or, "There's a bonny day."

Peg.   Ye dash the lad with constant slighting pride;   45
        Hatred for love is unco sair to bide:
        But ye'll repent ye, if his love grows cauld.
        What like's a dorty maiden when she's auld?
        Like dawted we'an that tarrows at its meat,
        That for some feckless whim will orp and greet.   50
        The lave laugh at it, till the dinner's past,
        And syne the fool thing is oblig'd to fast.
        Or scart anither's leavings at the last.
        Fy, Jenny, think, and dinna sit your time.

Jen.   I never thought a single life a crime.   55

Peg.   Nor I – but love in whispers lets us ken,
        That men were made for us, and we for men.

Jen.   If Roger is my jo, he kens himsell;
        For sic a tale I never heard him tell.
        He glowrs and sighs, and I can guess the cause,   60
        But wha's obliged to spell his 'Hums' and 'Haws'?
        When e'er he likes to tell his mind mair plain,
        I'se tell him frankly ne'er to do't again.
        They're fools that slavery like, and may be free:
        The cheils may a' knit up themsells for me.   65

Peg.   Be doing your ways; for me, I have a mind
        To be as yielding as my Patie's kind.

Jen.	Heh! Lass, how can ye loo that rattle-scull,	
	A very deel that ay maun hae his will?	
	We'll soon here tell what a poor fighting life	70
	You twa will lead, sae soon's ye're man and wife.	

Jen.   Heh! Lass, how can ye loo that rattle-scull,
         A very deel that ay maun hae his will?
         We'll soon here tell what a poor fighting life   70
         You twa will lead, sae soon's ye're man and wife.

Peg.   I'll rin the risk; nor have I ony fear,
         But rather think ilk langsome day a year,
         Till I with pleasure mount my bridal-bed,
         Where on my Patie's breast I'll lean my head.   75
         There we may kiss as lang as kissing's good,
         And what we do, there's nane dare call it rude.
         He's get his will: Why no? 'tis good my part
         To give him that; and he'll give me his heart.

Jen.   He may indeed, for ten or fifteen days,   80
         Mak meikle o' ye, with an unco fraise;
         And daut ye baith afore fowk and your lane:
         But soon as his newfangleness is gane,
         He'll look upon you as his tether-stake,
         And think he's tint his freedom for your sake.   85
         Instead then of lang days of sweet delite,
         Ae day be dumb, and a' the neist he'll flite:
         And may be, in his barlickhoods, ne'er stick
         To lend his loving wife a loundering lick.

Peg.   Sic coarse-spun thoughts as thae want pith to move   90
         My settl'd mind, I'm o'er far gane in love.
         Patie to me is dearer than my breath;
         But want of him I dred nae other skaith.
         There's nane of a' the herds that tread the green
         Has sic a smile, or sic twa glancing een.   95
         And then he speaks with sic a taking art,
         His words they thirle like musick thro' my heart.
         How blythly can he sport, and gently rave,
         And jest at feckless fears that fright the lave?
         Ilk day that he's alane upon the hill,   100
         He reads fell books that teach him meikle skill.
         He is – But what need I say that or this?
         I'd spend a month to tell you what he is!
         In a' he says or does, there's sic a gait,

The rest seem coofs compar'd with my dear Pate.　105
His better sense will lang his love secure:
Ill nature heffs in sauls are weak and poor.

Jen.　Hey! *bonny lass of Branksome*, or't be lang,
Your witty Pate will put you in a sang.
O! 'tis a pleasant thing to be a bride;　110
Syne whindging getts about your ingle-side,
Yelping for this or that with fasheous din,
To mak them brats then ye maun toil and spin.
Ae we'an fa's sick, ane scads it sell wi' broe,
Ane breaks his shin, anither tynes his shoe;　115
The deel gaes o'er John Wobster, hame grows hell,
When Pate misca's ye war than tongue can tell.

Peg.　Yes, 'tis a heartsome thing to be a wife,
When round the ingle-edge young sprouts are rife.
Gif I'm sae happy, I shall have delight,　120
To hear their little plaints, and keep them right.
Wow! Jenny, can there greater pleasure be,
Than see sic wee tots toolying at your knee;
When a' they ettle at – their greatest wish,
Is to be made of, and obtain a kiss?　125
Can there be toil in tenting day and night,
The like of them, when love makes care delight?

Jen.　But poortith, Peggy, is the warst of a',
Gif o'er your heads ill chance shou'd beggary draw:
But little love, or canty chear can come,　130
Frae duddy doublets, and a pantry toom.
Your nowt may die – the spate may bear away
Frae aff the howms your dainty rucks of hay. –
The thick blawn wreaths of snaw, or blashy thows,
May smoor your wathers, and may rot your ews.　135
A dyvour buys your butter, woo and cheese,
But, or the day of payment, breaks and flees.
With glooman brow the laird seeks in his rent:
'Tis no to gi'e; your merchant's to the bent;
His Honour mauna want, he poinds your gear:　140
Syne, driven frae house and hald, where will ye steer?

51

Dear Meg, be wise, and live a single life;
Troth 'tis nae mows to be a marry'd wife.

Peg.
May sic ill luck befa' that silly she,
Wha has sic fears; for that was never me.   145
Let fowk bode well, and strive to do their best;
Nae mair's requir'd, let heaven make out the rest.
I've heard my honest uncle aften say,
That lads shou'd a' for wives that's vertuous pray:
For the maist thrifty man cou'd never get   150
A well stor'd room, unless his wife wad let:
Wherefore nocht shall be wanting on my part,
To gather wealth to raise my Shepherd's heart.
What e'er he wins, I'll guide with canny care,
And win the vogue, at market, tron, or fair,   155
For halesome, clean, cheap and sufficient ware.
A flock of lambs, cheese, butter, and some woo,
Shall first be sald, to pay the laird his due;
Syne a' behind's our ain. – Thus, without fear,
With love and rowth we thro' the warld will steer: 160
And when my Pate in bairns and gear grows rife,
He'll bless the day he gat me for his wife.

Jen.
But what if some young giglit on the green,
With dimpled cheeks, and twa bewitching een,
Should gar your Patie think his haff-worn Meg,   165
And her kend kisses, hardly worth a feg?

Peg.
Nae mair of that; – dear Jenny, to be free,
There's some men constanter in love than we:
Nor is the ferly great, when nature kind
Has blest them with solidity of mind.   170
They'll reason calmly, and with kindness smile,
When our short passions wad our peace beguile.
Sae whensoe'er they slight their maiks at hame,
'Tis ten to ane the wives are maist to blame.
Then I'll employ with pleasure a' my art   175
To keep him chearfu' and secure his heart.
At even, when he comes weary frae the hill,
I'll have a' things made ready to his will.

In winter, when he toils thro' wind and rain,
A bleezing ingle, and a clean hearth-stane.   180
And soon as he flings by his plaid and staff,
The seething pot's be ready to take aff.
Clean hagabag I'll spread upon his board,
And serve him with the best we can afford.
Good humour and white bigonets shall be   185
Guards to my face, to keep his love for me.

Jen.   A dish of married love right soon grows cauld,
And dosens down to nane, as fowk grow auld.

Peg.   But we'll grow auld togither, and ne'er find
The loss of youth, when love grows on the mind.   190
Bairns, and their bairns, make sure a firmer ty,
Than ought in love the like of us can spy.
See yon twa elms that grow up side by side,
Suppose them, some years syne, bridegroom and bride;
Nearer and nearer ilka year they've prest,   195
Till wide their spreading branches are increast,
And in their mixture now are fully blest.
This shields the other frae the eastlin blast,
That in return defends it frae the west.
Sic as stand single, – a state sae liked by you!   200
Beneath ilk storm, frae ev'ry airth, maun bow.

Jen.   I've done, – I yield, dear lassie, I maun yield,
Your better sense has fairly won the field,
With the assistance of a little fae
Lyes darn'd within my breast this mony a day.   205

Peg.   Alake! Poor prisoner! Jenny, that's no fair,
That ye'll no let the wee thing tak the air:
Haste, let him out, we'll tent as well's we can,
Gif he be Bauldy's or poor Roger's man.

Jen.   Anither time's as good, – for see, the sun   210
Is right far up, and we're no yet begun
To freath the graith; – if cankered Madge our aunt
Come up the burn, she'll gie's a wicked rant:

But when we've done, I'll tell ye a' my mind;
For this seems true, – nae lass can be unkind.   215

Exeunt

End of the First Act

Act II, Scene I

A snug thack-house, before the door a green;
Hens on the midding, ducks in dubs are seen.
On this side stands a barn, on that a byre;
A peat-stack joins, and forms a rural square.
The house is Glaud's; – there you may see him lean,   5
And to his divot-seat invite his frien'.

Glaud and Symon

Glaud.   Good-morrow, nibour Symon – come sit down,
And gie's your cracks. – What's a' the news in town?
They tell me ye was in the ither day,
And sald your Crummock and her bassend quey.   10
I'll warrant ye've coft a pund of cut and dry;
Lug out your box, and gie's a pipe to try.

Sym.   With a' my heart – and tent me now, auld boy,
I've gather'd news will kittle your mind with joy.
I cou'dna rest till I came o'er the burn,   15
To tell ye things have taken sic a turn,
Will gar our vile oppressors stend like flaes,
And skulk in hidlings on the hether braes.

Glaud.   Fy, blaw! Ah! Symie, ratling chiels ne'er stand
To cleck and spread the grossest lies aff hand,   20
Whilk soon flies round like will-fire far and near:
But loose your poke, be't true or fause, let's hear.

Sym.   Seeing's believing, Glaud, and I have seen
Hab, that abroad has with our Master been;
Our brave good Master, wha right wisely fled,   25
And left a fair estate, to save his head:
Because ye ken fou well he bravely chose

54

To stand his liege's friend with great Montrose.
Now Cromwell's gane to Nick; and ane ca'd Monk
Has play'd the Rumple a right slee begunk,   30
Restor'd King Charles, and ilka thing's in tune:
And Habby says, we'll see Sir William soon.

Glaud. That makes me blyth indeed: – but dinna flaw:
Tell o'er your news again! and swear till't a';
And saw ye Hab! And what did Halbert say?   35
They have been e'en a dreary time away.
Now God be thanked that our laird's come hame,
And his estate, say, can he eithly claim?

Sym. They that hag-raid us till our guts did grane,
Like greedy bairs, dare nae mair do't again;   40
And good Sir William sall enjoy his ain.

Glaud. And may he lang; for never did he stent
Us in our thriving, with a racket rent:
Nor grumbl'd, if ane grew rich; or shor'd to raise
Our mailens, when we pat on Sunday's claiths.   45

Sym. Nor wad he lang, with senseless saucy air,
Allow our lyart noddles to be bare.
"Put on your bonnet, Symon; – Tak a seat. –
How's all at hame? – How's Elspa? How does Kate?
How sells black cattle? What gie's woo this year?" –   50
And sic like kindly questions wad he speer.

Glaud. Then wad he gar his butler bring bedeen
The nappy bottle ben, and glasses clean,
Whilk in our breast rais'd sic a blythsome flame,
As gart me mony a time gae dancing hame.   55
My heart's e'en raised! Dear nibour, will ye stay,
And tak your dinner here with me the day?
We'll send for Elspath too – and upo' sight,
I'll whistle Pate and Roger frae the height:
I'll yoke my sled, and send to the neist town,   60
And bring a draught of ale baith stout and brown,

And gar our cottars a', man, wife and we'an,
Drink till they tine the gate to stand their lane.

Sym.   I wad na bauk my friend his blyth design,
       Gif that it hadna first of a' been mine: 65
       For heer-yestreen I brew'd a bow of maut,
       Yestreen I slew twa wathers prime and fat;
       A firlot of good cakes my Elspa beuk,
       And a large ham hings reesting in the nook:
       I saw my sell, or I came o'er the loan,   70
       Our meikle pot that scads the whey put on,
       A mutton-bouk to boil: – and ane we'll roast;
       And on the haggies Elspa spares nae cost;
       Sma' are they shorn, and she can mix fu' nice
       The gusty ingans with a curn of spice: 75
       Fat are the puddings, – heads and feet well sung.
       And we've invited nibours auld and young,
       To pass this afternoon with glee and game,
       And drink our Master's health and welcome-hame.
       Ye mauna then refuse to join the rest,   80
       Since ye're my nearest friend that I like best.
       Bring wi' ye a' your family, and then,
       When e'er you please, I'll rant wi' you again.

Glaud. Spoke like ye'r sell, auld-birky, never fear
        But at your banquet I shall first appear.   85
        Faith we shall bend the bicker, and look bauld,
        Till we forget that we are fail'd or auld.
        Auld, said I! troth, I'm younger be a score,
        With your good news, than what I was before.
        I'll dance or een! Hey! Madge, come forth: D'ye
           hear?   90

                      Enter Madge

Mad.   The man's gane gyte! Dear Symon, welcome here.
        What wad ye, Glaud, with a' this haste and din?
        Ye never let a body sit to spin.

Glaud. Spin? Snuff! Gae break your wheel, and burn your tow,
        And set the meiklest peat-stack in a low.   95

                            56

Syne dance about the bane-fire till ye die,
Since now again we'll soon Sir William see.

Mad.   Blyth news indeed! And what was tald you o't?

Glaud.   What's that to you? Gae get my Sunday's coat;
        Wale out the whitest of my bobbit bands,   100
        My white-skin hose, and mittons for my hands;
        Then frae their washing cry the bairns in haste,
        And make your sells as trig, head, feet and waist,
        As ye were a' to get young lads or e'en;
        For we're gaun o'er to dine with Sym bedeen.   105

Sym.   Do, honest Madge: – and, Glaud, I'll o'er the gate,
        And see that a' be done as I wad hae't.

                                                    Exeunt

                      Act II, Scene II

        The open field. – A cottage in a glen,
        An auld wife spinning at the sunny end. –
        At a small distance, by a blasted tree,
        With falded arms, and haff rais'd look ye see –

                    Bauldy *his lane*

Baul.   What's this! – I canna bear't! 'tis war than Hell,   5
        To be sae burnt with love, yet darna tell!
        O Peggy, sweeter than the dawning day,
        Sweeter than gowany glens, or new mawn hay;
        Blyther than lambs that frisk out o'er the knows,
        Straighter than ought that in the forest grows: 10
        Her een the clearest blob of dew outshines;
        The lilly in her breast its beauty tines.
        Her legs, her arms, her cheeks, her mouth, her een,
        Will be my dead, that will be shortly seen!
        For Pate loes her, – wae's me! and she loes Pate;   15
        And I with Neps, by some unlucky fate,
        Made a daft vow: – O, but ane be a beast
        That makes rash aiths till he's afore the priest!

                            57

I dare na speak my mind, else a' the three,
But doubt, wad prove ilk ane my enemy.   20
'Tis sair to thole; I'll try some witchcraft art,
To break with ane, and win the other's heart.
Hear Mausy lives, a witch, that for sma' price
Can cast her cantraips, and give me advice.
She can o'ercast the night, and cloud the moon,   25
And mak the deils obedient to her crune.
At midnight hours, o'er the kirk-yards she raves,
And howks unchristened we'ans out of their graves;
Boils up their livers in a warlock's pow,
Rins withershins about the hemlock low;   30
And seven times does her prayers backward pray,
Till Plotcock comes with lumps of Lapland clay,
Mixt with the venom of black taids and snakes;
Of this unsonsy pictures aft she makes
Of ony ane she hates – and gars expire   35
With slaw and racking pains afore a fire;
Stuck fu' of prins, the devilish pictures melt,
The pain, by fowk they represent, is felt.
And yonder's Mause: Ay, ay, she kens fu' well
When ane like me comes rinning to the Deil.   40
She and her cat sit beeking in her yard,
To speak my errand, faith amaist I'm fear'd:
But I maun do't, tho' I should never thrive;
They gallop fast that deils and lasses drive.
                                                    Exit

Act II, Scene III

A green kail-yard, a little fount,
    Where water popilan springs;
There sits a wife with wrinkle-front.
    And yet she spins and sings.

Mause *sings*

"Peggy, now the King's come,   5
    Peggy, now the King's come;
Thou may dance, and I shall sing,

                    Peggy, since the King's come.
                    Nae mair the hawkies shalt thou milk,
                    But change thy plaiding-coat for silk,
                    And be a lady of that ilk,   10
                        Now, Peggy, since the King's come."

                        Enter Bauldy

Baul.   How does auld honest Lucky of the glen?
             Ye look baith hale and fere at threescore ten.

Maus.   E'en twining out a threed with little din,   15
             And beeking my cauld limbs afore the sun.
             What brings my bairn this gate sae air at morn?
             Is there nae muck to lead? – to thresh nae corn?

Baul.   Enough of baith: – But something that requires
             Your helping hand, employs now all my cares.   20

Maus.   My helping hand, alake! what can I do,
             That underneath baith eild and poortith bow?

Baul.   Ay, but ye're wise, and wiser far than we,
             Or maist part of the parish tells a lie.

Maus.   Of what kind wisdom think ye I'm possest,   25
             That lifts my character aboon the rest?

Baul.   The word that gangs, how ye're sae wise and fell,
             Ye'll may be take it ill gif I shou'd tell.

Maus.   What fowk says of me, Bauldy, let me hear;
             Keep nathing up, ye nathing have to fear.   30

Baul.   Well, since ye bid me, I shall tell ye a',
             That ilk ane talks about you, but a flaw.
             When last the wind made Glaud a roofless barn;
             When last the burn bore down my mither's yarn;
             When Brawny elf-shot never mair came hame;   35
             When Tibby kirn'd, and there nae butter came;
             When Bessy Freetock's chuffy-cheeked we'an

To a fairy turn'd, and cou'd na stand its lane;
When Watie wander'd ae night thro' the shaw,
And tint himself amaist amang the snaw;   40
When Mungo's mear stood still, and swat with fright,
When he brought east the howdy under night;
When Bawsy shot to dead upon the green,
And Sara tint a snood was nae mair seen:
You, Lucky, gat the wyte of a' fell out,   45
And ilka ane here dreads you round about.
And sae they may that mint to do ye skaith:
For me to wrang ye, I'll be very laith;
But, when I neist make grots, I'll strive to please
You with a firlot of them mixt with pease.   50

Maus.   I thank ye, lad; – now tell me your demand,
          And, if I can, I'll lend my helping hand.

Baul.   Then, I like Peggy, – Neps is fond of me; –
          Peggy likes Pate, – and Patie's bauld and slee,
          And loes sweet Meg. – But Neps I downa see. –   55
          Cou'd ye turn Patie's love to Neps, and than
          Peggy's to me, – I'd be the happiest man.

Maus.   I'll try my art to gar the bowls row right;
          Sae gang your ways, and come again at night:
          'Gainst that time I'll some simple things prepare, 60
          Worth all your pease and grots; tak ye nae care.

Baul.   Well, Mause, I'll come, gif I the road can find:
          But if ye raise the Deil, he'll raise the wind;
          Syne rain and thunder may be, when 'tis late,
          Will make the night sae rough, I'll tine the gate. 65
          We're a' to rant in Symie's at a feast,
          O! will ye come like badrans, for a jest;
          And there ye can our different haviours spy:
          There's nane shall ken o't there but you and I.

Maus.   'Tis like I may, – but let na on what's past   70
          'Tween you and me, else fear a kittle cast.

Baul.   If I ought of your secrets e'er advance,
          May ye ride on me ilka night to France.

                                        Exit Bauldy

                         Mause *her lane*

          Hard luck, alake! when poverty and eild,
          Weeds out of fashion, and a lanely beild,   75
          With a sma' cast of wiles, should in a twitch,
          Gi'e ane the hatefu' name a wrinkled witch.
          This fool imagines, as do mony sic,
          That I'm a wretch in compact with Auld Nick;
          Because by education I was taught   80
          To speak and act aboon their common thought.
          Their gross mistake shall quickly now appear;
          Soon shall they ken what brought, what keeps me here;
          Nane kens but me, – and if the morn were come,
          I'll tell them tales will gar them a' sing dumb.   85

                                        Exit

                         Act II, Scene IV

                 Behind a tree, upon the plain,
                    Pate and his Peggy meet;
                 In love, without a vicious stain,
                 The bonny lass and chearfu' swain
                    Change vows and kisses sweet.   5

                         Patie and Peggy

Peg.   O Patie, let me gang, I mauna stay,
          We're baith cry'd hame, and Jenny she's away.

Pat.   I'm laith to part sae soon; now we're alane,
          And Roger he's awa with Jenny gane:
          They're as content, for ought I hear or see,   10
          To be alane themsells, I judge, as we.
          Here, where primroses thickest paint the green,
          Hard by this little burnie let us lean.
          Hark how the lavrocks chant aboon our heads,
          How saft the westlin winds sough thro' the reeds.   15

                              61

Peg. The scented meadows, – birds, – and healthy breeze,
For ought I ken, may mair than Peggy please.

Pat. Ye wrang me sair, to doubt my being kind;
In speaking sae, ye ca' me dull and blind.
Gif I could fancy ought's sae sweet or fair
As my dear Meg, or worthy of my care.
Thy breath is sweeter than the sweetest brier,
Thy cheek and breast the finest flowers appear.
Thy words excel the maist delightfu' notes,
That warble through the merl or mavis' throats.
With thee I tent nae flowers that busk the field,
Or ripest berries that our mountains yield.
The sweetest fruits that hing upon the tree,
Are far inferior to a kiss of thee.

Peg. But Patrick, for some wicked end, may fleech,
And lambs should tremble when the foxes preach.
I dare na stay – ye joker, let me gang,
Anither lass may gar ye change your sang;
Your thoughts may flit, and I may thole the wrang.

Pat. Sooner a mother shall her fondness drap,
And wrang the bairn sits smiling on her lap;
The sun shall change, the moon to change shall cease,
The gaits to clim, – the sheep to yield the fleece,
Ere ought by me be either said or done,
Shall skaith our love; I swear by all aboon.

Peg. Then keep your aith: – But mony lads will swear,
And be mansworn to twa in haff a year.
Now I believe ye like me wonder well;
But if a fairer face your heart shou'd steal,
Your Meg forsaken, bootless might relate,
How she was dauted anes by faithless Pate.

Pat. I'm sure I canna change, ye needna fear.
Tho' we're but young, I've loo'd you mony a year.
I mind it well, when thou coud'st hardly gang,
Or lisp out words, I choos'd ye frae the thrang

Of a' the bairns, and led thee by the hand,
Aft to the Tansy-know, or Rashy strand.
Thou smiling by my side, – I took delite,
To pou the rashes green, with roots sae white,
Of which, as well as my young fancy cou'd,   55
For thee I plet the flowry belt and snood.

Peg.   When first thou gade with shepherds to the hill,
And I to milk the ews first try'd my skill:
To bear a leglen was nae toil to me,
When at the bught at e'en I met with thee.   60

Pat.   When corns grew yellow, and the hether-bells
Bloom'd bonny on the moor and rising fells,
Nae birns, or briers, or whins e'er troubled me,
Gif I cou'd find blae berries ripe for thee.

Peg.   When thou didst wrestle, run, or putt the stane,   65
And wan the day, my heart was flightering fain:
At all these sports thou still gave joy to me;
For nane can wrestle, run, or putt with thee.

Pat.   Jenny sings saft *The Broom of Cowden-knows*,
And Rosie lilts *The Milking of the Ews*;   70
There's nane like Nansie, *Jenny Nettles* sings;
At turns in *Maggy Lauder*, Marion dings:
But when my Peggy sings, with sweeter skill,
The Boat-man, or *The Lass of Patie's Mill*;
It is a thousand times mair sweet to me: 75
Tho' they sing well, they canna sing like thee.

Peg.   How eith can lasses trow what they desire!
And roos'd by them we love, blaws up that fire:
But wha loves best, let time and carriage try;
Be constant, and my love shall time defy.   80
Be still as now, and a' my care shall be,
How to contrive what pleasant is for thee.

Pat.   Wert thou a giglit gawky like the lave,
That little better than our nowt behave;

At nought they'll ferly; – senseless tales believe;   85
Be blyth for silly heghts, for trifles grieve: –
Sic ne'er cou'd win my heart, that kenna how,
Either to keep a prize, or yet prove true.
But thou, in better sense, without a flaw,
As in thy beauty far excells them a',   90
Continue kind; and a' my care shall be,
How to contrive what pleasing is for thee.

Peg.   Agreed; – But harken, yon's auld Aunty's cry;
I ken they'll wonder what can make us stay.

Pat.   And let them ferly. – Now, a kindly kiss,   95
Or fivescore good anes wad not be amiss;
And syne we'll sing the sang with tunefu' glee,
That I made up last owk on you and me.

Peg.   Sing first, syne claim your hire.

Pat.   Well, I agree.

Patie *sings*

By the delicious warmness of thy mouth,   100
And rowing eyes that smiling tell the truth,
I guess, my lassie, that as well as I,
You're made for love, and why should ye deny?

Peggy *sings*

But ken ye, lad, gin we confess o'er soon,
Ye think us cheap, and syne the wooing's done?   105
The maiden that o'er quickly tines her power,
Like unripe fruit, will taste but hard and sowr.

Patie *sings*

But gin they hing o'er lang upon the tree,
Their sweetness they may tine; and sae may ye.
Red-cheekèd you completely ripe appear;   110
And I have thol'd and woo'd a lang haff year.

Peggy, singing, falls into Patie's *arms*

Then dinna pu' me, gently thus I fa'
Into my Patie's arms, for good and a'.
But stint your wishes to this kind embrace;
And mint nae farther till we've got the grace.   115

Patie, *with his left hand about her waste*

O charming armfu', hence ye cares away,
I'll kiss my treasure a' the live lang day;
All night I'll dream my kisses o'er again,
Till that day come that ye'll be a' my ain.

Sung by both

Sun, gallop down the westlin skies,   120
Gang soon to bed, and quickly rise;
O lash your steeds, post time away,
And haste about our bridal day:
And if ye're wearied, honest light,
Sleep, gin ye like, a week that night.   125

End of the second Act

Act III, Scene I

Now turn your eyes beyond yon spreading lime,
And tent a man whase beard seems bleech'd with time;
An elvand fills his hand, his habit mean:
Nae doubt ye'll think he has a pedlar been.
But whisht! It is the knight in masquerade,   5
That comes hid in this cloud to see his lad.
Observe how pleased the loyal sufferer moves
Thro' his auld av'news, anes delightfu' groves.

Sir William *solus*

The gentleman thus hid in low disguise,
I'll for a space unknown delight mine eyes,   10
With a full view of every fertile plain,
Which once I lost, – which now are mine again.
Yet 'midst my joys, some prospects pain renew,
Whilst I my once fair seat in ruins view.

Yonder, ah me! it desolately stands,   15
Without a roof; the gates faln from their bands;
The casements all broke down; no chimney left;
The naked walls of tap'stry all bereft:
My stables and pavilions, broken walls!
That with each rainy blast decaying falls.   20
My gardens, once adorn'd the most compleat,
With all that nature, all that art makes sweet;
Where, round the figur'd green, and peeble walks,
The dewy flowers hung nodding on their stalks:
But, overgrown with nettles, docks and brier,   25
No jaccacinths or eglintines appear.
How do those ample walls to ruin yield,
Where peach and nect'rine branches found a beild,
And bask'd in rays, which early did produce
Fruit fair to view, delightfu' in the use!   30
All round in gaps, the most in rubbish ly,
And from what stands the wither'd branches fly.
    These soon shall be repair'd: – and now my joy
Forbids all grief, – when I'm to see my boy,
My only prop, and object of my care,   35
Since heaven too soon called hame his mother fair.
Him ere the rays of reason clear'd his thought,
I secretly to faithful Symon brought,
And charg'd him strictly to conceal his birth,
'Till we should see what changing times brought forth. 40
Hid from himself, he starts up by the dawn,
And ranges careless o'er the height and lawn,
After his fleecy charge, serenely gay,
With other shepherds whistling o'er the day.
Thrice happy life! that's from ambition free;   45
Remov'd from crowns and courts, how chearfully
A quiet contented mortal spends his time
In hearty health, his soul unstain'd with crime.
    Now tow'rds good Symon's house I'll bend my way,
And see what makes yon gamboling to-day,   50
All on the green, in a fair wanton ring
My youthful tenants gayly dance and sing.

                                                          Exit

'Tis Symon's house, please to step in,
  And vissy't round and round;
There's nought superfluous to give pain,
  Or costly to be found.
Yet all is clean: a clear peat-ingle   5
  Glances amidst the floor;
The green-horn spoons, beech-luggies mingle,
  On skelfs foregainst the door.
While the young brood sport on the green,
  The auld anes think it best,   10
With the brown cow to clear their een,
  Snuff, crack, and take their rest.

Symon, Glaud and Elspa

Glaud.	We anes were young our sells. – I like to see
	The bairns bob round with other merrilie.
	Troth, Symon, Patie's grown a strapan lad, 15
	And better looks than his I never bade.
	Amang our lads, he bears the gree awa',
	And tells his tale the cleverest of them a'.

Elsp.	Poor man! – he's a great comfort to us baith:
	God mak him good, and hide him ay frae skaith. 20
	He is a bairn, I'll say't, well worth our care,
	That ga'e us ne'er vexation late or air.

Glaud.	I trow, goodwife, if I be not mistane,
	He seems to be with Peggy's beauty tane,
	And troth, my niece is a right dainty we'an, 25
	As ye well ken: a bonnier needna be,
	Nor better, – be't she were nae kin to me.

Sym.	Ha! Glaud, I doubt that ne'er will be a match;
	My Patie's wild, and will be ill to catch:
	And or he were, for reasons I'll no tell, 30
	I'd rather be mixt with the mools my sell.

Glaud.	What reason can ye have? There's nane, I'm sure,
	Unless ye may cast up that she's but poor:

But gif the lassie marry to my mind,
I'll be to her as my ain Jenny kind.   35
Fourscore of breeding ews of my ain birn,
Five ky that at ae milking fills a kirn,
I'll gie to Peggy that day she's a bride;
By and attour, gif my good luck abide,
Ten lambs at spaining-time, as lang's I live,   40
And twa quey cawfs I'll yearly to them give.

Elsp.   Ye offer fair, kind Glaud; but dinna speer
What may be is not fit ye yet should hear.

Sym.   Or this day eight days likely he shall learn,
That our denial disna slight his bairn.   45

Glaud.   Well, nae mair o't, – come, gie's the other bend;
We'll drink their healths, whatever way it end.

Their healths gae round

Sym.   But will ye tell me, Glaud, – by some 'tis said,
Your niece is but a fundling that was laid
Down at your hallon-side, ae morn in May,   50
Right clean row'd up, and bedded on dry hay.

Glaud.   That clatteran Madge, my titty, tells sic flaws,
When e'er our Meg her cankart humour gaws.

Enter Jenny

Jen.   O Father! there's an auld man on the green,
The fellest fortune-teller e'er was seen: 55
He tents our loofs, and syne whops out a book,
Turns o'er the leaves, and gie's our brows a look;
Syne tells the oddest tales that e'er ye heard.
His head is gray, and lang and gray his beard.

Sym.   Gae bring him in; we'll hear what he can say: 60
Nane shall gang hungry by my house to-day.
                                       Exit Jenny

43 hear 1734) here.

But for his telling fortunes, troth I fear,
He kens nae mair of that than my gray mare.

Glaud.   Spae-men! the truth of a' their saws I doubt;
For greater liars never ran there out.   65

Returns Jenny, *bringing in* Sir William; *with them* Patie

Sym.   Ye're welcome, honest Carle; – here, take a seat.

S. Will.   I give ye thanks, goodman; I'se no be blate.

Glaud *drinks*

Come t'ye, friend: – How far came ye the day?

S. Will.   I pledge ye, nibour: – E'en but little way:
Rousted with eild, a wee piece gate seems lang;   70
Twa miles or three's the maist that I dow gang.

Sym.   Ye're welcome here to stay all night with me,
And take sic bed and board as we can gi' ye.

S. Will.   That's kind unsought. – Well, gin ye have a bairn
That ye like well, and wad his fortune learn,   75
I shall employ the farthest of my skill,
To spae it faithfully, be't good or ill.

Symon, *pointing to* Patie

Only that lad; – alake! I have nae mae,
Either to make me joyful now, or wae.

S. Will.   Young man, let's see your hand; – what gars ye sneer? 80

Pat.   Because your skill's but little worth I fear.

S. Will.   Ye cut before the point. – But, billy, bide,
I'll wager there's a mouse mark on your side.

Elsp.   Betooch-us-to! and well I wat that's true:
Awa, awa! the deil's o'er grit wi' you.   85

69

Four inch aneath his oxter is the mark,
Scarce ever seen since he first wore a sark.

S. Will.   I'll tell ye mair, if this young lad be spar'd
But a short while, he'll be a braw rich laird.

Elsp.   A laird! – Hear ye, goodman! What think ye now?   90

Sym.   I dinna ken: Strange auld man! What art thou?
Fair fa' your heart; 'tis good to bode of wealth:
Come turn the timmer to Laird Patie's health.

Patie's health gaes round

Pat.   A laird of twa good whistles, and a kent,
Twa curs, my trusty tenants, on the bent,   95
Is all my great estate – and like to be:
Sae, cunning carle, ne'er break your jokes on me.

Sym.   Whisht, Patie, – let the man look o'er your hand,
Aftimes as broken a ship has come to land.

    Sir William *looks a little at* Patie's *hand, then
counterfeits falling into a trace, while they endeavour
to lay him right.*

Elsp.   Preserve's! The man's a warlock, or possesst   100
With some nae good – or second sight, at least:
Where is he now?

Glaud.   He's seeing a' that's done
In ilka place, beneath or yont the moon.

Elsp.   These second-sighted fowk, his peace be here!
See things far aff, and things to come, as clear   105
As I can see my thumb – Wow, Can he tell
(Speer at him, soon as he comes to himsell)
How soon we'll see Sir William? Whisht, he heaves,
And speaks out broken words like ane that raves.

Sym.   He'll soon grow better; – Elspa, haste ye, gae,   110
And fill him up a tass of usquebae.

Sir William *starts up, and speaks*

> A knight that for a Lyon fought,
> Against a herd of bears,
> Was to lang toil and trouble brought,
> In which some thousands shares.   115
> But now again the Lyon rares,
> And joy spreads o'er the plain:
> The Lyon has defeat the bears,
> The knight returns again.
> That knight, in a few days, shall bring   120
> A shepherd frae the fauld,
> And shall present him to his king,
> A subject true and bauld.
> He Mr. Patrick shall be call'd:
> All you that hear me now,   125
> May well believe what I have tald;
> For it shall happen true.

Sym.   Friend, may your spaeing happen soon and weel;
     But, faith, I'm redd you've bargain'd with the deil,
     To tell some tales that fowks wad secret keep: 130
     Or do ye get them tald you in your sleep?

S. Will.   Howe'er I get them, never fash your beard;
     Nor come I to redd fortunes for reward:
     But I'll lay ten to ane with ony here,
     That all I prophesy shall soon appear.   135

Sym.   You prophesying fowks are odd kind men!
     They're here that ken, and here that disna ken,
     The wimpled meaning of your unco tale,
     Whilk soon will mak a noise o'er moor and dale.

Glaud.   'Tis nae sma' sport to hear how Sym believes,   140
     And takes't for gospel what the spae-man gives
     Of flawing fortunes, whilk he evens to Pate:
     But what we wish, we trow at ony rate.

S. Will.   Whisht, doubtfu' carle; for ere the sun
     Has driven twice down to the sea,   145

| | What I have said he shall see done | |
| | In part, or nae mair credit me. | |

Glaud.   Well, be't sae, friend, I shall say nathing mair;
            But I've twa sonsy lasses young and fair,
            Plump ripe for men: I wish ye cou'd foresee   150
            Sic fortunes for them might prove joy to me.

S. Will.   Nae mair thro' secrets can I sift
                Till darkness black the bent:
            I have but anes a day that gift;
                Sae rest a while content.   155

Sym.   Elspa, cast on the claith, fetch butt some meat,
            And, of your best, gar this auld stranger eat.

S. Will.   Delay a while your hospitable care;
            I'd rather enjoy this evening calm and fair,
            Around yon ruin'd tower, to fetch a walk   160
            With you, kind friend, to have some private talk.

Sym.   Soon as you please I'll answer your desire: –
            And, Glaud, you'll take your pipe beside the fire;
            We'll but gae round the Place, and soon be back,
            Syne sup together, and tak our pint, and crack.   165

Glaud.   I'll out a while, and see the young anes play.
            My heart's still light, abeit my locks be gray.
                                                    Exeunt

Act III, Scene III

Jenny pretends an errand hame,
    Young Roger draps the rest,
To whisper out his melting flame,
    And thow his lassie's breast.
Behind a bush, well hid frae sight, they meet: 5
    See Jenny's laughing; Roger's like to greet.
        Poor Shepherd!

72

Roger and Jenny

Rog. Dear Jenny, I wad speak to ye, wad ye let;
And yet I ergh, ye're ay sae scornfu' set.

Jen. And what would Roger say, if he could speak? 10
Am I oblig'd to guess what ye're to seek?

Rog. Yes, ye may guess right eith for what I grein,
Baith by my service, sighs, and langing een.
And I maun out wi't, tho' I risk your scorn;
Ye're never frae my thoughts baith ev'n and morn. 15
Ah! cou'd I loo ye less, I'd happy be;
But happier far, cou'd ye but fancy me.

Jen. And wha kens, honest lad, but that I may;
Ye canna say that e'er I said ye nay.

Rog. Alake! my frighted heart begins to fail, 20
When e'er I mint to tell ye out my tale,
For fear some tighter lad, mair rich than I,
Has win your love, and near your heart may ly.

Jen. I loo my father, cousin Meg I love;
But to this day, nae man my mind could move: 25
Except my kin, ilk lad's alike to me;
And frae ye all I best had keep me free.

Rog. How lang, dear Jenny? – Sayna that again;
What pleasure can ye tak in giving pain?
I'm glad, however, that ye yet stand free: 30
Wha kens but ye may rue, and pity me?

Jen. Ye have my pity else, to see ye set
On that whilk makes our sweetness soon foryet.
Wow! but we're bonny, good, and every thing;
How sweet we breathe, when e'er we kiss, or sing! 35
But we're nae sooner fools to give consent,
Than we our daffine and tint power repent:
When prison'd in four waws, a wife right tame,
Altho' the first, the greatest drudge at hame.

73

Rog.	That only happens when, for sake of gear,	40
	Ane wales a wife, as he wad buy a mear;	
	Or when dull parents bairns together bind	
	Of different tempers, that can ne'er prove kind.	
	But love, true downright love, engages me,	
	Tho' thou should scorn, – still to delight in thee.	45

Jen.	What suggar'd words frae woers lips can fa'!	
	But girning marriage comes and ends them a'.	
	I've seen with shining fair the morning rise,	
	And soon the sleety clouds mirk a' the skies.	
	I've seen the silver spring a while rin clear,	50
	And soon in mossy puddles disappear.	
	The bridegroom may rejoice, the bride may smile;	
	But soon contentions a' their joys beguile.	

Rog.	I've seen the morning rise with fairest light,	
	The day unclouded sink in calmest night.	55
	I've seen the spring rin wimpling thro' the plain,	
	Increase and join the ocean without stain.	
	The bridegroom may be blyth, the bride may smile;	
	Rejoice thro' life, and all your fears beguile.	

Jen.	Were I but sure you lang wou'd love maintain,	60
	The fewest words my easy heart could gain:	
	For I maun own, since now at last you're free,	
	Altho' I jok'd, I lov'd your company;	
	And ever had a warmness in my breast,	
	That made ye dearer to me than the rest.	65

Rog.	I'm happy now! o'er happy! had my head! –	
	This gush of pleasure's like to be my dead.	
	Come to my arms! or strike me! I'm all fir'd	
	With wond'ring love! Let's kiss till we be tir'd.	
	Kiss, kiss! We'll kiss the sun and starns away,	70
	And ferly at the quick return of day!	
	O Jenny! Let my arms about thee twine,	
	And briss thy bonny breasts and lips to mine.	

| Jen. | With equal joy my easy heart gi'es way, | |
| | To own thy well try'd love has won the day. | 75 |

74

Now by these warmest kisses thou has tane,
Swear thus to love me, when by vows made ane.

Rog.   I swear by fifty thousand yet to come,
Or may the first ane strike me deaf and dumb,
There shall not be a kindlier dawted wife,   80
If you agree with me to lead your life.

Jen.   Well, I agree: – Neist, to my parent gae,
Get his consent; – he'll hardly say ye nay.
Ye have what will commend ye to him well,
Auld fowks like them that wants na milk and meal.   85

Rog.   My faulds contain twice fifteen forrow nowt,
As mony newcal in my byers rowt;
Five pack of woo I can at Lammas sell,
Shorn frae my bob-tail'd bleeters on the fell:
Good twenty pair of blankets for our bed,   90
With meikle care, my thrifty mither made.
Ilk thing that makes a heartsome house and tight,
Was still her care, my father's great delight.
They left me all; which now gi'es joy to me,
Because I can give a', my dear, to thee: 95
And had I fifty times as meikle mair,
Nane but my Jenny should the samen skair.
My love and all is yours; now had them fast,
And guide them as ye like, to gar them last.

Jen.   I'll do my best – But see wha comes this way,   100
Patie and Meg; – besides, I mauna stay:
Let's steal frae ither now, and meet the morn;
If we be seen, we'll drie a deal of scorn.

Rog.   To where the saugh-trees shades the mennin-pool,
I'll frae the hill come down, when day grows cool: 105
Keep triste, and meet me there; – there let us meet,
To kiss, and tell our love; – there's nought sae sweet.

This scene presents the knight and Sym
   Within a gallery of the Place,
Where all looks ruinous and grim;
   Nor has the baron shown his face,
But joking with his shepherd leel,   5
   Aft speers the gate he kens fu' well.

Sir William and Symon

S. Will.	To whom belongs this house so much decay'd?

Sym.   To ane that lost it, lending generous aid,
To bear the head up, when rebellious tail
Against the laws of nature did prevail.   10
Sir William Worthy is our Master's name,
Whilk fills us all with joy, now he's come hame.

(Sir William *draps his masking beard,*
   Symon *transported sees*
The welcome knight, with fond regard,   15
   And grasps him round the knees.)

My Master! My dear Master! – do I breathe,
To see him healthy, strong, and free frae skaith;
Return'd to chear his wishing tenants' sight,
To bless his son, my charge, the world's delight!   20

S. Will.   Rise, faithful Symon; in my arms enjoy
A place, thy due, kind guardian of my boy:
I came to view thy care in this disguise,
And am confirm'd thy conduct has been wise;
Since still the secret thou'st securely seal'd,   25
And ne'er to him his real birth reveal'd.

Sym.   The due obedience to your strict command
Was the first lock; – neist, my ain judgment fand
Out reasons plenty; since, without estate,
A youth, tho' sprung frae kings, looks baugh and
    blate.   30

S. *Will.*	And aften vain and idly spend their time,
	'Till grown unfit for action, past their prime,
	Hang on their friends – which gie's their sauls a cast
	That turns them downright beggars at the last.

Sym.	Now well I wat, Sir, ye have spoken true;	35
	For there's Laird Kytie's son, that's loo'd by few:	
	His father steght his fortune in his wame,	
	And left his heir nought but a gentle name.	
	He gangs about sornan frae place to place,	
	As scrimp of manners, as of sense and grace;	40
	Oppressing all as punishment of their sin,	
	That are within his tenth degree of kin;	
	Rins in ilk trader's debt, wha's sae unjust	
	To his ain fam'ly, as to give him trust.	

S. *Will.*	Such useless branches of a common-wealth	45
	Should be lopt off, to give a state mair health.	
	Unworthy bare reflection. – Symon, run	
	O'er all your observations on my son;	
	A parent's fondness easily finds excuse:	
	But do not with indulgence truth abuse.	50

Sym.	To speak his praise, the langest simmer day	
	Wad be o'er short, – could I them right display.	
	In word and deed he can sae well behave,	
	That out of sight he runs before the lave;	
	And when there's e'er a quarrel or contest,	55
	Patrick's made judge to tell whase cause is best.	
	And his decreet stands good; – he'll gar it stand:	
	Wha dares to grumble finds his correcting hand;	
	With a firm look, and a commanding way,	
	He gars the proudest of our herds obey.	60

S. *Will.*	Your tale much pleases; – my good friend, proceed:
	What learning has he? Can he write and read?

Sym.	Baith wonder well; for, troth, I didna spare	
	To gi'e him at the school enough of lair;	
	And he delites in books: – he reads, and speaks	65
	With fowks that ken them, Latin words and Greeks.	

77

S. Will.	Where gets he books to read? – And of what kind?
	Tho' some give light, some blindly lead the blind.
Sym.	Whene'er he drives our sheep to Edinburgh Port,
	He buys some books of history, sangs or sport: 70
	Nor does he want of them a rowth at will,
	And carries ay a poutchfu' to the hill.
	About ane Shakspear, and a famous Ben,
	He aften speaks, and ca's them best of men.
	How sweetly Hawthrenden and Stirling sing, 75
	And ane ca'd Cowley, loyal to his King,
	He kens fu' well, and gars their verses ring.
	I sometimes thought he made o'er great a frase
	About fine poems, histories and plays.
	When I reproved him anes, – a book he brings, 80
	"With this," quoth he, "on braes I crack with kings."
S. Will.	He answer'd well; and much ye glad my ear
	When such accounts I of my shepherd hear.
	Reading such books can raise a peasant's mind
	Above a lord's that is not thus inclin'd. 85
Sym.	What ken we better, that sae sindle look,
	Except on rainy Sundays, on a book;
	When we a leaf or twa haff read haff spell,
	Till a' the rest sleep round, as well's our sell?
S. Will.	Well jested, Symon. – But one question more 90
	I'll only ask ye now, and then give o'er.
	The youth's arriv'd the age when little loves
	Flighter around young hearts like cooing doves:
	Has nae young lassie, with inviting mien,
	And rosy cheek, the wonder of the green, 95
	Engag'd his look, and caught his youthfu' heart?
Sym.	I fear'd the warst, but kend the smallest part,
	Till late I saw him twa three times mair sweet,
	With Glaud's fair neice, than I thought right or meet:
	I had my fears, but now have nought to fear, 100
	Since like your sell your son will soon appear.

A gentleman, enrich'd with all these charms,
May bless the fairest best born lady's arms.

S. Will. This night must end his unambitious fire,
When higher views shall greater thoughts inspire.   105
Go, Symon, bring him quickly here to me;
None but your self shall our first meeting see.
Yonder's my horse and servants nigh at hand,
They come just at the time I gave command;
Straight in my own apparel I'll go dress: 110
Now ye the secret may to all confess.

Sym. With how much joy I on this errand flee!
There's nane can know, that is not downright me.
                                        Exit Symon

                Sir William *solus*

When the event of hopes successfully appears,
One happy hour cancells the toil of years.   115
A thousand toils are lost in Lethe's stream,
And cares evanish like a morning dream;
When wish'd for pleasures rise like morning light,
The pain that's past enhanses the delight.
These joys I feel that words can ill express,   120
I ne'er had known without my late distress.
But from his rustick business and love,
I must in haste my Patrick soon remove,
To courts and camps that may his soul improve.
Like the rough diamond, as it leaves the mine,   125
    Only in little breakings shew its light,
Till artfu' polishing has made it shine:
    Thus education makes the genius bright.

                End of the Third Act

The scene describ'd in former page:
Glaud's onset. – Enter Mause and Madge.

Maus.	Our laird's come hame! And owns young Pate his heir!
	That's news indeed!

Mad.   As true as ye stand there.
As they were dancing all in Symon's yard,   5
Sir William, like a warlock, with a beard
Five nives in length, and white as driven snaw,
Amang us came, cry'd, "Had ye merry a'."
We ferly'd meikle at his unco look,
While frae his pouch he whirled forth a book.   10
As we stood round about him on the green
He view'd us a', but fixed on Pate his een;
Then pawkily pretended he cou'd spae,
Yet for his pains and skill wad nathing ha'e.

Maus.   Then sure the lasses, and ilk gaping coof,
Wad rin about him, and had out their loof.

Mad.   As fast as flaes skip to the tate of woo,
Whilk slee Tod Lawrie hads without his mow,
When he to drown them, and his hips to cool,
In simmer days slides backward in a pool: 20
In short he did, for Pate, braw things fortell,
Without the help of conjuring or spell.
At last, when well diverted, he withdrew,
Pow'd aff his beard to Symon, Symon knew
His welcome Master; – round his knees he gat,   25
Hang at his coat, and syne for blythness grat.
Patrick was sent for; – happy lad is he!
Symon tald Elspa, Elspa tald it me.
Ye'll hear out a' the secret story soon;
And troth 'tis e'en right odd when a' is done,   30
To think how Symon ne'er afore wad tell,
Na, no sae meikle as to Pate himsell.
Our Meg, poor thing, alake! has lost her jo.

Maus.	It may be sae; wha kens? and may be no.
	To lift a love that's rooted, is great pain; 35
	Even kings have tane a queen out of the plain:
	And what has been before, may be again.
Mad.	Sic nonsense! Love tak root, but tocher-good,
	'Tween a herd's bairn, and ane of gentle blood:
	Sic fashions in King Bruce's days might be; 40
	But siccan ferlies now we never see.
Maus.	Gif Pate forsakes her, Bauldy she may gain;
	Yonder he comes, and wow but he looks fain!
	Nae doubt he thinks that Peggy's now his ain.
Mad.	He get her! Slaverin doof; it sets him weil 45
	To yoke a plough where Patrick thought to till.
	Gif I were Meg, I'd let young Master see –
Maus.	Ye'd be as dorty in your choice as he:
	And so wad I. But whisht, here Bauldy comes.

Enter Bauldy singing

Jenny said to Jocky, "Gin ye winna tell,   50
Ye shall be the lad, I'll be the lass my sell.
Ye're a bonny lad, and I'm a lassie free;
Ye're welcomer to tak me than to let me be."
I trow sae. – Lasses will come to at last,
Though for a while they maun their snaw-ba's cast.   55

Maus.	Well, Bauldy, how gaes a'?
Bauld.	Faith, unco right:
	I hope we'll a' sleep sound but ane this night.
Mad.	And wha's the unlucky ane, if we may ask?
Bauld.	To find out that, is nae difficult task;
	Poor bonny Peggy, wha maun think nae mair 60
	On Pate, turn'd Patrick, and Sir William's heir.
	Now, now, good Madge, and honest Mause, stand be,

While Meg's in dumps, put in a word for me.
I'll be as kind as ever Pate could prove;
Less wilful, and ay constant in my love.   65

Mad.   As Neps can witness, and the bushy thorn,
Where mony a time to her your heart was sworn:
Fy! Bauldy, blush, and vows of love regard;
What other lass will trow a mansworn herd?
The curse of heaven hings ay aboon their heads,   70
That's ever guilty of sic sinfu' deeds.
I'll ne'er advise my niece sae gray a gate;
Nor will she be advis'd, fu' well I wate.

Bauld.   Sae gray a gate! Mansworn! and a' the rest:
Ye leed, auld roudes – and, in faith, had best   75
Eat in your words; else I shall gar ye stand
With a het face afore the haly band.

Mad.   Ye'll gar me stand! Ye sheveling-gabit brock;
Speak that again, and, trembling, dread my rock,
And ten sharp nails, that when my hands are in,   80
Can flyp the skin o' ye'r cheeks out o'er your chin.

Bauld.   I tak ye witness, Mause, ye heard her say
That I'm mansworn: – I winna let it gae.

Mad.   Ye're witness to, he ca'd me bonny names,
And should be served as his good breeding claims. 85
Ye filthy dog!

Flees to his hair like a Fury. – A stout battle –
Mause *endeavours to redd them.*

Maus.   Let gang your grips, fy, Madge! howt, Bauldy leen:
I wadna wish this tulzie had been seen;
'Tis sae daft like.

Bauldy *gets out of* Madge's *clutches with a bleeding nose.*

Mad.   'Tis dafter like to thole
An ether-cap, like him, to blaw the coal: 90
It sets him well, with vile unscrapit tongue,

82

To cast up whether I be auld or young;
They're aulder yet than I have married been,
And or they died their bairns' bairns have seen.

Maus.   That's true; and Bauldy, ye was far to blame,   95
To ca' Madge ought but her ain christen'd name.

Bauld.   My lugs, my nose, and nodle finds the same.

Mad.   Auld roudes! Filthy fallow; I shall auld ye.

Maus.   Howt no! – Ye'll e'en be friends with honest Bauldy.
Come, come, shake hands; this maun nae farder gae: 100
Ye maun forgie'm. I see the lad looks wae.

Bauld.   In troth now, Mause, I have at Madge nae spite;
But she abusing first, was a' the wite
Of what has happen'd; And should therefore crave
My pardon first, and shall acquittance have.   105

Mad.   I crave your pardon! Gallows-face, gae greet,
And own your faut to her that ye wad cheat,
Gae, or be blasted in your health and gear,
'Till ye learn to perform, as well as swear.
Vow and lowp back! – Was e'er the like heard tell? 110
Swith, tak him Deil; he's o'er lang out of hell!

Bauldy running off

His Presence be about us! Curst were he
That were condemn'd for life to live with thee.
Exit Bauldy

Madge laughing

I think I've towzl'd his harigalds a wee;
He'll no soon grein to tell his love to me.   115
He's but a rascal that wad mint to serve
A lassie sae, he does but ill deserve.

Maus.   Ye towin'd him tightly – I commend ye for't;
His blooding snout gave me nae little sport:

For this forenoon he had that scant of grace,   120
And breeding baith, – to tell me to my face,
He hop'd I was a witch, and wadna stand,
To lend him in this case my helping hand.

Mad.   A witch! – How had ye patience this to bear,
         And leave him een to see, or lugs to hear?   125

Maus.   Auld wither'd hands, and feeble joints like mine,
         Obliges fowk resentment to decline;
         Till aft 'tis seen, when vigour fails, then we
         With cunning can the lake of pith supplie.
         Thus I pat aff revenge till it was dark,   130
         Syne bade him come, and we should gang to wark:
         I'm sure he'll keep his triste; and I came here
         To seek your help, that we the fool may fear.

Mad.   And special sport we'll have, as I protest;
         Ye'll be the witch, and I shall play the ghaist,   135
         A linen sheet wond round me like ane dead,
         I'll cawk my face, and grane, and shake my head.
         We'll fleg him sae, he'll mint nae mair to gang
         A conjuring, to do a lassie wrang.

Maus.   Then let us go; for see, 'tis hard on night,   140
         The westlin cloud shines red with setting light.
                                                Exeunt

Act IV, Scene II

When birds begin to nod upon the bough,
And the green swaird grows damp with falling dew,
While good Sir William is to rest retir'd,
The gentle shepherd, tenderly inspir'd,
Walks through the broom with Roger ever leel,   5
To meet, to comfort Meg, and tak farewell.

Rog.   Wow! But I'm cadgie, and my heart lowps light
         O, Mr. Patrick! Ay your thoughts were right:

84

Sure gentle fowk are farther seen than we,
That naithing ha'e to brag of pedigree.   10
My Jenny now, wha brak my heart this morn,
Is perfect yielding, – sweet, and nae mair scorn.
I spake my mind – she heard – I spake again,
She smil'd – I kiss'd – I woo'd, nor woo'd in vain.

Pat.   I'm glad to hear't – But O my change this day   15
Heaves up my joy, and yet I'm sometimes wae.
I've found a father, gently kind as brave,
And an estate that lifts me 'boon the lave.
With looks all kindness, words that love confest;
He all the father to my soul exprest,   20
While close he held me to his manly breast.
Such were the eyes, he said, thus smil'd the mouth
Of thy lov'd mother, blessing of my youth;
Who set too soon! – And while he praise bestow'd,
Adown his graceful cheek a torrent flow'd.   25
My new-born joys, and this his tender tale,
Did, mingled thus, o'er a' my thoughts prevail:
That speechless lang, my late kend sire I view'd,
While gushing tears my panting breast bedew'd.
Unusual transports made my head turn round,   30
Whilst I myself with rising raptures found
The happy son of ane sae much renown'd.
But he has heard! too faithful Symon's fear
Has brought my love for Peggy to his ear;
Which he forbids. – Ah! this confounds my peace,   35
While thus to beat, my heart shall sooner cease.

Rog.   How to advise ye, troth I'm at a stand:
But were't my case, ye'd clear it up aff hand.

Pat.   Duty, and haflen reason plead his cause:
But what cares love for reason, rules and laws?   40
Still in my heart my shepherdess excells,
And part of my new happiness repells.

Rog.   Enjoy them baith. – Sir William will be won:
Your Peggy's bonny; – you're his only son.

Pat.	She's mine by vows, and stronger ties of love; 45
	And frae these bands nae change my mind shall move.
	I'll wed nane else; thro' life I will be true:
	But still obedience is a parent's due.
Rog.	Is not our Master and your sell to stay
	Amang us here? – or are ye gawn away 50
	To London Court, or ither far aff parts,
	To leave your ain poor us with broken hearts?
Pat.	To Edinburgh straight to-morrow we advance,
	To London neist, and afterwards to France,
	Where I must stay some years, and learn – to dance, 55
	And twa three other monky-tricks. – That done,
	I come hame struting in my red-heel'd shoon.
	Then 'tis design'd, when I can well behave,
	That I maun be some petted thing's dull slave,
	For some few bags of cash, that I wat weel 60
	I nae mair need nor carts do a third wheel.
	But Peggy, dearer to me than my breath,
	Sooner than hear sic news, shall hear my death.
Rog.	'They wha have just enough, can soundly sleep;
	The o'ercome only fashes fowk to keep.' – 65
	Good Mr. Patrick, tak your ain tale hame.
Pat.	What was my morning thought, at night's the same.
	The poor and rich but differ in the name.
	Content's the greatest bliss we can procure
	Frae 'boon the lift. – Without it kings are poor. 70
Rog.	But an estate like yours yields braw content,
	When we but pick it scantly on the bent:
	Fine claiths, saft beds, sweet houses, and red wine,
	Good chear, and witty friends, whene'er ye dine;
	Obeysant servants, honour, wealth and ease: 75
	Wha's no content with these, are ill to please.
Pat.	Sae Roger thinks, and thinks not far amiss;
	But mony a cloud hings hovering o'er the bliss.

The passions rule the roast; – and, if they're sowr,
Like the lean ky, will soon the fat devour.   80
The spleen, tint honour, and affronted pride,
Stang like the sharpest goads in gentry's side,
The gouts and gravels, and the ill disease,
Are frequentest with fowk o'erlaid with ease;
While o'er the moor the shepherd, with less care,   85
Enjoys his sober wish, and halesome air.

Rog. Lord, man! I wonder ay, and it delights
My heart, whene'er I hearken to your flights.
How gat ye a' that sense, I fain wad lear,
That I may easier disappointments bear.   90

Pat. Frae books, the wale of books, I gat some skill;
These best can teach what's real good and ill.
Ne'er grudge ilk year to ware some stanes of cheese,
To gain these silent friends that ever please.

Rog. I'll do't, and ye shall tell me which to buy: 95
Faith, I'se hae books, tho' I should sell my ky.
But now let's hear how you're design'd to move,
Between Sir William's will, and Peggy's love.

Pat. Then here it lyes; – his will maun be obey'd;
My vows I'll keep, and she shall be my bride: 100
But I some time this last design maun hide.
Keep you the secret close, and leave me here;
I sent for Peggy, yonder comes my dear.

Rog. Pleas'd that ye trust me with the secret, I
To wyle it frae me a' the deils defy.   105
                                        Exit Roger

                    Patie *solus*

With what a struggle must I now impart
My father's will to her that hads my heart!
I ken she loves, and her saft saul will sink,
While it stands trembling on the hated brink
Of disappointment. – Heaven! support my fair,   110

And let her comfort claim your tender care.
Her eyes are red!

Enter Peggy

My Peggy, why in tears?
Smile as ye wont, allow nae room for fears:
Tho' I'm nae mair a shepherd, yet I'm thine.

Peg.   I dare not think sae high: I now repine   115
At the unhappy chance, that made not me
A gentle match, or still a herd kept thee.
Wha can, withoutten pain, see frae the coast
The ship that bears his all like to be lost?
Like to be carry'd, by some rever's hand,   120
Far frae his wishes, to some distant land?

Pat.   Ne'er quarrel fate, whilst it with me remains,
To raise thee up, or still attend these plains.
My father has forbid our loves, I own:
But love's superior to a parent's frown.   125
I falshood hate: come, kiss thy cares away;
I ken to love, as well as to obey.
Sir William's generous; leave the task to me,
To make strict duty and true love agree.

Peg.   Speak on! – Speak ever thus, and still my grief;   130
But short I dare to hope the fond relief.
New thoughts a gentler face will soon inspire,
That with nice air swims round in silk attire:
Then I, poor me! – With sighs may ban my fate,
When the young laird's nae mair my heartsome Pate, 135
Nae mair again to hear sweet tales exprest,
By the blyth shepherd that excell'd the rest:
Nae mair be envy'd by the tattling gang
When Patie kiss'd me, when I danc'd or sang:
Nae mair, alake! we'll on the meadow play!   140
And rin haff breathless round the rucks of hay;
As aftimes I have fled from thee right fain,
And fawn on purpose, that I might be tane.
Nae mair around the Foggy-know I'll creep

	To watch and stare upon thee, while asleep.	145
	But hear my vow – 'twill help to give me ease;	
	May sudden death, or deadly sair disease,	
	And warst of ills attend my wretched life,	
	If e'er to ane, but you, I be a wife.	

Pat. Sure, heaven approves – and be assur'd of me, 150
I'll ne'er gang back of what I've sworn to thee:
And time, tho' time maun interpose a while,
And I maun leave my Peggy and this isle;
Yet time, nor distance, nor the fairest face,
If there's a fairer, e'er shall fill thy place. 155
I'd hate my rising fortune, should it move
The fair foundation of our faithful love.
If at my foot were crowns and scepters laid,
To bribe my soul frae thee, delightful maid;
For thee I'd soon leave these inferior things 160
To sic as have the patience to be kings.
Wherefore that tear? Believe, and calm thy mind.

Peg. I greet for joy, to hear thy words sae kind.
When hopes were sunk, and nought but mirk despair
Made me think life was little worth my care, 165
My heart was like to burst; but now I see
Thy generous thoughts will save thy love for me.
With patience then I'll wait each wheeling year,
Hope time away, till thou with joy appear;
And all the while I'll study gentler charms, 170
To make me fitter for my traveller's arms:
I'll gain on Uncle Glaud – he's far frae fool,
And will not grudge to put me thro' ilk school;
Where I may manners learn.

Pat.   That's wisely said,
And what he wares that way shall be well paid. 175
Tho' without a' the little helps of art,
Thy native sweets might gain a prince's heart:
Yet now, lest in our station, we offend,
We must learn modes, to innocence unkend;
Affect aftimes to like the thing we hate, 180

And drap serenity, to keep up state:
Laugh, when we're sad; speak, when we've nought
   to say;
And, for the fashion, when we're blyth, seem wae:
Pay compliments to them we aft have scorn'd;
Then scandalize them, when their backs are turn'd.   185

Peg.   If this is gentry, I had rather be
What I am still – But I'll be ought with thee.

Pat.   No, no, my Peggy, I but only jest
With gentry's apes; for still amangst the best,
Good manners give integrity a bleez,   190
When native vertues join the arts to please.

Peg.   Since with nae hazard, and sae small expence,
My lad frae books can gather siccan sense;
Then why, ah! why should the tempestuous sea,
Endanger thy dear life, and frighten me?   195
Sir William's cruel, that wad force his son,
For watna-whats, sae great a risk to run.

Pat.   There is nae doubt but travelling does improve,
Yet I would shun it for thy sake, my love.
But soon as I've shook aff my landwart cast   200
In foreign cities, hame to thee I'll haste.

Peg.   With every setting day, and rising morn,
I'll kneel to heaven, and ask thy safe return.
Under that tree, and on the Suckler Brae,
Where aft we wont, when bairns, to run and play;   205
And to the hissel-shaw where first ye vow'd
Ye wad be mine, and I as eithly trow'd,
I'll aften gang, and tell the trees and flowers,
With joy, that they'll bear witness I am yours.

Pat.   My dear, allow me, frae thy temples fair,   210
A shining ringlet of thy flowing hair;
Which, as a sample of each lovely charm,
I'll aften kiss, and wear about my arm.

Peg. Were't in my power with better boons to please,
I'd give the best I could with the same ease; 215
Nor wad I, if thy luck had faln to me,
Been in ae jot less generous to thee.

Pat. I doubt it not; but since we've little time
To ware't on words, wad border on a crime:
Love's safter meaning better is exprest, 220
When 'tis with kisses on the heart imprest.

Exeunt

End of the Fourth Act

Act V, Scene I

*See how poor Bauldy stares like ane possest,
And roars up Symon frae his kindly rest.
Bare leg'd, with night-cap, and unbutton'd coat,
See, the auld man comes forward to the sot.*

Sym. What want ye, Bauldy, at this early hour, 5
While drowsy sleep keeps a' beneath its pow'r?
Far to the north, the scant approaching light
Stands equal 'twixt the morning and the night.
What gars ye shake and glowr, and look sae wan?
Your teeth they chitter, hair like bristles stand. 10

Baul. O len me soon some water, milk or ale,
My head's grown giddy, – legs with shaking fail;
I'll ne'er dare venture forth at night my lane:
Alake! I'll never be my sell again.
I'll ne'er o'erput it! Symon! O Symon! O! 15

Symon gives him a drink

Sym. What ails thee, gowk! – to make sae loud ado?
You've waked Sir William, he has left his bed;
He comes, I fear ill-pleas'd: I hear his tred.

Enter Sir William

S. Will.   How goes the night? Does day-light yet appear?
          Symon, you're very timeously asteer.   20

Sym.   I'm sorry, sir, that we've disturb'd your rest:
          But some strange thing has Bauldy's sp'rit opprest;
          He's seen some witch, or wrestl'd with a ghaist.

Baul.   O ay, – dear sir, in troth 'tis very true;
          And I am come to make my plaint to you.   25

                   Sir William *smiling*

I lang to hear't.

Baul.   Ah! Sir, the witch ca'd Mause,
          That wins aboon the mill amang the haws,
          First promis'd that she'd help me with her art,
          To gain a bonny thrawart lassie's heart.
          As she had tristed, I met wi'er this night;   30
          But may nae friend of mine get sic a fright!
          For the curs'd hag, instead of doing me good,
          (The very thought o't's like to freeze my blood!)
          Rais'd up a ghaist or deil, I kenna whilk,
          Like a dead corse in sheet as white as milk;   35
          Black hands it had, and face as wan as death,
          Upon me fast the witch and it fell baith,
          And gat me down; while I, like a great fool,
          Was laboured as I wont to be at school.
          My heart out of its hool was like to lowp;   40
          I pithless grew with fear, and had nae hope,
          Till, with an elritch laugh, they vanish'd quite:
          Syne I, haff dead with anger, fear and spite,
          Crap up, and fled straight frae them, sir, to you,
          Hoping your help, to gi'e the Deil his due.   45
          I'm sure my heart will ne'er gi'e o'er to dunt,
          Till in a fat tar-barrel Mause be burnt.

S. Will.   Well, Bauldy, whate'er's just shall granted be;
          Let Mause be brought this morning down to me.

Baul.	Thanks to your Honour; soon shall I obey:	50

Baul.   Thanks to your Honour; soon shall I obey: 50
But first I'll Roger raise, and twa three mae,
To catch her fast, or she get leave to squeel,
And cast her cantraips that bring up the Deil.

Exit Bauldy

S. *Will.*   Troth, Symon, Bauldy's more afraid than hurt,
The witch and ghaist have made themselves good
    sport.   55
What silly notions crowd the clouded mind,
That is thro' want of education blind!

Sym.   But does your Honour think there's nae sic thing
As witches raising deils up thro' a ring?
Syne playing tricks, a thousand I cou'd tell,   60
Cou'd never be contriv'd on this side hell.

S. *Will.*   Such as the Devil's dancing in a moor
Amongst a few old women craz'd and poor,
Who are rejoic'd to see him frisk and lowp
O'er braes and bogs, with candles in his dowp;   65
Appearing sometimes like a black-horn'd cow,
Aftimes like bawty, badrans, or a sow:
Then with his train thro' airy paths to glide,
While they on cats, or clowns, or broom-staffs ride;
Or in the egg-shell skim out o'er the main,   70
To drink their leader's health in France or Spain:
Then aft by night, bumbaze hare-hearted fools,
By tumbling down their cupboard, chairs and stools.
Whate'er's in spells, or if there witches be,
Such whimsies seem the most absurd to me.   75

Sym.   'Tis true enough, we ne'er heard that a witch
Had either meikle sense, or yet was rich.
But Mause, tho' poor, is a sagacious wife,
And lives a quiet and very honest life;
That gars me think this hobleshew that's past   80
Will land in naithing but a joke at last.

S. Will.	I'm sure it will: – But see increasing light
	Commands the imps of darkness down to night;
	Bid raise my servants, and my horse prepare, 85
	Whilst I walk out to take the morning air.

Act V, Scene II

While Peggy laces up her bosom fair,
With a blew snood Jenny binds up her hair;
Glaud by his morning ingle takes a beek,
The rising sun shines motty thro' the reek,
A pipe his mouth; the lasses please his een,   5
And now and than his joke maun interveen.

Glaud.	I wish, my bairns, it may keep fair till night;
	Ye do not use sae soon to see the light.
	Nae doubt now ye intend to mix the thrang,
	To take your leave of Patrick or he gang. 10
	But do ye think that now, when he's a laird,
	That he poor landwart lasses will regard?

Jen.	Though he's young Master now, I'm very sure
	He has mair sense than slight auld friends, tho' poor.
	But yesterday he ga'e us mony a tug, 15
	And kiss'd my cousin there frae lug to lug.

Glaud.	Ay, ay, nae doubt o't, and he'll do't again;
	But, be advis'd, his company refrain:
	Before he, as a shepherd, sought a wife,
	With her to live a chast and frugal life; 20
	But now grown gentle, soon he will forsake
	Sic godly thoughts, and brag of being a rake.

Peg.	A rake! – What's that? – sure if it means ought ill,
	He'll never be't; else I have tint my skill.

Glaud.	Daft lassie, ye ken nought of the affair, 25
	Ane young and good and gentle's unco' rare.

A rake's a graceless spark, that thinks nae shame,
To do what like of us thinks sin to name:
Sic are sae void of shame, they'll never stap
To brag how aften they have had the clap.   30
They'll tempt young things, like you, with youdith
    flush'd;
Syne make ye a' their jest, when ye're debauch'd.
Be warry then, I say, and never gi'e
Encouragement, or bourd with sic as he.

Peg.   Sir William's vertuous, and of gentle blood;   35
And may not Patrick too, like him, be good?

Glaud.   That's true, and mony gentry mae than he,
As they are wiser, better are than we;
But thinner sawn: they're sae puft up with pride,
There's mony of them mocks ilk haly guide,   40
That shaws the gate to heaven. – I've heard my sell,
Some of them laugh at doomsday, sin and hell.

Jen.   Watch o'er us, father! Heh! that's very odd;
Sure him that doubts a doomsday, doubts a God.

Glaud.   Doubt! why, they neither doubt, nor judge, nor
    think,
                                       45
Nor hope, nor fear; but curse, debauch and drink!
But I'm no saying this, as if I thought
That Patrick to sic gates will e'er be brought.

Peg.   The Lord forbid! Na, he kens better things:
But here comes Aunt; her face some ferly brings.   50

Enter Madge

Haste, haste ye; we're a' sent for o'er the gate,
To hear, and help to redd some odd debate
'Tween Mause and Bauldy, 'bout some witchcraft
    spell,
At Symon's house: the knight sits judge himsell.

95

| Glaud. | Lend me my staff; – Madge, lock the outer-door, | 55 |
| | And bring the lasses wi' ye; I'll step before. | |

Exit Glaud

Mad.	Poor Meg! – Look, Jenny, was the like e'er seen,	
	How bleer'd and red with greeting look her een?	
	This day her brankan wooer takes his horse,	
	To strute a gentle spark at Edinburgh Cross;	60
	To change his kent, cut frae the branchy plain,	
	For a nice sword, and glancing-headed cane;	
	To leave his ram-horn spoons, and kitted whey,	
	For gentler tea, that smells like new won hay;	
	To leave the green-swaird dance, when we gae milk,	65
	To rustle amang the beauties clad in silk.	
	But Meg, poor Meg! maun with the shepherd stay,	
	And tak what God will send, in hodden-gray.	

Peg.	Dear Aunt, what need ye fash us wi' your scorn?	
	That's no my faut that I'm nae gentler born.	70
	Gif I the daughter of some laird had been,	
	I ne'er had notic'd Patie on the green:	
	Now since he rises, why should I repine?	
	If he's made for another, he'll ne'er be mine:	
	And then, the like has been, if the decree	75
	Designs him mine, I yet his wife may be.	

| Mad. | A bonny story, trowth! – But we delay: | |
| | Prin up your aprons baith, and come away. | |

Exeunt

Act V, Scene III

Sir William fills the twa-arm'd chair,
  While Symon, Roger, Glaud and Mause,
Attend, and with loud laughter hear
  Daft Bauldy bluntly plead his cause:
For now 'tis tell'd him that the taz   5
  Was handled by revengefu' Madge,
Because he brak good breeding's laws,
  And with his nonsense rais'd their rage.

S. Will.	And was that all? Well, Bauldy, ye was serv'd
	No otherwise than what ye well deserv'd. 10
	Was it so small a matter, to defame,
	And thus abuse an honest woman's name?
	Besides your going about to have betray'd
	By perjury an innocent young maid.
Baul.	Sir, I confess my faut thro' a' the steps, 15
	And ne'er again shall be untrue to Neps.
Maus.	Thus far, sir, he oblig'd me on the score;
	I kend not that they thought me sic before.
Bau..	An't like your Honour, I believ'd it well;
	But trowth I was e'en doilt to seek the Deil: 20
	Yet, with your Honour's leave, tho' she's nae witch,
	She's baith a slee and a revengefu' bitch,
	And that my some-place finds; but I had best
	Had in my tongue; for yonder comes the ghaist,
	And the young bonny witch, whase rosy cheek 25
	Sent me, without my wit, the Deil to seek.

Enter Madge, Peggy, *and* Jenny

Sir William, *looking at* Peggy

	Whose daughter's she that wears th' *Aurora* gown,
	With face so fair, and locks a lovely brown?
	How sparkling are her eyes! What's this? I find
	The girl brings all my sister to my mind. 30
	Such were the features once adorn'd a face,
	Which death too soon depriv'd of sweetest grace.
	Is this your daughter, Glaud?
Glaud.	Sir, she's my niece; –
	And yet she's not: – But I should hald my peace.
S. Will.	This is a contradiction: what d'ye mean? 35
	She is, and is not! Pray thee, Glaud, explain.
Glaud.	Because I doubt, if I should make appear
	What I have kept a secret thirteen year.

Maus.	You may reveal what I can fully clear.
S. Will.	Speak soon – I'm all impatience! 40
Pat.	So am I! For much I hope, and hardly yet know why.
Glaud.	Then, since my Master orders, I obey. This bonny fundling, ae clear morn of May, Close by the lee-side of my door I found, All sweet and clean, and carefully hapt round, 45 In infant-weeds of rich and gentle make. What cou'd they be, thought I, did thee forsake? Wha, warse than brutes, cou'd leave expos'd to air Sae much of innocence sae sweetly fair, Sae hopeless young? For she appear'd to me 50 Only about twa towmands auld to be. I took her in my arms; the bairnie smil'd With sic a look wad made a savage mild. I hid the story: she has past sincesyne As a poor orphan, and a niece of mine. 55 Nor do I rue my care about the we'an, For she's well worth the pains that I have tane. Ye see she's bonny, I can swear she's good, And am right sure she's come of gentle blood: Of whom I kenna. – Nathing ken I mair, 60 Than what I to your Honour now declare.
S. Will.	This tale seems strange!
Pat.	The tale delights my ear;
S. Will.	Command your joys, young man, till truth appear.
Maus.	That be my task. – Now, sir, bid all be hush; Peggy may smile; – thou hast nae cause to blush. 65 Long have I wish'd to see this happy day, That I might safely to the truth give way; That I may now Sir William Worthy name, The best and nearest friend that she can claim:

| | He saw't at first, and with quick eye did trace | 70 |
| | His sister's beauty in her daughter's face. |

S. *Will.*   Old woman, do not rave, – prove what you say;
'Tis dangerous in affairs like this to play.

Pat.   What reason, sir, can an old woman have
To tell a lie, when she's sae near her grave?   75
But how, or why, it should be truth, I grant,
I every thing looks like a reason want.

Omnes.   The story's odd! we wish we heard it out.

S. *Will.*   Mak haste, good woman, and resolve each doubt.

Mause *goes forward, leading* Peggy *to* Sir William

Maus.   Sir, view me well: has fifteen years so plow'd   80
A wrinkled face that you have often view'd,
That here I as an unknown stranger stand,
Who nurs'd her mother that now holds my hand?
Yet stronger proofs I'll give, if you demand.

S. *Will.*   Ha! Honest nurse, where were my eyes before!   85
I know thy faithfulness, and need no more;
Yet, from the lab'rinth to lead out my mind,
Say, to expose her who was so unkind?

Sir William *embraces* Peggy, *and makes her sit by him*

Yes, surely thou'rt my niece; truth must prevail:
But no more words, till Mause relate her tale.   90

Pat.   Good nurse, go on; nae musick's haff sae fine,
Or can give pleasure like these words of thine.

Maus.   Then, it was I that sav'd her infant-life,
Her death being threat'ned by an uncle's wife.
The story's lang; but I the secret knew,   95
How they pursu'd, with avaritious view,
Her rich estate, of which they're now possest:
All this to me a confident confest.

99

I heard with horror, and with trembling dread,
They'd smoor the sakeless orphan in her bed! 100
That very night, when all were sunk in rest,
At midnight hour, the floor I saftly prest,
And staw the sleeping innocent away;
With whom I travel'd some few miles e'er day:
All day I hid me, – when the day was done, 105
I kept my journey, lighted by the moon,
Till eastward fifty miles I reach'd these plains,
Where needful plenty glads your chearful swains;
Afraid of being found out, I, to secure
My charge, e'en laid her at this shepherd's door, 110
And took a neighbouring cottage here, that I,
Whate'er should happen to her, might be by.
Here honest Glaud himsell, and Symon may
Remember well, how I that very day
Frae Roger's father took my little crove. 115

 Glaud, *with tears of joy happing down his beard*

I well remember't. Lord reward your love:
Lang have I wish'd for this; for aft I thought,
Sic knowledge sometime should about be brought.

Pat.   'Tis now a crime to doubt, – my joys are full,
With due obedience to my parent's will. 120
Sir, with paternal love survey her charms,
And blame me not for rushing to her arms.
She's mine by vows; and would, tho' still unknown,
Have been my wife, when I my vows durst own.

S. Will. My niece, my daughter, welcome to my care, 125
Sweet image of thy mother good and fair,
Equal with Patrick: now my greatest aim
Shall be to aid your joys, and well-match'd flame.
My boy, receive her from your father's hand,
With as good will as either would demand. 130

Patie *and* Peggy *embrace, and kneel to* Sir William

Pat.   With as much joy this blessing I receive,
As ane wad life, that's sinking in a wave.

I give you both my blessing: may your love
Produce a happy race, and still improve.

Peg.   My wishes are compleat, my joys arise,   135
        While I'm haff dizzy with the blest surprise.
        And am I then a match for my ain lad,
        That for me so much generous kindness had?
        Lang may Sir William bless these happy plains,
        Happy while heaven grant he on them remains.   140

Pat.   Be lang our guardian, still our Master be;
        We'll only crave what you shall please to gi'e:
        The estate be yours, my Peggy's ane to me.

Glaud. I hope your Honour now will take amends
        Of them that sought her life for wicked ends.   145

S. Will. The base unnatural villain soon shall know,
        That eyes above watch the affairs below.
        I'll strip him soon of all to her pertains,
        And make him reimburse his ill got gains.

Peg.   To me the views of wealth and an estate,   150
        Seem light when put in ballance with my Pate!
        For his sake only, I'll ay thankful bow
        For such a kindness, best of men, to you.

Sym.   What double blythness wakens up this day!
        I hope now, sir, you'll no soon haste away.   155
        Sall I unsadle your horse, and gar prepare
        A dinner for ye of hale country fare?
        See how much joy unwrinkles every brow;
        Our looks hing on the twa, and doat on you!
        Even Bauldy the bewitch'd has quite forgot   160
        Fell Madge's taz, and pawky Mause's plot.

S. Will. Kindly old man, remain with you this day,
        I never from these fields again will stray:
        Masons and wrights shall soon my house repair.

	And bussy gardners shall new planting rear;	165
	My father's hearty table you soon shall see	
	Restor'd, and my best friends rejoyce with me.	

Sym.   That's the best news I heard this twenty year;
          New day breaks up, rough times begin to clear.

Glaud.   God save the King, and save Sir William lang,   170
          To enjoy their ain, and raise the shepherds' sang.

Rog.   Wha winna dance? Wha will refuse to sing?
          What shepherd's whistle winna lilt the spring?

Baul.   I'm friends with Mause, – with very Madge I'm 'greed,
          Although they skelpit me when woodly fleid.   175
          I'm now fu' blyth, and frankly can forgive,
          To join and sing, "Lang may Sir William live."

Mad.   Lang may he live: – And, Bauldy, learn to steek
          Your gab a wee, and think before ye speak;
          And never ca' her auld that wants a man,   180
          Else ye may yet some witches' fingers ban.
          This day I'll wi' the youngest of ye rant,
          And brag for ay, that I was ca'd the aunt
          Of our young lady, – my dear bonny bairn!

Peg.   No other name I'll ever for you learn. –   185
          And, my good nurse, how shall I gratefu' be,
          For a' thy matchless kindness done for me?

Maus.   The flowing pleasures of this happy day
          Does fully all I can require repay.

S. Will.   To faithful Symon and, kind Glaud, to you,   190
          And to your heirs I give in endless feu,
          The mailens ye possess, as justly due,
          For acting like kind fathers to the pair,
          Who have enough besides, and these can spare.
          Mause, in my house in calmness close your days,   195
          With nought to do, but sing your Maker's praise.

| Omnes. | The Lord of Heaven return your Honour's love, |
| | Confirm your joys, and a' your blessings roove. |

Patie, *presenting* Roger *to* Sir William

Sir, here's my trusty friend, that always shar'd
My bosom secrets, ere I was a laird;   200
Glaud's daughter Janet (Jenny, thinkna shame)
Rais'd, and maintains in him a lover's flame:
Lang was he dumb, at last he spake, and won,
And hopes to be our honest uncle's son:
Be pleas'd to speak to Glaud for his consent,   205
That nane may wear a face of discontent.

S. Will.	My son's demand is fair, – Glaud, let me crave,
	That trusty Roger may your daughter have,
	With frank consent; and while he does remain
	Upon these fields, I make him chamberlain. 210

Glaud.	You crowd your bounties, sir, what can we say,
	But that we're dyvours that can ne'er repay?
	Whate'er your Honour will, I shall obey.
	Roger, my daughter, with my blessing, take,
	And still our master's right your business make, 215
	Please him, be faithful, and this auld gray head
	Shall nod with quietness down amang the dead.

Rog.	I ne'er was good a speaking a' my days,
	Or ever loo'd to make o'er great a fraise:
	But for my master, father, and my wife, 220
	I will employ the cares of all my life.

S. Will.	My friends, I'm satisfied you'll all behave,
	Each in his station, as I'd wish or crave.
	Be ever vertuous, soon or late you'll find
	Reward, and satisfaction to your mind. 225
	The maze of life sometimes looks dark and wild;
	And oft, when hopes are highest, we're beguil'd.
	Aft, when we stand on brinks of dark despair,
	Some happy turn with joy dispells our care.
	Now all's at rights, who sings best let me hear. 230

103

Peg.　　　When you demand, I readiest should obey:
　　　　　I'll sing you ane, the newest that I ha'e.

　　　Sings to the tune of Corn-riggs Are Bonny

　　　My Patie is a lover gay,
　　　　His mind is never muddy;
　　　His breath is sweeter than new hay,　　　　　235
　　　　His face is fair and ruddy:
　　　His shape is handsome, middle size;
　　　　He's comely in his wauking:
　　　The shining of his een surprise;
　　　　'Tis heaven to hear him tawking.　　　　　240
　　　Last night I met him on a bawk,
　　　　Where yellow corn was growing,
　　　There mony a kindly word he spake,
　　　　That set my heart a-glowing.
　　　He kiss'd, and vow'd he wad be mine,　　　　245
　　　　And loo'd me best of ony,
　　　That gars me like to sing since syne,
　　　　O corn-riggs are bonny.
　　　Let lasses of a silly mind
　　　　Refuse what maist they're wanting;　　　　250
　　　Since we for yielding were design'd,
　　　　We chastly should be granting.
　　　Then I'll comply, and marry Pate,
　　　　And syne my cockernonny
　　　He's free to touzel air or late,　　　　　255
　　　　Where corn-riggs are bonny.

　　　　　　　　　　　　　　　　Exeunt omnes

THE MONK AND THE MILLER'S WIFE

A TALE

Now lend your lugs, ye benders fine,
Wha ken the benefit of wine;
And you wha laughing scud brown ale,
Leave jinks a wee, and hear a tale.
  An honest miller wond in Fife,   5
That had a young and wanton wife,
Wha sometimes thol'd the parish priest
To make her man a twa-horn'd beast:
He paid right mony visits till her;
And to keep in with Hab the miller,   10
He endeavour'd aft to mak him happy,
Where e'er he kend the ale was nappy.
Sic condescension in a pastor,
Knit Halbert's love to him the faster;
And by his converse, troth 'tis true,   15
Hab learn'd to preach when he was fou.
Thus all the three were wonder pleas'd,
The wife well serv'd, the men well eas'd.
This ground his corns, and that did cherish
Himsell with dining round the parish.   20
Bess the good-wife thought it nae skaith,
Since she was able to serve them baith.
  When equal is the night and day,
And Ceres gives the schools the play,
A youth sprung frae a gentle *pater*,   25
Bred at Saint Andro's *Alma Mater*,
Ae day gawn hameward, it fell late,
And him benighted by the gate:
To ly without, pit-mirk did shore him;
He couldna see his thumb before him: 30
But, clack, – clack, – clack, he heard a mill,

Whilk led him be the lugs theretill.
To tak the threed of tale alang,
This mill to Halbert did belang.
Not less this note your notice claims,   35
The scholar's name was Master James.
    Now, smiling Muse, the prelude past,
Smoothly relate a tale shall last
As lang as Alps and Grampian Hills,
As lang as wind or water-mills.   40
    In enter'd James, Hab saw and kend him,
And offer'd kindly to befriend him
With sic good chear as he cou'd make,
Baith for his ain and father's sake.
The scholar thought himsell right sped,   45
And gave him thanks in terms well bred.
Quoth Hab: "I canna leave my mill
As yet; – but step ye west the kill
A bow-shot, and ye'll find my hame:
Gae warm ye, and crack with our dame,   50
Till I set aff the mill; syne we
Shall tak what Bessy has to gi'e."
James, in return, what's handsome said,
O'er lang to tell; and aff he gade.
Out of the house some light did shine,   55
Which led him till't as with a line:
Arriv'd, he knock'd; for doors were steekit;
Straight throw a window Bessy keekit,
And cries: "Wha's that gie's fowk a fright
At sic untimous time of night?"   60
James with good humour, maist discreetly,
Tald her his circumstance completely.
"I dinna ken ye," quoth the wife,
"And up and down the thieves are rife:
Within my lane, I'm but a woman;   65
Sae I'll unbar my door to nae man.
But since 'tis very like, my dow,
That all ye're telling may be true,
Hae there's a key, gang in your way
At the neist door, there's braw ait strae;   70
Streek down upon't, my lad, and learn

106

They're no ill-lodg'd that get a barn."
Thus after meikle clitter-clatter,
James fand he couldna mend the matter;
And since it might not better be,   75
With resignation took the key,
Unlocked the barn, – clam up the mou,
Where there was an opening near the hou,
Throw whilk he saw a glent of light,
That gave diversion to his sight: 80
By this he quickly cou'd discern
A thin wa' separate house and barn,
And throw this rive was in the wa',
All done within the house he saw:
He saw (what ought not to be seen,   85
And scarce gave credit to his een)
The parish priest of reverend fame
In active courtship with the dame. –
To lengthen out description here,
Wou'd but offend the modest ear,   90
And beet the lewder youthfu' flame,
That we by satyre strive to tame.
Suppose the wicked action o'er,
And James continuing still to glowre;
Wha saw the wife, as fast as able,   95
Spread a clean servite on the table,
And syne, frae the ha' ingle, bring ben
A pyping het young roasted hen,
And twa good bottles stout and clear,
Ane of strong ale, and ane of beer.   100
   But wicked luck, just as the priest
Shot in his fork in chucky's breast,
Th'unwelcome miller ga'e a roar,
Cry'd: "Bessy, haste ye open the door!"
With that the haly letcher fled,   105
And darn'd himsell behind a bed;
While Bessy huddl'd a' things by,
That nought the cuckold might espy;
Syne loot him in; – but, out of tune,
Speer'd why he left the mill sae soon.   110
"I come," said he, "as manners claims,

To crack and wait on Master James,
Whilk I shou'd do, tho' ne'er sae bissy:
I sent him here, goodwife, where is he?"
"Ye sent him here!," quoth Bessy, grumbling;   115
"Kend I this James? A chiel came rumbling:
But how was I assur'd, when dark,
That he had been nae thievish spark,
Or some rude wencher, gotten a dose,
That a weak wife cou'd ill oppose?"   120
"And what came of him? Speak nae langer,"
Crys Halbert in a Highland anger.
"I sent him to the barn," quoth she.
"Gae quickly bring him in," quoth he.
    James was brought in; – the wife was bawked;   125
The priest stood close; the miller cracked: –
Then ask'd his sunkan gloomy spouse,
What supper had she in the house,
That might be suitable to gi'e
Ane of their lodger's qualitie?   130
Quoth she, "Ye may well ken, goodman,
Your feast comes frae the pottage-pan:
The stov'd or roasted we afford
Are aft great strangers on our board."
"Pottage," quoth Hab, "ye senseless tawpie!   135
Think ye this youth's a gilly-gawpy;
And that his gentle stamock's master
To worry up a pint of plaister,
Like our mill knaves that lift the laiding,
Whase kytes can streek out like raw plaiding?   140
Swith roast a hen, or fry some chickens,
And send for ale frae Maggy Pickens."
"Hout I," quoth she, "ye may well ken
'Tis ill brought butt that's no there ben;
When but last owk, nae farder gane,   145
The laird got a' to pay his kain."
    Then James, wha had as good a guess
Of what was in the house as Bess,
With pawky smile, this plea to end,
To please himsell, and ease his friend,   150
First open'd with a slee oration

His wond'rous skill in conjuration.
Said he: "By this fell art I'm able
To whop aff any great man's table
Whate'er I like, to make a mail of,   155
Either in part, or yet the haill off;.
And if ye please, I'll shaw my art."
Crys Halbert, "Faith, with a' my heart!"
Bess sain'd herself, – cryed, "LORD be here!"
And near hand fell a swoon for fear.   160
James leugh, and bade her nathing dread,
Syne to his conjuring went with speed;
And first he draws a circle round,
Then utters mony a magick sound,
Of words part Latin, Greek and Dutch,   165
Enow to fright a very witch:
That done, he says, "Now, now 'tis come,
And in the boal beside the lum:
Now set the board; goodwife, gae ben,
Bring frae yon boal a roasted hen."   170
She wadna gang, but Haby ventur'd,
And soon as he the ambrie enter'd,
It smell'd sae well, he short time sought it,
And, wondring, 'tween his hands he brought it.
He view'd it round, and thrice he smell'd it,   175
Syne with a gentle touch he felt it.
Thus ilka sense he did conveen,
Lest glamour had beguil'd his een:
They all, in an united body,
Declar'd it a fine fat how-towdy.   180
"Nae mair about it," quoth the miller,
"The fowl looks well, and we'll fa' till her."
"Sae be't," says James, and in a doup,
They snapt her up baith stoup and roup.
    "Neist, O!" crys Halbert, "cou'd your skill,   185
But help us to a waught of ale,
I'd be oblig'd t' ye a' my life,
And offer to the Deel my wife,
To see if he'll discreeter make her,
But that I'm fleed he winna take her."   190
Said James, "Ye offer very fair:

The bargain's hadden, say nae mair."
Then thrice he shook a willow wand,
With kittle words thrice gave command;
That done, with look baith learn'd and grave,   195
Said: "Now ye'll get what ye wad have;
Twa bottles of as nappy liquor
As ever reamed in horn or bicquor,
Behind the ark that hads your meal,
Ye'll find twa standing corkit well."   200
He said, and fast the miller flew,
And frae their nest the bottles drew;
Then first the scholar's health he toasted,
Whase art had gart him feed on roasted;
His father's neist, – and a' the rest   205
Of his good friends that wish'd him best,
Which were o'er langsome at the time,
On a short tale, to put in rhime.
Thus while the miller and the youth
Were blythly slock'ning of their drowth,   210
Bess, fretting, scarcely held frae greeting,
The priest enclos'd stood vex'd and sweating.
"O wow!" said Hab, "if ane might speer,
Dear Master James, wha brought our chear?
Sic laits appear to us sae awfu',   215
We hardly think your learning lawfu'."
"To bring your doubts to a conclusion,"
Says James, "ken I'm a Rosiecrucian,
Ane of the set that never carries
On traffick with black deels or fairies: 220
There's mony a sp'rit that's no a deel,
That constantly around us wheel.
There was a sage called Albumazor,
Whase wit was gleg as ony razor.
Frae this great man we learn'd the skill   225
To bring these gentry to our will;
And they appear when we've a mind,
In ony shape of humane kind:
Now, if you'll drap your foolish fear,
I'll gar my Pacolet appear."   230
Hab fidg'd and leugh, his elbuck clew,

Baith fear'd and fond a sp'rit to view:
At last his courage wan the day,
He to the scholar's will gave way.
   Bessy be this began to smell   235
A rat, but kept her mind to'r sell:
She pray'd like howdy in her drink,
But meantime tipt young James a wink.
James frae his eye an answer sent,
Which made the wife right well content,   240
Then turn'd to Hab, and thus advis'd,
"Whate'er ye see, be nought surpriz'd;
But for your saul move not your tongue,
And ready stand with a great rung;
Syne as the sp'rit gangs marching out,   245
Be sure to lend him a sound rout.
I bidna this be way of mocking;
For nought delytes him mair than knocking."
   Hab got a kent, – stood by the hallan;
And straight the wild mischievous callan,   250
Cries: "Radamanthus, Husky, Mingo,
Monk-horner, Hipock, Jinko, Jingo,
Appear in likeness of a priest,
No like a deel in shape of beast,
With gaping chafts to fleg us a'.   255
Wauk forth; the door stands to the wa'."
   Then frae the hole where he was pent,
The priest approach'd right well content,
With silent pace strade o'er the floor,
Till he was drawing near the door;   260
Then, to escape the cudgel, ran;
But was not miss'd by the goodman,
Wha lent him on the neck a lounder,
That gart him o'er the threshold founder.
Darkness soon hid him frae their sight;   265
Ben flew the miller in a fright:
"I trow," quoth he, "I laid well on;
But wow he's like our ain Mess John!"

III

POLWART ON THE GREEN

At Polwart on the Green
If you'll meet me the morn,
Where lasses do conveen
To dance about the thorn;
A kindly welcome you shall meet   5
  Frae her wha likes to view
A lover and a lad complete,
  The lad and lover you.

Let dorty dames say Na,
As lang as e'er they please,   10
Seem caulder than the sna',
While inwardly they bleeze;
But I will frankly shaw my mind,
  And yield my heart to thee;
Be ever to the captive kind,   15
  That langs na to be free.

At Polwart on the Green,
Amang the new-maun hay,
With sangs and dancing keen
We'll pass the heartsome day,   20
At night, if beds be o'er thrang laid,
  And thou be twin'd of thine,
Thou shalt be welcome, my dear lad,
  To take a part of mine.

UP IN THE AIR

Now the sun's gane out o' sight,
Beet the ingle, and snuff the light:
In glens the fairies skip and dance,
And witches wallop o'er to France,

Up in the air
On my bonny grey mare. 5
And I see her yet, and I see her yet,
Up in, &c.

The wind's drifting hail and sna'
O'er frozen hags like a foot ba', 10
Nae starns keek throw the azure slit,
'Tis cauld and mirk as ony pit,
The Man i' the Moon
Is carowsing aboon,
D'ye see, d'ye see, d'ye see him yet. 15
The Man, &c.

Take your glass to clear your een,
'Tis the elixir hales the spleen,
Baith wit and mirth it will inspire,
And gently puffs the lover's fire, 20
Up in the air,
It drives away care,
Ha'e wi' ye, ha'e wi' ye, and ha'e wi' ye lads yet,
Up in, &c.

Steek the doors, keep out the frost, 25
Come Willy gi'es about ye'r tost,
Til't lads, and lilt it out,
And let us ha'e a blythsom bowt,
Up wi't there, there!
Dinna cheat, but drink fair, 30
Huzza, Huzza, and Huzza lads yet,
Up wi't, &c.

I'LL NEVER LEAVE THEE

Jonny

Tho' for seven years and mair honour shou'd reave me,
To fields where cannons rair, thou need na grieve thee;
For deep in my spirit thy sweets are indented,

And love shall preserve ay what love has imprinted.
Leave thee, leave thee, I'll never leave thee,   5
Gang the warld as it will, dearest believe me.

Nelly

O Jonny I'm jealous, when e'er ye discover
My sentiments yielding, ye'll turn a loose rover;
And nought i' the warld wa'd vex my heart sairer,
If you prove unconstant, and fancy ane fairer.   10
Grieve me, grieve me, Oh it wad grieve me!
A' the lang night and day, if you deceive me.

Jonny

My Nelly let never sic fancies oppress ye,
For while my blood's warm I'll kindly caress ye.
Your blooming saft beauties first beeted love's fire,   15
Your virtue and wit make it ay flame the hyer:
Leave thee, leave thee, I'll never leave thee,
Gang the warld as it will, dearest believe me.

Nelly

Then Jonny I frankly this minute allow ye
To think me your mistress, for love gars me trow ye,   20
And gin ye prove fa'se, to ye'r sel be it said then,
Ye'll win but sma' honour to wrang a kind maiden.
Reave me, reave me, Heav'ns! it wad reave me,
Of my rest night and day, if ye deceive me.

Jonny

Bid iceshogles hammer red gauds on the study,   25
And fine simmer mornings nae mair appear ruddy;
Bid Britons think ae gate, and when they obey ye,
But never till that time, believe I'll betray ye:
Leave thee, leave thee, I'll never leave thee;
The starns shall gang withershins e'er I deceive thee.   30

THE WIDOW

The widow can bake, and the widow can brew,
The widow can shape, and the widow can shew,
And mony braw things the widow can do;
   Then have at the widow, my laddie.
With courage attack her baith early and late,   5
To kiss her and clap her ye mauna be blate:
Speak well, and do better; for that's the best gate
   To win a young widow, my laddie.

The widow she's youthfu', and never ae hair
The war of the wearing, and has a good skair   10
Of every thing lovely; she's witty and fair,
   And has a rich jointure, my laddie.
What cou'd ye wish better your pleasure to crown,
Than a widow, the bonniest toast in the town,
With nathing, but draw in your stool, and sit down,   15
   And sport with the widow, my laddie.

Then till her, and kill her with courtesy dead,
Tho' stark love and kindness be all ye can plead;
Be heartsome and airy, and hope to succeed
   With a bonny gay widow, my laddie.   20
Strike iron while 'tis het, if ye'd have it to wald,
For fortune ay favours the active and bauld,
But ruines the woer that's thowless and cauld,
   Unfit for the widow, my laddie.

On seeing a stroling congregation going to a
field meeting, May 9th, 1738.

To the tune of: *Fy let us a' to the bridal.*

O fy, let us a' to the meeting,
    For there will be canting there,
Where some will be laughing, some greeting,
    At the preaching of Erskine and Mair.
Then rouze ye up, Robie and Willy!   5
    The lasies are raiking awa,
In petty-coats white as the lilly,
    And biggonets prind on fou braw.

And there will be blinkan eyed Bessy,
    Blyth Baby, and sweet lipet Megg,   10
And mony a rosie cheek'd lassie
    With coats kiltet to their mid-legg.
To gar them gang clever and lightly,
    We'll carry their hose and their shoon;
Syne kiss them and clap them fou tightly,   15
    As soon as the sermon is done.

The sun will be sunk in the west
    Before they have finished the wark:
Then behind a whin bush we can rest,
    Ther's mekle good done in the dark.   20
There Tammy to Tibby may creep,
    Slee Sandy may mool in with Kate;
While other dowf sauls are asleep,
    We'll handle deep matters of state.

And shou'd we deserve the black stools,   25
    For geting a gamphrell with wean,
We'll answer we're no siccan fools
    To obey them that have the oaths tane.
When the lave's to the parish kirk gawn,

On Sundays – we'll rest us at hame, 30
An' runing to hills now and than
    Makes it nowther a sin nor a shame.

Then up with the brethren true blew,
    Wha lead us to siccan delight,
And can prove it, altho they be few, 35
    That ther is naebody else wha is right.
And doun with all government laws,
    That are made by the Bishops of Baal,
And the thieves wha climb o'er the kirk waws
    And come not in by a right call. 40

POEMS BY ROBERT FERGUSSON

THE DAFT-DAYS

Now mirk December's dowie face
Glours our the rigs wi' sour grimace,
While, thro' his *minimum* of space,
       The bleer-ey'd sun,
Wi' blinkin light and stealing pace,   5
       His race doth run.

From naked groves nae birdie sings;
To shepherd's pipe nae hillock rings;
The breeze nae od'rous flavour brings
       From Borean cave;   10
And dwyning Nature droops her wings,
       Wi' visage grave.

Mankind but scanty pleasure glean
Frae snawy hill or barren plain,
Whan Winter, 'midst his nipping train,   15
       Wi' frozen spear,
Sends drift owr a' his bleak domain,
       And guides the weir.

Auld Reikie! thou'rt the canty hole,
A bield for mony caldrife soul,   20
Wha snugly at thine ingle loll,
       Baith warm and couth;
While round they gar the bicker roll
       To weet their mouth.

When merry Yule-day comes, I trow,   25
You'll scantlins find a hungry mou;
Sma' are our cares, our stamacks fou
       O' gusty gear,

And kickshaws, strangers to our view,
          Sin fairn-year.   30

Ye browster wives, now busk ye bra,
And fling your sorrows far awa';
Then, come and gies the tither blaw
          Of reaming ale,
Mair precious than the well of Spa,   35
          Our hearts to heal.

Then, tho' at odds wi' a' the warl',
Amang oursells we'll never quarrel;
Tho' Discord gie a canker'd snarl
          To spoil our glee,   40
As lang's there's pith into the barrel
          We'll drink and 'gree.

Fidlers, your pins in temper fix,
And roset weel your fiddlesticks,
But banish vile Italian tricks   45
          From out your *quorum*,
Nor *fortes* wi' *pianos* mix,
          Gie's *Tulloch Gorum*.

For nought can cheer the heart sae weil
As can a canty Highland reel;   50
It even vivifies the heel
          To skip and dance:
Lifeless is he wha canna feel
          Its influence.

Let mirth abound, let social cheer   55
Invest the dawning of the year;
Let blithesome innocence appear
          To crown our joy;
Nor envy wi' sarcastic sneer,
          Our bliss destroy.   60

And thou, great god of *Aqua Vitæ*!
Wha sways the empire of this city,

When fou we're sometimes capernoity,
       Be thou prepar'd
To hedge us frae that black banditti,   65
       The City-Guard.

ELEGY, ON THE DEATH OF SCOTS MUSIC

Mark it, Cæsario; it is old and plain,
The spinsters and the knitters in the sun,
And the free maids that weave their thread with bones,
Do use to chant it.
          Shakespeare's *Twelfth Night*

On Scotia's plains, in days of yore,
When lads and lasses tartan wore,
Saft Music rang on ilka shore,
       In hamely weid;
But harmony is now no more,   5
       And music dead.

Round her the feather'd choir would wing,
Sae bonnily she wont to sing,
And sleely wake the sleeping string,
       Their sang to lead,   10
Sweet as the zephyrs of the spring;
       But now she's dead.

Mourn ilka nymph and ilka swain,
Ilk sunny hill and dowie glen;
Let weeping streams and Naiads drain   15
       Their fountain head;
Let echo swell the dolefu' strain,
       Since music's dead.

Whan the saft vernal breezes ca'
The grey-hair'd Winter's fogs awa',
Naebody then is heard to blaw,
        Near hill or mead,
On chaunter or on aiten straw,
          Since music's dead.

Nae lasses now, on simmer days,
Will lilt at bleaching of their claes;
Nae herds on *Yarrow*'s bonny braes,
        Or banks of *Tweed*,
Delight to chant their hameil lays,
          Since music's dead.

At glomin now the bagpipe's dumb,
Whan weary owsen hameward come;
Sae sweetly as it wont to bum,
        And pibrachs skreed;
We never hear its warlike hum;
          For music's dead.

Macgibbon's gane: Ah! waes my heart!
The man in music maist expert,
Wha cou'd sweet melody impart,
        And tune the reed,
Wi' sic a slee and pawky art;
          But now he's dead.

Ilk carline now may grunt and grane,
Ilk bonny lassie make great mane,
Since he's awa', I trow there's nane
        Can fill his stead;
The blythest sangster on the plain!
          Alake, he's dead!

Now foreign sonnets bear the gree,
And crabbit queer variety
Of sound fresh sprung frae Italy,
        A bastard breed!
Unlike that saft-tongu'd melody
          Which now lies dead.

Could lav'rocks at the dawning day,   55
Could linties chirming frae the spray,
Or todling burns that smoothly play
        O'er gowden bed,
Compare wi' *Birks of Invermay*?
        But now they're dead.   60

O Scotland! that cou'd yence afford
To bang the pith of Roman sword,
Winna your sons, wi' joint accord,
        To battle speed?
And fight till Music be restor'd,   65
        Which now lies dead.

THE KING'S BIRTH-DAY IN EDINBURGH

Oh! qualis hurly-burly fuit, si forte vidisses.
        Polemo-Middinia

I sing the day sae aften sung,
Wi' which our lugs hae yearly rung,
In whase loud praise the Muse has dung
        A' kind o' print;
But wow! the limmer's fairly flung;   5
        There's naething in't.

I'm fain to think the joys the same
In London town as here at hame,
Whare fock of ilka age and name,
        Baith blind and cripple,   10
Forgather aft, O fy for shame!
        To drink and tipple.

O Muse, be kind, and dinna fash us,
To flee awa' beyont Parnassus,
Nor seek for Helicon to wash us,   15
        That heath'nish spring;

Wi' Highland whisky scour our hawses,
        And gar us sing.

Begin then, dame, ye've drunk your fill,
You wouldna hae the tither gill?   20
You'll trust me, mair would do you ill,
        And ding you doitet;
Troth 'twould be sair agains my will
        To hae the wyte o't.

Sing then, how, on the fourth of June,   25
Our bells screed aff a loyal tune,
Our antient castle shoots at noon,
        Wi' flag-staff buskit,
Frae which the soldier blades come down
        To cock their musket.   30

Oh willawins! Mons Meg, for you,
'Twas firing crack'd thy muckle mou;
What black mishantar gart ye spew
        Baith gut and ga'?
I fear they bang'd thy belly fu'   35
        Against the law.

Right seldom am I gi'en to bannin,
But, by my saul, ye was a cannon,
Cou'd hit a man had he been stannin
        In shire o' Fife,   40
Sax lang Scots miles ayont Clackmannan,
        And tak his life.

The hills in terror wou'd cry out,
And echo to thy dinsome rout;
The herds wou'd gather in their nowt,   45
        That glowr'd wi' wonder,
Haflins afraid to bide thereout
        To hear thy thunder.

Sing likewise, Muse, how blue-gown bodies,
Like scar-craws new ta'en down frae woodies,   50

Come here to cast their clouted duddies,
                    And get their pay:
Than them, what magistrate mair proud is
                    On king's birth-day?

On this great day, the city-guard,   55
In military art well lear'd,
Wi' powder'd pow and shaven beard,
                    Gang thro' their functions,
By hostile rabble seldom spar'd
                    Of clarty unctions.   60

O soldiers! for your ain dear sakes,
For Scotland's, alias Land of Cakes,
Gie not her bairns sic deadly pakes,
                    Nor be sae rude,
Wi' firelock or Lochaber aix,   65
                    As spill their blude.

Now round and round the serpents whiz,
Wi' hissing wrath and angry phiz;
Sometimes they catch a gentle gizz,
                    Alake the day!   70
And singe, wi' hair-devouring bizz,
                    Its curls away.

Shou'd th' owner patiently keek round,
To view the nature of his wound,
Dead pussie, dragled thro' the pond,   75
                    Takes him a lounder,
Which lays his honour on the ground
                    As flat's a flounder.

The Muse maun also now implore
Auld wives to steek ilk hole and bore;   80
If baudrins slip but to the door,
                    I fear, I fear,
She'll no lang shank upon all-four
                    This time o' year.

127

Next day each hero tells his news   85
O' crackit crowns and broken brows,
And deeds that here forbid the Muse
        Her theme to swell,
Or time mair precious abuse
        Their crimes to tell.   90

She'll rather to the fields resort,
Whare music gars the day seem short,
Whare doggies play, and lambies sport
        On gowany braes,
Whare peerless Fancy hads her court,   95
        And tunes her lays.

CALLER OYSTERS

Happy the man who, free from care and strife,
In silken or in leathern purse retains
A splendid shilling. He nor hears with pain
New oysters cry'd, nor sighs for chearful ale.
                  Phillips

Of a' the waters that can hobble
A fishin yole or salmon coble,
And can reward the fishers trouble,
        Or south or north,
There's nane sae spacious and sae noble   5
        As Firth o' Forth.

In her the skate and codlin sail,
The eil fou souple wags her tail,
Wi' herrin, fleuk, and mackarel,
        And whitens dainty: 10
Their spindle-shanks the labsters trail,
        Wi' partans plenty.

Auld Reikie's sons blyth faces wear;
September's merry month is near,
That brings in Neptune's caller chere, 15
   New oysters fresh;
The halesomest and nicest gear
   Of fish or flesh.

O! then we needna gie a plack
For dand'ring mountebank or quack, 20
Wha o' their drogs sae bauldly crack,
   And spred sic notions,
As gar their feckless patient tak
   Their stinkin potions.

Come prie, frail man! for gin thou art sick, 25
The oyster is a rare cathartic,
As ever doctor patient gart lick
   To cure his ails;
Whether you hae the head or heart-ake,
   It ay prevails. 30

Ye tiplers, open a' your poses,
Ye wha are faush'd wi' plouky noses,
Fling owr your craig sufficient doses,
   You'll thole a hunder,
To fleg awa' your simmer roses, 35
   And naething under.

Whan big as burns the gutters rin,
Gin ye hae catcht a droukit skin,
To Luckie Middlemist's loup in,
   And sit fu snug 40
O'er oysters and a dram o' gin,
   Or haddock lug.

When auld Saunt Giles, at aught o'clock,
Gars merchant lowns their chopies lock,
There we adjourn wi' hearty fock 45
   To birle our bodles,
And get wharewi' to crack our joke,
   And clear our noddles.

Whan Phœbus did his windocks steek,
How aften at that ingle cheek   50
Did I my frosty fingers beek,
            And taste gude fare?
I trow there was nae hame to seek
            Whan steghin there.

While glakit fools, o'er rife o' cash,   55
Pamper their weyms wi' fousom trash,
I think a chiel may gayly pass;
            He's no ill boden
That gusts his gabb wi' oyster sauce,
            And hen weel soden.   60

At Musselbrough, and eke Newhaven,
The fisher wives will get top livin,
When lads gang out on Sunday's even
            To treat their joes,
And tak of fat pandours a prieven,   65
            Or mussel brose:

Then sometimes 'ere they flit their doup,
They'll ablins a' their siller coup
For liquor clear frae cutty stoup,
            To weet their wizen,   70
And swallow o'er a dainty soup,
            For fear they gizzen.

A' ye wha canna stand sae sicker,
Whan twice you've toom'd the big ars'd bicker,
Mix caller oysters wi' your liquor,   75
            And I'm your debtor,
If greedy priest or drouthy vicar
            Will thole it better.

BRAID CLAITH

Ye wha are fain to hae your name
Wrote in the bonny book of fame,
Let merit nae pretension claim
        To laurel'd wreath,
But hap ye weel, baith back and wame,   5
        In gude Braid Claith.

He that some ells o' this may fa,
An' slae-black hat on pow like snaw,
Bids bauld to bear the gree awa'
        Wi' a' this graith,   10
Whan bienly clad wi' shell fu' braw
        O' gude Braid Claith.

Waesuck for him wha has nae fek o't!
For he's a gowk they're sure to geck at,
A chield that ne'er will be respekit   15
        While he draws breath,
Till his four quarters are bedeckit
        Wi' gude Braid Claith.

On Sabbath-days the barber spark,
Whan he has done wi' scrapin wark,   20
Wi' siller broachie in his sark,
        Gangs trigly, faith!
Or to the Meadow, or the Park,
        In gude Braid Claith.

Weel might ye trow, to see them there,   25
That they to shave your haffits bare,
Or curl an' sleek a pickle hair,
        Wou'd be right laith,
Whan pacing wi' a gawsy air
        In gude Braid Claith.   30

If ony mettl'd stirrah green
For favour frae a lady's ein,

He maunna care for being seen
           Before he sheath
His body in a scabbard clean   35
           O' gude Braid Claith.

For, gin he come wi' coat thread-bare,
A feg for him she winna care,
But crook her bony mou' fu' sair,
           An' scald him baith.   40
Wooers shou'd ay their travel spare
           Without Braid Claith.

Braid Claith lends fock an unco heese,
Makes mony kail-worms butter-flies,
Gies mony a doctor his degrees   45
           For little skaith:
In short, you may be what you please
           Wi' gude Braid Claith.

For thof ye had as wise a snout on
As Shakespeare or Sir Isaac Newton,   50
Your judgment fouk wou'd hae a doubt on,
           I'll tak my aith,
Till they cou'd see ye wi' a suit on
           O' gude Braid Claith.

HALLOW-FAIR

At Hallowmas, whan nights grow lang,
   And starnies shine fu' clear,
Whan fock, the nippin cald to bang,
   Their winter hap-warms wear,
Near Edinbrough a fair there hads,   5
   I wat there's nane whase name is,
For strappin dames and sturdy lads,
   And cap and stoup, mair famous
           Than it that day.

Upo' the tap o' ilka lum 10
  The sun began to keek,
And bad the trig made maidens come
  A sightly joe to seek
At Hallow-fair, where browsters rare
  Keep gude ale on the gantries, 15
And dinna scrimp ye o' a skair
  O' kebbucks frae their pantries,
          Fu' saut that day.

Here country John in bonnet blue,
  An' eke his Sunday's claise on, 20
Rins after Meg wi' rokelay new,
  An' sappy kisses lays on;
She'll tauntin say, "Ye silly coof!
  Be o' your gab mair spairin";
He'll tak the hint, and criesh her loo 25
  Wi' what will buy her fairin,
          To chow that day.

Here chapmen billies tak their stand,
  An' shaw their bonny wallies;
Wow, but they lie fu' gleg aff hand 30
  To trick the silly fallows:
Heh, sirs! what cairds and tinklers come,
  An' ne'er-do-weel horse-coupers,
An' spae-wives fenzying to be dumb,
  Wi' a' siclike landloupers, 35
          To thrive that day.

Here Sawny cries, frae Aberdeen;
  "Come ye to me fa need:
The brawest shanks that e'er were seen
  I'll sell ye cheap an' guid. 40
I wyt they are as protty hose
  As come frae weyr or leem:
Here tak a rug and shaw's your pose:
  Forseeth, my ain's but teem
          An' light this day." 45

Ye wives, as ye gang thro' the fair,
　　O mak your bargains hooly!
Of a' thir wylie lowns beware,
　　Or fegs they will ye spulzie,
For fairn-year Meg Thamson got,　　　　　　　50
　　Frae thir mischievous villains,
A scaw'd bit o' a penny note,
　　That lost a score o' shillins
　　　　　　To her that day.

The dinlin drums alarm our ears,　　　　　　　55
　　The serjeant screechs fu' loud,
"A' gentlemen and volunteers
　　That wish your country gude,
Come here to me, and I sall gie
　　Twa guineas and a crown,　　　　　　　60
A bowl o' punch, that like the sea
　　Will soum a lang dragoon
　　　　　　Wi' ease this day."

Without, the cuissers prance and nicker,
　　An' owr the ley-rig scud;　　　　　　　65
In tents the carles bend the bicker,
　　An' rant an' roar like wud.
Then there's sic yellowchin and din,
　　Wi' wives and wee-anes gablin,
That ane might true they were a-kin　　　　　　70
　　To a' the tongues at Babylon,
　　　　　　Confus'd that day.

Whan Phœbus ligs in Thetis lap,
　　Auld Reikie gies them shelter,
Whare cadgily they kiss the cap,　　　　　　　75
　　An' ca't round helter-skelter.
Jock Bell gaed furth to play his freaks,
　　Great cause he had to rue it,
For frae a stark Lochaber aix
　　He got a clamihewit,　　　　　　　80
　　　　　　Fu' sair that night.

"Ohon!" quo' he, "I'd rather be
  By sword or bagnet stickit,
Than hae my crown or body wi'
  Sic deadly weapons nicket."   85
Wi' that he gat anither straik,
  Mair weighty than before,
That gar'd his feckless body aik,
  An' spew the reikin gore,
              Fu' red that night.   90

He peching on the cawsey lay,
  O' kicks and cuffs weel sair'd;
A Highland aith the serjeant gae,
  "She maun pe see our guard."
Out spak the weirlike corporal,   95
  "Pring in ta drunken sot."
They trail'd him ben, an' by my saul,
  He paid his drunken groat
              For that neist day.

Good fock, as ye come frae the fair,   100
  Bide yont frae this black squad;
There's nae sic savages elsewhere
  Allow'd to wear cockade.
Than the strong lion's hungry maw,
  Or tusk o' Russian bear,   105
Frae their wanruly fellin paw
  Mair cause ye hae to fear
              Your death that day.

A wee soup drink dis unco weel
  To had the heart aboon;
It's gude as lang's a canny chiel   110
  Can stand steeve in his shoon.
But gin a birkie's owr weel sair'd,
  It gars him aften stammer
To pleys that bring him to the guard,   115
  An' eke the Council-chawmir,
              Wi' shame that day.

ELEGY, ON THE DEATH OF
MR DAVID GREGORY,

late Professor of Mathematics in the University of St Andrews

Now mourn, ye college masters a'!
And frae your ein a tear lat fa',
Fam'd Gregory death has taen awa'
          Without remeid;
The skaith ye've met wi's nae that sma',   5
          Sin Gregory's dead.

The students too will miss him sair,
To school them weel his eident care,
Now they may mourn for ever mair,
          They hae great need;   10
They'll hip the maist fek o' their lear,
          Sin Gregory's dead.

He could, by Euclid, prove lang sine
A ganging point compos'd a line;
By numbers too he cou'd divine,   15
          Whan he did read,
That three times three just made up nine;
          But now he's dead.

In algebra weel skill'd he was,
An' kent fu' well proportion's laws;   20
He cou'd make clear baith B's and A's
          Wi' his lang head;
Rin owr surd roots, but cracks or flaws;
          But now he's dead.

Weel vers'd was he in architecture,   25
An' kent the nature o' the sector,
Upon baith globes he weel cou'd lecture,
          An' gar's tak heid;
Of geometry he was the Hector;
          But now he's dead.   30

Sae weel's he'd fley the students a',
Whan they war skelpin at the ba',
They took leg bail and ran awa',
                    Wi' pith and speid;
We winna get a sport sae braw   35
                    Sin Gregory's dead.

Great 'casion hae we a' to weep,
An' cleed our skins in mourning deep,
For Gregory death will fairly keep
                    To take his nap;   40
He'll till the resurrection sleep
                    As sound's a tap.

AN ECLOGUE

Twas e'ening whan the spreckled gowdspink sang,
Whan new-fa'an dew in blobs o' chrystal hang;
Than Will and Sandie thought they'd wrought eneugh,
And loos'd their sair toil'd owsen frae the pleugh:
Before they ca'd their cattle to the town,   5
The lads to draw thir breath e'en sat them down:
To the stiff sturdy aik they lean'd their backs,
While honest Sandie thus began the cracks.

Sandie

Yence I could hear the laverock's shrill-tun'd throat,
And listen to the clattering gowdspink's note;   10
Yence I cou'd whistle cantilly as they,
To owsen, as they till'd my raggit clay;
But now I wou'd as leive maist lend my lugs
To tuneless puddocks croakin i' the boggs;
I sigh at hame, a-field am dowie too,   15
To sowf a tune, I'll never crook my mou.

137

Willie

Foul fa me gif your bridal had na been
Nae langer bygane than sin Hallow-e'en,
I cou'd hae tell'd you but a warlock's art,
That some daft lightlyin quean had stow'n your heart;   20
Our beasties here will take their e'ening pluck,
An' now sin Jock's gane hame the byres to muck,
Fain wou'd I houp my friend will be inclin'd
To gie me a' the secrets o' his mind:
Heh! Sandie, lad, what dool's come owr ye now,   25
That you to whistle ne'er will crook your mou.

Sandie

Ah! Willie, Willie, I may date my wae,
Frae what beted me on my bridal day;
Sair may I rue the hour in which our hands
Were knit thegither in the haly bands;   30
Sin that I thrave sae ill, in troth I fancy,
Some fiend or fairy, nae sae very chancy,
Has driven me by pauky wiles uncommon,
To wed this flyting fury of a woman.

Willie

Ah! Sandie, aften hae I heard you tell,   35
Amang the lasses a' she bure the bell;
And say, the modest glances o' her ein
Far dang the brightest beauties o' the green;
You ca'd her ay sae innocent, sae young,
I thought she kent na how to use her tongue.   40

Sandie

Before I married her, I'll take my aith,
Her tongue was never louder than her breath;
But now its turn'd sae souple and sae bauld,
That Job himsell cou'd scarcely thole the scauld.

138

Willie

Lat her yelp on, be you as calm's a mouse,   45
Nor lat your whisht be heard into the house;
Do what she can, or be as loud's she please,
Ne'er mind her flytes but set your heart at ease,
Sit down and blaw your pipe, nor faush your thumb,
An' there's my hand she'll tire, and soon sing dumb;   50
Sooner shou'd winter cald confine the sea,
An' lat the sma'est o' our burns rin free;
Sooner at Yule-day shall the birk be drest,
Or birds in sapless busses big their nest,
Before a tonguey woman's noisy plea   55
Shou'd ever be a cause to dantan me.

Sandie

Weel cou'd I this abide, but oh! I fear
I'll soon be twin'd o' a' my warldly gear;
My kirnstaff now stands gizzand at the door,
My cheese-rack toom that ne'er was toom before;   60
My ky may now rin rowtin to the hill,
And on the nakit yird their milkness spill;
She seenil lays her hand upon a turn,
Neglects the kebbuck, and forgets the kirn;
I vow my hair-mould milk would poison dogs,   65
As it stands lapper'd in the dirty cogs.
Before the seed I sell'd my ferra cow,
An' wi' the profit coft a stane o' woo':
I thought, by priggin, that she might hae spun
A plaidie, light, to screen me frae the sun;   70
But though the siller's scant, the cleedin dear,
She has na ca'd about a wheel the year.
Last ouk but ane I was frae hame a day,
Buying a threave or twa o' bedding strae:
O' ilka thing the woman had her will,   75
Had fouth o' meal to bake, and hens to kill;
But hyn awa' to Edinbrough scoured she
To get a making o' her fav'rite tea;
And 'cause I left her not the weary clink,
She sell't the very trunchers frae my bink.   80

Willie

Her tea! ah! wae betide sic costly gear,
Or them that ever wad the price o't spear.
Sin my auld gutcher first the warld knew,
Fouk had na fund the Indies, whare it grew.
I mind mysell, its nae sae lang sin syne,   85
Whan Auntie Marion did her stamack tyne,
That Davs our gardiner came frae Apple-bogg,
An' gae her tea to tak by way o' drog.

Sandie

Whan ilka herd for cauld his fingers rubbs,
An' cakes o' ice are seen upo' the dubbs;   90
At morning, whan frae pleugh or fauld I come,
I'll see a braw reek rising frae my lum,
An' ablins think to get a rantin blaze
To fley the frost awa' an' toast my taes;
But whan I shoot my nose in, ten to ane   95
If I weelfardly see my ane hearthstane;
She round the ingle with her gimmers sits,
Crammin their gabbies wi' her nicest bits,
While the gudeman out-by maun fill his crap
Frae the milk coggie, or the parritch cap.   100

Willie

Sandie, gif this were ony common plea,
I shou'd the lealest o' my counsel gie;
But mak or meddle betwixt man and wife,
Is what I never did in a' my life.
It's wearin on now to the tail o' May,   105
An' just between the bear seed and the hay;
As lang's an orrow morning may be spar'd,
Stap your wa's east the haugh, an' tell the laird;
For he's a man weel vers'd in a' the laws,
Kens baith their outs and ins, their cracks and flaws,   110
An' ay right gleg, whan things are out o' joint,
At sattlin o' a nice or kittle point.
But yonder's Jock, he'll ca' your owsen hame,

And tak thir tidings to your thrawart dame,
That ye're awa' ae peacefu' meal to prie,   115
And take your supper kail or sowens wi' me.

THE LEE RIGG

Will ye gang o'er the lee-rigg,
   My ain kind deary O!
And cuddle there sae kindly
   Wi' me, my kind deary O?

At thornie-dike and birken-tree   5
   We'll daff, and ne'er be weary O;
They'll scug ill een frae you and me,
   Mine ain kind deary O.

Nae herds wi' kent or colly there,
   Shall ever come to fear ye O;   10
But lav'rocks, whistling in the air,
   Shall woo, like me, their deary O!

While others herd their lambs and ewes,
   And toil for warld's gear, my jo,
Upon the lee my pleasure grows,   15
   Wi' you, my kind dearie O!

AULD REIKIE, A POEM

Auld Reikie! wale o' ilka town
That Scotland kens beneath the moon;
Whare couthy chiels at e'ening meet
Their bizzing craigs and mou's to weet:

And blythly gar auld Care gae bye   5
Wi' blinkit and wi' bleering eye:
O'er lang frae thee the Muse has been
Sae frisky on the simmer's green,
Whan flowers and gowans wont to glent
In bonny blinks upo' the bent;   10
But now the leaves a yellow die,
Peel'd frae the branches, quickly fly;
And now frae nouther bush nor brier
The spreckl'd mavis greets your ear;
Nor bonny blackbird skims and roves   15
To seek his love in yonder groves.
    Then, Reikie, welcome! Thou canst charm
Unfleggit by the year's alarm;
Not Boreas, that sae snelly blows,
Dare here pap in his angry nose: 20
Thanks to our dads, whase biggin stands
A shelter to surrounding lands.
    Now morn, with bonny purpie-smiles,
Kisses the air-cock o' St. Giles;
Rakin their ein, the servant lasses   25
Early begin their lies and clashes;
Ilk tells her friend of saddest distress,
That still she brooks frae scouling mistress;
And wi' her joe in turnpike stair
She'd rather snuff the stinking air,   30
As be subjected to her tongue,
When justly censur'd in the wrong.
    On stair wi' tub, or pat in hand,
The barefoot housemaids looe to stand,
That antrin fock may ken how snell   35
Auld Reikie will at morning smell:
Then, with an inundation big as
The burn that 'neath the Nore Loch Brig is,
They kindly shower Edina's roses,
To quicken and regale our noses.   40
Now some for this, wi' satyr's leesh,
Ha'e gi'en auld Edinburgh a creesh:
But without souring nocht is sweet;
The morning smells that hail our street,

Prepare, and gently lead the way   45
To simmer canty, braw and gay;
Edina's sons mair eithly share
Her spices and her dainties rare,
Than he that's never yet been call'd
Aff frae his plaidie or his fauld.   50
    Now stairhead critics, senseless fools,
Censure their aim, and pride their rules,
In Luckenbooths, wi' glouring eye,
Their neighbours sma'est faults descry:
If ony loun should dander there,   55
Of aukward gate, and foreign air,
They trace his steps, till they can tell
His pedigree as weel's himsell.
    When Phœbus blinks wi' warmer ray,
And schools at noonday get the play,   60
Then bus'ness, weighty bus'ness comes;
The trader glours; he doubts, he hums:
The lawyers eke to Cross repair,
Their wigs to shaw, and toss an air;
While busy agent closely plies,   65
And a' his kittle cases tries.
    Now Night, that's cunzied chief for fun,
Is wi' her usual rites begun;
Thro' ilka gate the torches blaze,
And globes send out their blinking rays.   70
The usefu' cadie plies in street,
To bide the profits o' his feet;
For by thir lads Auld Reikie's fock
Ken but a sample, o' the stock
O' thieves, that nightly wad oppress,   75
And make baith goods and gear the less.
Near him the lazy chairman stands,
And wats na how to turn his hands,
Till some daft birky, ranting fu',
Has matters somewhere else to do;   80
The chairman willing, gi'es his light
To deeds o' darkness and o' night:
    It's never sax pence for a lift
That gars thir lads wi' fu'ness rift;

For they wi' better gear are paid,   85
And whores and culls support their trade.
    Near some lamp-post, wi' dowy face,
Wi' heavy een, and sour grimace,
Stands she that beauty lang had kend,
Whoredom her trade, and vice her end.
But see wharenow she wuns her bread,   90
By that which Nature ne'er decreed;
And sings sad music to the lugs,
'Mang burachs o' damn'd whores and rogues.
Whane'er we reputation loss,
Fair chastity's transparent gloss!   95
Redemption seenil kens the name
But a's black misery and shame.
    Frae joyous tavern, reeling drunk,
Wi' fiery phizz, and ein half sunk,   100
Behald the bruiser, fae to a'
That in the reek o' gardies fa':
Close by his side, a feckless race
O' macaronies shew their face,
And think they're free frae skaith or harm,   105
While pith befriends their leaders arm:
Yet fearfu' aften o' their maught,
They quatt the glory o' the faught
To this same warrior wha led
Thae heroes to bright honour's bed;   110
And aft the hack o' honour shines
In bruiser's face wi' broken lines:
Of them sad tales he tells anon,
Whan ramble and whan fighting's done;
And, like Hectorian, ne'er impairs   115
The brag and glory o' his sairs.
    Whan feet in dirty gutters plash,
And fock to wale their fitstaps fash;
At night the macaroni drunk,
In pools or gutters aftimes sunk: 120
Hegh! what a fright he now appears,
Whan he his corpse dejected rears!
Look at that head, and think if there
The pomet slaister'd up his hair!

The cheeks observe, where now cou'd shine 125
The scancing glories o' carmine?
Ah, legs! in vain the silk-worm there
Display'd to view her eidant care;
For stink, instead of perfumes, grow,
And clarty odours fragrant flow, 130
   Now some to porter, some to punch,
Some to their wife, and some their wench,
Retire, while noisy ten-hours drum
Gars a' your trades gae dandring home.
Now mony a club, jocose and free, 135
Gie a' to merriment and glee;
Wi' sang and glass, they fley the pow'r
O' care that wad harrass the hour:
For wine and Bacchus still bear down
Our thrawart fortunes wildest frown: 140
It maks you stark, and bauld, and brave,
Ev'n whan descending to the grave.
   Now some, in Pandemonium's shade,
Resume the gormandizing trade;
Whare eager looks, and glancing ein, 145
Forespeak a heart and stamack keen.
Gang on, my lads; it's lang sin syne
We kent auld Epicurus' line;
Save you, the board wad cease to rise;
Bedight wi' daintiths to the skies; 150
And salamanders cease to swill
The comforts of a burning gill.
   But chief, O Cape! we crave thy aid,
To get our cares and poortith laid:
Sincerity, and genius true, 155
Of Knights have ever been the due:
Mirth, music, porter deepest dy'd,
Are never here to worth deny'd:
And health, o' happiness the queen,
Blinks bonny, wi' her smile serene. 160
   Tho' joy maist part Auld Reikie owns,
Eftsoons she kens sad sorrows frowns;
What group is yon sae dismal grim,
Wi' horrid aspect, cleeding dim?

Says Death, "They'r mine, a dowy crew,   165
To me they'll quickly pay their last adieu."
   How come mankind, whan lacking woe,
In saulie's face their heart to show,
As if they were a clock, to tell
That grief in them had rung her bell?   170
Then, what is man? why a' this phraze?
Life's spunk decay'd, nae mair can blaze.
Let sober grief alone declare
Our fond anxiety and care:
Nor let the undertakers be   175
The only waefu' friends we see.
   Come on, my Muse, and then rehearse
The gloomiest theme in a' your verse:
In morning, when ane keeks about,
Fu' blyth and free frae ail, nae doubt   180
He lippens not to be misled
Amang the regions of the dead:
But straight a painted corp he sees,
Lang streekit 'neath its canopies.
Soon, soon will this his mirth controul,   185
And send damnation to his soul:
Or when the dead-deal, (awful shape!)
Makes frighted mankind girn and gape,
Reflection then his reason sours,
For the niest dead-deal may be ours.   190
Whan Sybil led the Trojan down
To haggard Pluto's dreary town,
Shapes war nor thae, I freely ween,
Cou'd never meet the soldier's ein.
   If kail sae green, or herbs delight,   195
Edina's street attracts the sight;
Not Covent-garden, clad sae braw,
Mair fouth o' herbs can eithly shaw:
For mony a yeard is here sair sought,
That kail and cabbage may be bought;   200
And healthfu' sallad to regale,
Whan pamper'd wi' a heavy meal.
Glour up the street in simmer morn,
The birks sae green, and sweet brier-thorn,

Wi' sprangit flow'rs that scent the gale,   205
Ca' far awa' the morning smell,
Wi' which our ladies flow'r-pat's fill'd,
And every noxious vapour kill'd.
O Nature! canty, blyth and free,
Whare is there keeking-glass like thee?   210
Is there on earth that can compare
Wi' Mary's shape, and Mary's air,
Save the empurpled speck, that grows
In the saft faulds of yonder rose?
How bonny seems the virgin breast,   215
Whan by the lillies here carest,
And leaves the mind in doubt to tell
Which maist in sweets and hue excel?
    Gillespies' snuff should prime the nose
Of her that to the market goes,   220
If they wad like to shun the smells
That buoy up frae markest cells;
Whare wames o' paunches sav'ry scent
To nostrils gi'e great discontent.
Now wha in Albion could expect   225
O' cleanliness sic great neglect?
Nae Hottentot that daily lairs
'Mang tripe, or ither clarty wares,
Hath ever yet conceiv'd, or seen
Beyond the Line, sic scenes unclean.   230
    On Sunday here, an alter'd scene
O' men and manners meets our ein:
Ane wad maist trow some people chose
To change their faces wi' their clo'es,
And fain wad gar ilk neighbour think   235
They thirst for goodness, as for drink:
But there's an unco dearth o' grace,
That has nae mansion but the face,
And never can obtain a part
In benmost corner of the heart.   240
Why should religion make us sad,
If good frae virtue's to be had?
Na, rather gleefu' turn your face;
Forsake hypocrisy, grimace;

147

And never have it understood 245
You fleg mankind frae being good.
   In afternoon, a' brawly buskit,
The joes and lasses loe to frisk it:
Some take a great delight to place
The modest bongrace o'er the face; 250
Tho' you may see, if so inclin'd,
The turning o' the leg behind.
Now Comely-Garden and the Park
Refresh them after forenoon's wark;
Newhaven, Leith or Canonmills, 255
Supply them in their Sunday's gills;
Whare writers aften spend their pence,
To stock their heads wi' drink and sense.
   While dandring cits delight to stray
To Castlehill, or public way, 260
Whare they nae other purpose mean,
Than that fool cause o' being seen;
Let me to Arthur's Seat pursue,
Whare bonny pastures meet the view;
And mony a wild-lorn scene accrues, 265
Befitting Willie Shakespeare's muse:
If Fancy there would join the thrang,
The desart rocks and hills amang,
To echoes we should lilt and play,
And gie to mirth the lee-lang day. 270
   Or shou'd some canker'd biting show'r
The day and a' her sweets deflour,
To Holy-rood-house let me stray,
And gie to musing a' the day;
Lamenting what auld Scotland knew, 275
Bien days for ever frae her view:
O Hamilton, for shame! the Muse
Would pay to thee her couthy vows,
Gin ye wad tent the humble strain,
And gie's our dignity again: 280
For O, waes me! the thistle springs
In domicile of ancient kings,
Without a patriot to regrete
Our palace, and our ancient state.

Blest place! whare debtors daily run,   285
To rid themselves frae jail and dun;
Here, tho' sequester'd frae the din
That rings Auld Reikie's waas within,
Yet they may tread the sunny braes,
And brook Apollo's cheery rays;   290
Glour frae St. Anthon's grassy hight,
O'er vales in simmer claise bedight,
Nor ever hing their head, I ween,
Wi' jealous fear o' being seen.
May I, whanever duns come nigh,   295
And shake my garret wi' their cry,
Scour here wi' haste, protection get,
To screen mysell frae them and debt;
To breathe the bliss of open sky,
And Simon Fraser's bolts defy.   300
    Now gin a lown should ha'e his clase
In thread-bare autumn o' their days,
St. Mary, brokers' guardian saint,
Will satisfy ilk ail and want;
For mony a hungry writer, there   305
Dives down at night, wi' cleading bare,
And quickly rises to the view
A gentleman, perfyte and new.
Ye rich fock, look no wi' disdain
Upo' this ancient brokage lane!   310
For naked poets are supplied
With what you to their wants deny'd.
    Peace to thy shade, thou wale o' men,
Drummond! relief to poortith's pain:
To thee the greatest bliss we owe;   315
And tribute's tear shall grateful flow:
The sick are cur'd, the hungry fed,
And dreams of comfort tend their bed:
As lang as Forth weets Lothians shore,
As lang's on Fife her billows roar,   320
Sae lang shall ilk whase country's dear,
To thy remembrance gie a tear.
By thee Auld Reikie thrave, and grew
Delightfu' to her childer's view:

149

Nae mair shall Glasgow striplings threap   325
Their city's beauty and its shape,
While our new city spreads around
Her bonny wings on fairy ground.
    But Provosts now that ne'er afford
The smaest dignity to 'Lord',   330
Ne'er care tho' every scheme gae wild
That Drummond's sacred hand has cull'd:
The spacious Brig neglected lies,
Tho' plagu'd wi' pamphlets, dunn'd wi' cries;
They heed not tho' destruction come   335
To gulp us in her gaunting womb.
O shame! that safety canna claim
Protection from a provost's name,
But hidden danger lies behind
To torture and to fleg the mind;   340
I may as weel bid Arthur's Seat
To Berwick-Law make gleg retreat,
As think that either will or art
Shall get the gate to win their heart;
For politics are a' their mark,   345
Bribes latent, and corruption dark:
If they can eithly turn the pence,
Wi' city's good they will dispense;
Nor care tho' a' her sons were lair'd
Ten fathom i' the aulk kirk-yard.   350
    To sing yet meikle does remain,
Undecent for a modest strain;
And since the poet's daily bread is
The favour of the Muse or ladies,
He downa like to gie offence   355
To delicacy's bonny sense;
Therefore the stews remain unsung,
And bawds in silence drop their tongue.
    Reikie, farewell! I ne'er cou'd part
Wi' thee but wi' a dowy heart;   360
Aft frae the Fifan coast I've seen
Thee tow'ring on thy summit green;
So glowr the saints when first is given,
A fav'rite keek o' glore and heaven;

On earth nae mair they bend their ein,
But quick assume angelic mein;
So I on Fife wad glowr no more,
But gallop'd to Edina's shore.

TO THE TRON-KIRK BELL

Wanwordy, crazy, dinsome thing,
As e'er was fram'd to jow or ring,
What gar'd them sic in steeple hing
   They ken themsel',
But weel wat I they coudna bring   5
   War sounds frae hell.

What de'il are ye? that I shud ban,
Your neither kin to pat nor pan;
Not uly pig, nor master-cann,
   But weel may gie   10
Mair pleasure to the ear o' man
   Than stroak o' thee.

Fleece merchants may look bald, I trow,
Sin a' Auld Reikie's childer now
Maun stap their lugs wi' teats o' woo,   15
   Thy sound to bang,
And keep it frae gawn thro' and thro'
   Wi' jarrin' twang.

Your noisy tongue, there's nae abideint,
Like scaulding wife's, there is nae guideint;   20
Whan I'm 'bout ony bus'ness eident,
   It's sair to thole;
To deave me, than, ye tak' a pride in't
   Wi' senseless knoll.

O! war I provost o' the town,   25
I swear by a' the pow'rs aboon,

I'd bring ye wi' a reesle down;
        Nor shud you think
(Sae sair I'd crack and clour your crown)
        Again to clink.   30

For whan I've toom'd the muckle cap,
An' fain wud fa' owr in a nap,
Troth I cud doze as sound's a tap,
        Wer't na for thee,
That gies the tither weary chap   35
        To waukin me.

I dreamt ae night I saw Auld Nick;
Quo he, "this bell o' mine's a trick,
A wylie piece o' politic,
        A cunnin snare   40
To trap fock in a cloven stick,
        'Ere they're aware.

As lang's my dautit bell hings there,
A' body at the kirk will skair;
Quo they, 'gif he that preaches there   45
        Like it can wound,
We douna care a single hair
        For joyfu' sound.'"

If magistrates wi' me wud 'gree,
For ay tongue-tackit shud you be,   50
Nor fleg wi' antimelody
        Sic honest fock,
Whase lugs were never made to dree
        Thy doolfu' shock.

But far frae thee the bailies dwell,   55
Or they wud scunner at your knell,
Gie the foul thief his riven bell,
        And than, I trow,
The by-word hads, 'the de'il himsel'
        Has got his due.'   60

MUTUAL COMPLAINT OF PLAINSTANES AND CAUSEY, IN THEIR MOTHER-TONGUE

Since Merlin laid Auld Reikie's causey,
And made her o' his wark right saucy,
The spacious street and plainstanes
Were never kend to crack but anes,
Whilk happened on the hinder night,   5
Whan Fraser's ulie tint its light.
Of Highland sentries nane were waukin,
To hear thir cronies glibbly taukin;
For them this wonder might hae rotten,
And, like night robb'ry, been forgotten,   10
Had na' a cadie, wi' his lanthorn,
Been gleg enough to hear them bant'rin,
Wha came to me neist morning early,
To gi'e me tidings o' this ferly.

    Ye taunting lowns trow this nae joke,   15
For anes the ass of Balaam spoke,
Better than lawyers do, forsooth,
For it spake naething but the truth:
Whether they follow its example,
You'll ken best whan you hear the sample.   20

Plainstanes

    My friend, thir hunder years and mair,
We've been forfoughen late and air,
In sun-shine, and in weety weather,
Our thrawart lot we bure thegither.
I never growl'd, but was content   25
Whan ilk ane had an equal stent,
But now to flyte I'se e'en be bauld,
Whan I'm wi' sic a grievance thrall'd.
How haps it, say, that mealy bakers,
Hair-kaimers, crieshy gezy-makers,   30
Shou'd a' get leave to waste their powders
Upon my beaux and ladies shoulders?

153

My travellers are fley'd to deid
Wi' creels wanchancy, heap'd wi' bread,
Frae whilk hing down uncanny nicksticks,   35
That aften gie the maidens sic licks,
As make them blyth to skreen their faces
Wi' hats and muckle maun bon-graces,
And cheat the lads that fain wad see
The glances o' a pauky eie,   40
Or gie their loves a wylie wink,
That erst might lend their hearts a clink.
Speak, was I made to dree the laidin
Of Gallic chairman heavy treadin,
Wha in my tender buke bore holes   45
Wi' waefu' tackets i' the soals
O' broags, whilk on my body tramp,
And wound like death at ilka clamp.

Causey

Weil crackit friend – It aft hads true,
Wi' naething fock make maist ado;   50
Weel ken ye, tho' ye doughtna tell,
I pay the sairest kain mysell;
Owr me ilk day big waggons rumble,
And a' my fabric birze and jumble;
Owr me the muckle horses gallop,   55
Enough to rug my very saul up;
And coachmen never trow they're sinning,
While down the street his wheels are spinning.
Like thee, do I not bide the brunt
O' Highland chairman's heavy dunt?   60
Yet I hae never thought o' breathing
Complaint, or making din for naething.

Plainstanes

Had sae, and lat me get a word in,
Your back's best fitted for the burden;
And I can eithly tell you why,   65
Ye're doughtier by far than I;
For whin-stanes, howkit frae the craigs,

154

May thole the prancing feet of naigs,
Nor ever fear uncanny hotches
Frae clumsy carts or hackney-coaches,   70
While I, a weak and feckless creature,
Am moulded by a safter nature.
Wi' mason's chissel dighted neat,
To gar me look baith clean and feat,
I scarce can bear a sairer thump   75
Than comes frae sole of shoe or pump.
I grant, indeed, that, now and than,
Yield to a paten's pith I maun;
But patens, tho' they're aften plenty,
Are ay laid down wi' feet fou tenty,   80
And stroaks frae ladies, tho' they're teazing,
I freely maun avow are pleasing.
    For what use was I made, I wonder,
It was na tamely to chap under
The weight of ilka codroch chiel,   85
That does my skin to targits peel;
But gin I guess aright, my trade is
To fend frae skaith the bonny ladies,
To keep the bairnies free frae harms
Whan airing in their nurses arms,   90
To be a safe and canny bield
For growing youth or drooping eild.
    Take then frae me the heavy load
Of burden-bearers heavy shod,
Or, by my troth, the gude auld town shall   95
Hae this affair before their council.

Causey

    I dinna care a single jot,
Tho' summon'd by a shelly-coat,
Sae leally I'll propone defences,
As get ye flung for my expences;   100
Your libel I'll impugn *verbatim*,
And hae a *magnum damnum datum*;
For tho' frae Arthur's-seat I sprang,
And am in constitution strang,

155

Wad it no fret the hardest stane   105
Beneath the Luckenbooths to grane?
Tho' magistrates the Cross discard,
It makes na whan they leave the Guard,
A lumbersome and stinkin bigging,
That rides the sairest on my rigging.   110
Poor me owr meikle do ye blame,
For tradesmen tramping on your wame,
Yet a' your advocates and braw fock
Come still to me 'twixt ane and twa clock,
And never yet were kend to range   115
At Charlie's Statue or Exchange.
Then tak your beaux and macaronies
Gie me trades-fock and country Johnies;
The deil's in't gin ye dinna sign
Your sentiments conjunct wi' mine.   120

Plainstanes

Gin we twa cou'd be as auld-farrant
As gar the council gie a warrant,
Ilk lown rebellious to tak,
Wha walks not in the proper track,
And o' three shilling Scottish suck him,   125
Or in the water-hole sair douk him;
This might assist the poor's collection,
And gie baith parties satisfaction.

Causey

Bur first, I think it will be good
To bring it to the Robinhood,   130
Whare we shall hae the question stated,
And keen and crabbitly debated,
Whether the provost and the baillies,
For the town's good whase daily toil is,
Shou'd listen to our joint petitions,   135
And see obtemper'd the conditions.

Plainstanes

Content am I – But east the gate is
The sun, wha taks his leave of Thetis,
And comes to wauken honest fock,
That gang to wark at sax o'clock;   140
It sets us to be dumb a while,
And let our words gie place to toil.

THE RISING OF THE SESSION

To a' men living be it kend,
The Session now is at an end:
Writers, your finger-nebbs unbend,
             And quat the pen,
Till Time wi' lyart pow shall send   5
             Blythe June again.

Tir'd o' the law, and a' its phrases,
The wylie writers, rich as Crœsus,
Hurl frae the town in hackney chaises,
             For country cheer: 10
The powny that in spring-time grazes,
             Thrives a' the year.

Ye lawyers, bid fareweel to lies,
Fareweel to din, fareweel to fees,
The canny hours o' rest may please   15
             Instead o' siller:
Hain'd multer hads the mill at ease,
             And finds the miller.

Blyth they may be wha wanton play
In fortune's bonny blinkin ray,   20
Fu' weel can they ding dool away
             Wi' comrades couthy,
And never dree a hungert day,
             Or e'ening drouthy.

Ohon the day for him that's laid,   25
In dowie poortith's caldrife shade,
Ablins o'er honest for his trade,
                    He racks his wits,
How he may get his buick weel clad,
                    And fill his guts.   30

The farmers' sons, as yap as sparrows,
Are glad, I trow, to flee the barras,
And whistle to the plough and harrows
                    At barley seed:
What writer wadna gang as far as   35
                    He cou'd for bread.

After their yokin, I wat weel
They'll stoo the kebbuck to the heel;
Eith can the plough-stilts gar a chiel
                    Be unco vogie,   40
Clean to lick aff his crowdy-meal,
                    And scart his cogie.

Now mony a fallow's dung adrift
To a' the blasts beneath the lift,
And tho' their stamack's aft in tift   45
                    In vacance time,
Yet seenil do they ken the rift
                    O' stappit weym.

Now gin a Notar shou'd be wanted,
You'll find the pillars gayly planted;   50
For little thing *protests* are granted
                    Upo' a bill,
And weightiest matters covenanted
                    For haf a gill.

Nae body takes a morning dribb   55
O' Holland gin frae Robin Gibb;
And tho' a dram to Rob's mair sib
                    Than is his wife,
He maun take time to daut his Rib
                    Till siller's rife.   60

This vacance is a heavy doom
On Indian Peter's coffee-room,
For a' his china pigs are toom;
                    Nor do we see
In wine the sucker biskets soom   65
                    As light's a flee.

But stop, my Muse, nor make a main,
Pate disna fend on that alane;
He can fell twa dogs wi' ae bane,
                    While ither fock   70
Maun rest themselves content wi' ane,
                    Nor farer trock.

Ye change-house keepers never grumble,
Tho' you a while your bickers whumble,
Be unco patientfu' and humble,   75
                    Nor make a din,
Tho' gude joot binna kend to rumble
                    Your weym within.

You needna grudge to draw your breath
For little mair than haf a reath,   80
Than, gin we a' be spar'd frae death,
                    We'll gladly prie
Fresh noggans o' your reaming graith
                    Wi' blythsome glee.

ODE TO THE BEE

Herds, blythsome tune your canty reeds,
And welcome to the gowany meads
The pride o' a' the insect thrang,
A stranger to the green sae lang.
Unfald ilk buss and ilka brier,   5

The bounties o' the gleesome year,
To him whase voice delights the spring,
Whase soughs the saftest slumbers bring.
　　The trees in simmer-cleething drest,
The hillocks in their greenest vest,　　　　　　10
The brawest flow'rs rejoic'd we see,
Disclose their sweets, and ca' on thee,
Blythly to skim on wanton wing
Thro' a' the fairy haunts o' spring.
　　Whan fields ha'e got their dewy gift,　　　15
And dawnin breaks upo' the lift,
Then gang ye're wa's thro' hight and how,
Seek caller haugh or sunny know,
Or ivy'd craig, or burnbank brae,
Whare industry shall bid ye gae,　　　　　　20
For hiney or for waxen store,
To ding sad poortith frae your door,
　　Cou'd feckless creature, man, be wise,
The simmer o' his life to prize,
In winter he might fend fu' bald,　　　　　　25
His eild unkend to nippin' cald,
Yet thir, alas! are antrin fock
That lade their scape wi' winter stock.
Auld age maist feckly glowrs right dour
Upo' the ailings of the poor,　　　　　　　　30
Wha hope for nae comforting, save
That dowie dismal house, the grave.
Then feeble man, be wise, take tent
How industry can fetch content:
Behad the bees whare'er they wing,　　　　　35
Or thro' the bonny bow'rs of spring,
Whare vi'lets or whare roses blaw,
And siller dew-draps nightly fa',
Or whan on open bent they're seen,
On hether-bell or thristle green;　　　　　　40
The hiney's still as sweet that flows
Frae thistle cald or kendling rose.
　　Frae this the human race may learn
Reflection's hiney'd draps to earn,
Whither they tramp life's thorny way,　　　　45

Or thro' the sunny vineyard stray.
    Instructive bee! attend me still,
O'er a' my labours sey your skill:
For thee shall hiney-suckles rise,
With lading to your busy thighs,   50
And ilka shrub surround my cell,
Whereon ye like to hum and dwell:
My trees in bourachs o'er my ground
Shall fend ye frae ilk blast o' wind;
Nor e'er shall herd, wi' ruthless spike,   55
Delve out the treasures frae your bike,
But in my fence be safe, and free
To live, and work, and sing like me.
    Like thee, by fancy wing'd, the Muse
Scuds ear' and heartsome o'er the dews,   60
Fu' vogie, and fu' blyth to crap
The winsome flow'rs frae Nature's lap,
Twining her living garlands there,
That lyart time can ne'er impair.

THE FARMER'S INGLE

Et multo in primis hilarans convivia Baccho,
Ante focum, si frigus erit.

                                              Virgil. *Buc.*

Whan gloming grey out o'er the welkin keeks,
    Whan Batie ca's his owsen to the byre,
Whan Thrasher John, sair dung, his barn-door steeks,
    And lusty lasses at the dighting tire:
What bangs fu' leal the e'enings coming cauld,   5
    And gars snaw-tapit winter freeze in vain;
Gars dowie mortals look baith blyth and bauld,
    Nor fley'd wi' a' the poortith o' the plain;
    Begin my Muse, and chant in hamely strain.

Frae the big stack, weel winnow't on the hill,   10
   Wi' divets theekit frae the weet and drift,
Sods, peats, and heath'ry trufs the chimley fill,
   And gar their thick'ning smeek salute the lift;
The gudeman, new come hame, is blyth to find,
   Whan he out o'er the halland flings his een,   15
That ilka turn is handled to his mind,
   That a' his housie looks sae cosh and clean,
   For cleanly house looes he, tho' e'er sae mean.

Weel kens the gudewife that the pleughs require
   A heartsome meltith, and refreshing synd   20
O' nappy liquor, o'er a bleezing fire:
   Sair wark and poortith douna weel be join'd.
Wi' butter'd bannocks now the girdle reeks,
   I' the far nook the bowie briskly reams;
The readied kail stand by the chimley cheeks,   25
   And had the riggin het wi' welcome steams,
   Whilk than the daintiest kitchen nicer seems.

Frae this lat gentler gabs a lesson lear;
   Wad they to labouring lend an eidant hand,
They'd rax fell strang upo' the simplest fare,   30
   Nor find their stamacks ever at a stand.
Fu' hale and healthy wad they pass the day,
   At night in calmest slumbers dose fu' sound,
Nor doctor need their weary life to spae,
   Nor drogs their noddle and their sense confound,   35
   Till death slip sleely on, and gi'e the hindmost wound.

On sicken food has mony a doughty deed
   By Caledonia's ancestors been done;
By this did mony wight fu' weirlike bleed
   In brulzies frae the dawn to set o' sun: 40
'Twas this that brac'd their gardies, stiff and strang,
   That bent the deidly yew in antient days,
Laid Denmark's daring sons on yird alang,
   Gar'd Scottish thristles bang the Roman bays;
   For near our crest their heads they doughtna raise.   45

The couthy cracks begin whan supper's o'er,
  The cheering bicker gars them glibly gash
O' simmer's showery blinks and winters sour,
  Whase floods did erst their mailins produce hash:
'Bout kirk and market eke their tales gae on,   50
  How Jock woo'd Jenny here to be his bride,
And there how Marion, for a bastard son,
  Upo' the cutty-stool was forced to ride,
  The waefu' scald o' our Mess John to bide.

The fient a chiep's amang the bairnies now;   55
  For a' their anger's wi' their hunger gane:
Ay maun the childer, wi' a fastin mou',
  Grumble and greet, and make an unco mane,
In rangles round before the ingle's low:
  Frae gudame's mouth auld warld tale they hear,   60
O' warlocks louping round the wirrikow,
  O' gaists that win in glen and kirk-yard drear,
  Whilk touzles a' their tap, and gars them shak wi' fear.

For weel she trows that fiends and fairies be
  Sent frae the de'il to fleetch us to our ill;   65
That ky hae tint their milk wi' evil eie,
  And corn been scowder'd on the glowing kill.
O mock na this, my friends! but rather mourn,
  Ye in life's brawest spring wi' reason clear,
Wi' eild our idle fancies a' return,   70
  And dim our dolefu' days wi' bairnly fear;
  The mind's ay cradled whan the grave is near.

Yet thrift, industrious, bides her latest days,
  Tho' age her sair dow'd front wi' runcles wave,
Yet frae the russet lap the spindle plays,   75
  Her e'enin stent reels she as weel's the lave.
On some feast-day, the wee-things buskit braw
  Shall heeze her heart up wi' a silent joy,
Fu' cadgie that her head was up and saw
  Her ain spun cleething on a darling oy,   80
  Careless tho' death shou'd make the feast her foy.

In its auld lerroch yet the deas remains,
    Where the gudeman aft streeks him at his ease,
A warm and canny lean for weary banes
    O' lab'rers doil'd upo' the wintry leas: 85
Round him will badrins and the colly come,
    To wag their tail, and cast a thankfu' eie
To him wha kindly flings them mony a crum
    O' kebbuck whang'd, and dainty fadge to prie;
    This a' the boon they crave, and a' the fee.   90

Frae him the lads their morning counsel tak,
    What stacks he wants to thrash, what rigs to till;
How big a birn maun lie on bassie's back,
    For meal and multure to the thirling mill.
Niest the gudewife her hireling damsels bids   95
    Glowr thro' the byre, and see the hawkies bound,
Take tent case Crummy tak her wonted tids,
    And ca' the leglin's treasure on the ground,
    Whilk spills a kebbuck nice, or yellow pound.

Then a' the house for sleep begin to grien,   100
    Their joints to slack frae industry a while;
The leaden god fa's heavy on their ein,
    And hafflins steeks them frae their daily toil;
The cruizy too can only blink and bleer,
    The restit ingle's done the maist it dow;   105
Tacksman and cottar eke to bed maun steer,
    Upo' the cod to clear their drumly pow,
    Till wauken'd by the dawning's ruddy glow.

Peace to the husbandman and a' his tribe,
    Whase care fells a' our wants frae year to year;   110
Lang may his sock and couter turn the gleyb,
    And bauks o' corn bend down wi' laded ear.
May Scotia's simmers ay look gay and green,
    Her yellow har'sts frae scowry blasts decreed;
May a' her tenants sit fu' snug and bien,   115
    Frae the hard grip of ails and poortith freed,
    And a lang lasting train o' peaceful hours succeed.

164

THE GHAISTS: A KIRK-YARD ECLOGUE

Did you not say, in good Ann's day,
And vow and did protest, Sir,
That when Hanover should come o'er,
We surely should be blest, Sir?
            An auld Sang made new again.

Whare the braid planes in dowy murmurs wave
Their antient taps out o'er the cald, clad grave,
Whare Geordie Girdwood, mony a lang-spun day,
Houkit for gentlest banes the humblest clay,
Twa sheeted ghaists, sae grizly and sae wan,   5
'Mang lanely tombs their douff discourse began.

Watson

  Cauld blaws the nippin north wi' angry sough,
And showers his hailstanes frae the Castle Cleugh
O'er the Greyfriars, whare, at mirkest hour,
Bogles and spectres wont to tak their tour,   10
Harlin' the pows and shanks to hidden cairns,
Amang the hamlocks wild, and sun-burnt fearns,
But nane the night save you and I hae come
Frae the dern mansions of the midnight tomb.
Now whan the dawning's near, whan cock maun craw,   15
And wi' his angry bougil gar's withdraw,
Ayont the kirk we'll stap, and there tak bield,
While the black hours our nightly freedom yield.

Herriot

  I'm weel content; but binna cassen down,
Nor trow the cock will ca' ye hame o'er soon,   20
For tho' the eastern lift betakens day,
Changing her rokely black for mantle grey,
Nae weirlike bird our knell of parting rings,
Nor sheds the caller moisture frae his wings.
Nature has chang'd her course; the birds o' day   25
Dosin' in silence on the bending spray,

While owlets round the craigs at noon-tide flee,
And bludey bawks sit singand on the tree.
Ah, Caledon! the land I yence held dear,
Sair mane mak I for thy destruction near;   30
And thou, Edina! anes my dear abode,
Whan royal Jamie sway'd the sovereign rod,
In thae blest days, weel did I think bestow'd,
To blaw thy poortith by wi' heaps o' gowd;
To mak thee sonsy seem wi' mony a gift,   35
And gar thy stately turrets speel the lift:
In vain did Danish Jones, wi' gimcrack pains,
In Gothic sculpture fret the pliant stanes:
In vain did he affix my statue here,
Brawly to busk wi' flow'rs ilk coming year;   40
My tow'rs are sunk, my lands are barren now,
My fame, my honour, like my flow'rs maun dow.

Watson

Sure Major Weir, or some sic warlock wight,
Has flung beguilin' glamer o'er your sight;
Or else some kittle cantrup thrown, I ween,   45
Has bound in mirlygoes my ain twa ein,
If ever aught frae sense cou'd be believ'd
(And seenil hae my senses been deceiv'd),
This moment, o'er the tap of Adam's tomb,
Fu' easy can I see your chiefest dome: 50
Nae corbie fleein' there, nor croupin' craws,
Seem to forspeak the ruin of thy haws,
But a' your tow'rs in wonted order stand,
Steeve as the rocks that hem our native land.

Herriot

Think na I vent my well-a-day in vain,   55
Kent ye the cause, ye sure wad join my mane.
Black be the day that e'er to England's ground
Scotland was eikit by the Union's bond;
For mony a menzie of destructive ills
The country now maun brook frae *mortmain bills*,   60
That void our test'ments, and can freely gie

166

Sic will and scoup to the ordain'd trustee,
That he may tir our stateliest riggins bare,
Nor acres, houses, woods, nor fishins spare,
Till he can lend the stoitering state a lift   65
Wi' gowd in gowpins as a grassum gift;
In lieu o' whilk, we maun be weel content
To tyne the capital at *three per cent*.
A doughty sum indeed, whan now-a-days
They raise provisions as the stents they raise,   70
Yoke hard the poor, and lat the rich chiels be,
Pamper'd at ease by ither's industry.
    Hale interest for my fund can scantly now
Cleed a' my callants' backs, and stap their mou'.
How maun their weyms wi' sairest hunger slack,   75
Their duds in targets flaff upo' their back,
Whan they are doom'd to keep a lasting Lent,
Starving for England's weel at *three per cent*.

Watson

    Auld Reikie than may bless the gowden times,
Whan honesty and poortith baith are crimes;   80
She little kend, when you and I endow'd
Our hospitals for back-gaun burghers gude,
That e'er our siller or our lands shou'd bring
A gude bien living to a back-gaun king,
Wha, thanks to ministry! is grown sae wise,   85
He douna chew the bitter cud of vice;
For gin, frae Castlehill to Netherbow,
Wad honest houses baudy-houses grow,
The crown wad never spier the price o' sin,
Nor hinder younkers to the de'il to rin;   90
But gif some mortal grien for pious fame,
And leave the poor man's pray'r to sane his name,
His geer maun a' be scatter'd by the claws
O' ruthless, ravenous, and harpy laws.
Yet, shou'd I think, altho' the bill tak place,   95
The council winna lack sae meikle grace
As lat our heritage at wanworth gang,
Or the succeeding generations wrang

167

O' braw bien maintenance and walth o' lear,
Whilk else had drappit to their children's skair;   100
For mony a deep, and mony a rare engyne
Ha'e sprung frae Herriot's wark, and sprung frae mine,

Herriot

I find, my friend, that ye but little ken,
There's einow on the earth a set o' men,
Wha, if they get their private pouches lin'd,   105
Gie na a winnelstrae for a' mankind;
They'll sell their country, flae their conscience bare,
To gar the weigh-bauk turn a single hair.
The government need only bait the line
Wi' the prevailing flee, the gowden coin,   110
Then our executors, and wise trustees,
Will sell them fishes in forbidden seas,
Upo' their dwining country girn in sport,
Laugh in their sleeve, and get a place at court.

Watson

'Ere that day come, I'll 'mang our spirits pick   115
Some ghaist that trokes and conjures wi' Auld Nick,
To gar the wind wi' rougher rumbles blaw,
And weightier thuds than ever mortal saw:
Fire-flaught and hail, wi' tenfald fury's fires,
Shall lay yird-laigh Edina's airy spires: 120
Tweed shall rin rowtin' down his banks out o'er,
Till Scotland's out o' reach o' England's pow'r;
Upo' the briny Borean jaws to float,
And mourn in dowy saughs her dowy lot.

Herriot

Yonder's the tomb of wise Mackenzie fam'd,   125
Whase laws rebellious bigotry reclaim'd,
Freed the hail land frae covenanting fools,
Wha erst ha'e fash'd us wi' unnumber'd dools;
Till night we'll tak the swaird aboon our pows,
And than, whan she her ebon chariot rows,   130

We'll travel to the vaut wi' stealing stap,
And wauk Mackenzie frae his quiet nap:
Tell him our ails, that he, wi' wonted skill,
May fleg the schemers o' the *mortmain-bill.*

ON SEEING A BUTTERFLY IN THE STREET

Daft gowk, in macaroni dress,
Are ye come here to shew your face,
Bowden wi' pride o' simmer gloss,
To cast a dash at Reikie's cross;
And glowr at mony twa-legg'd creature,   5
Flees braw by art, tho' worms by nature?
  Like country laird in city cleeding,
Ye're come to town to lear' good breeding;
To bring ilk darling toast and fashion,
In vogue amang the flee creation,   10
That they, like buskit belles and beaus,
May crook their mou' fu' sour at those
Whase weird is still to creep, alas!
Unnotic'd 'mang the humble grass;
While you, wi' wings new buskit trim,   ·15
Can far frae yird and reptiles skim;
Newfangle grown wi' new got form,
You soar aboon your mither worm.
  Kind Nature lent but for a day
Her wings to make ye sprush and gay;   20
In her habuliments a while
Ye may your former sel' beguile,
And ding awa' the vexing thought
Of hourly dwining into nought,
By beenging to your foppish brithers,   25
Black corbies dress'd in peacocks feathers;
Like thee they dander here an' there,
Whan simmer's blinks are warm an' fair,
An' loo to snuff the healthy balm

Whan ev'nin' spreads her wing sae calm;   30
But whan she girns an' glowrs sae dowr
Frae Borean houff in angry show'r,
Like thee they scoug frae street or field,
An' hap them in a lyther bield;
For they war' never made to dree   35
The adverse gloom o' Fortune's eie,
Nor ever pried life's pining woes,
Nor pu'd the prickles wi' the rose.
    Poor butterfly! thy case I mourn,
To green kail-yeard and fruits return: 40
How cou'd you troke the mavis' note
For "penny pies all-piping hot"?
Can lintie's music be compar'd
Wi' gruntles frae the city-guard?
Or can our flow'rs at ten hours bell   45
The gowan or the spink excel.
    Now shou'd our sclates wi' hailstanes ring,
What cabbage fald wad screen your wing?
Say, fluttering fairy! wer't thy hap
To light beneath braw Nany's cap,   50
Wad she, proud butterfly of May!
In pity lat you skaithless stay;
The furies glancing frae her ein
Wad rug your wings o' siller sheen,
That, wae for thee! far, far outvy   55
Her Paris artist's finest dye;
Then a' your bonny spraings wad fall,
An' you a worm be left to crawl.
    To sic mishanter rins the laird
Wha quats his ha'-house an' kail-yard,   60
Grows politician, scours to court,
Whare he's the laughing-stock and sport
Of Ministers, wha jeer an' jibe,
And heeze his hopes wi' thought o' bribe,
Till in the end they flae him bare,   65
Leave him to poortith, and to care.
Their fleetching words o'er late he sees,
He trudges hame, repines and dies.
    Sic be their fa' wha dirk thir ben

In blackest business no their ain; 70
And may they scad their lips fu' leal,
That dip their spoons in ither's kail.

HAME CONTENT. A SATIRE

To all whom it may concern.

Some fock, like bees, fu' glegly rin
To bykes bang'd fu' o' strife and din,
And thieve and huddle crumb by crumb,
Till they have scrapt the dautit plumb,
Then craw fell crously o' their wark, 5
Tell o'er their turners mark by mark,
Yet darna think to lowse the pose,
To aid their neighbours ails and woes.
  Gif gowd can fetter thus the heart,
And gar us act sae base a part, 10
Shall man, a niggard near-gawn elf!
Rin to the tether's end for pelf;
Learn ilka cunzied scoundrel's trick,
Whan a's done sell his saul to Nick:
I trow they've coft the purchase dear, 15
That gang sic lengths for warldly gear.
  Now whan the Dog-day heats begin
To birsel and to peel the skin,
May I lie streekit at my ease,
Beneath the caller shady trees, 20
(Far frae the din o' Borrowstown,)
Whar water plays the haughs bedown,
To jouk the simmer's rigor there,
And breath a while the caller air
'Mang herds, an' honest cottar fock, 25
That till the farm and feed the flock;
Careless o' mair, wha never fash
To lade their kist wi' useless cash,

171

But thank the gods for what they've sent
O' health eneugh, and blyth content,   30
An' pith, that helps them to stravaig
Owr ilka cleugh and ilka craig,
Unkend to a' the weary granes
That aft arise frae gentler banes,
On easy-chair that pamper'd lie,   35
Wi' banefu' viands gustit high,
And turn and fald their weary clay,
To rax and gaunt the live-lang day.
  Ye sages, tell, was man e'er made
To dree this hatefu' sluggard trade?   40
Steekit frae Nature's beauties a'
That daily on his presence ca';
At hame to girn, and whinge, and pine
For fav'rite dishes, fav'rite wine:
Come then, shake off thir sluggish ties,   45
An' wi' the bird o' dawning rise;
On ilka bauk the clouds hae spread
Wi' blobs o' dew a pearly bed;
Frae faulds nae mair the owsen rout,
But to the fatt'ning clever lout,   50
Whare they may feed at heart's content,
Unyokit frae their winter's stent.
  Unyoke then, man, an' binna sweer
To ding a hole in ill-haind gear:
O think that eild, wi' wyly fitt,   55
Is wearing nearer bit by bit;
Gin yence he claws you wi' his paw,
What's siller for? Fiend haet awa,
But gowden playfair, that may please
The second sharger till he dies.   60
  Some daft chiel reads, and takes advice;
The chaise is yokit in a trice;
Awa drives he like huntit de'il,
And scarce tholes time to cool his wheel,
Till he's Lord kens how far awa,   65
At Italy, or Well o' Spaw,
Or to Montpelier's safter air;
For far aff fowls hae feathers fair.

172

There rest him weel; for eith can we
Spare mony glakit gouks like he;   70
They'll tell whare Tibur's waters rise;
What sea receives the drumly prize,
That never wi' their feet hae mett
The marches o' their ain estate.

    The Arno and the Tibur lang   75
Hae run fell clear in Roman sang;
But, save the reverence of schools!
They're baith but lifeless dowy pools.
Dought they compare wi' bonny Tweed,
As clear as ony lammer-bead?   80
Or are their shores mair sweet and gay
Than Fortha's haughs or banks o' Tay?
Tho' there the herds can jink the show'rs
'Mang thriving vines an' myrtle bow'rs,
And blaw the reed to kittle strains,   85
While echo's tongue commends their pains,
Like ours, they canna warm the heart
Wi' simple, saft, bewitching art.
On *Leader haughs an' Yarrow braes*,
Arcadian herds wad tyne their lays,   90
To hear the mair melodious sounds
That live on our poetic grounds.

    Come, Fancy, come, and let us tread
The simmer's flow'ry velvet bed,
And a' your springs delightfu' lowse   95
On *Tweeda's banks* or *Cowdenknows*,
That, ta'en wi' thy inchanting sang,
Our Scottish lads may round ye thrang,
Sae pleas'd, they'll never fash again
To court you on Italian plain;   100
Soon will they guess ye only wear
The simple garb o' Nature here;
Mair comely far, an' fair to sight
Whan in her easy cleething dight,
Than in disguise ye was before   105
On Tibur's, or on Arno's shore.

    O Bangour! now the hills and dales
Nae mair gi'e back thy tender tales!

The birks on Yarrow now deplore
Thy mournfu' muse has left the shore:
Near what bright burn or chrystal spring
Did you your winsome whistle hing?
The muse shall there, wi' wat'ry eie,
Gi'e the dunk swaird a tear for thee;
And Yarrow's genius, dowy dame!
Shall there forget her blude-stain'd stream,
On thy sad grave to seek repose,
Wha mourn'd her fate, condol'd her woes.

LEITH RACES

In July month, ae bonny morn,
   Whan Nature's rokelay green
Was spread o'er ilka rigg o' corn,
   To charm our roving een;
Glouring about I saw a quean,   5
   The fairest 'neath the lift;
Her een ware o' the siller sheen,
   Her skin like snawy drift,
         Sae white that day.

Quod she, "I ferly unco sair,   10
   That ye sud musand gae,
Ye wha hae sung o' Hallow-Fair,
   Her winter's pranks and play:
Whan on Leith-Sands the racers rare,
   Wi' Jocky louns are met,   15
Their orro pennies there to ware,
   And drown themsel's in debt
         Fu' deep that day."

"And wha are ye, my winsome dear,
   That takes the gate sae early?
Whare do ye win, gin ane may spier,   20

For I right meikle ferly,
That sic braw buskit laughing lass
  Thir bonny blinks shou'd gi'e,
An' loup like Hebe o'er the grass,   25
  As wanton and as free,
              Frae dule this day?"

"I dwall amang the caller springs
  That weet the Land o' Cakes,
And aften tune my canty strings   30
  At bridals and late-wakes:
They ca' me Mirth; I ne'er was kend
  To grumble or look sour,
But blyth wad be a lift to lend,
  Gif ye wad sey my pow'r   35
              An' pith this day."

"A bargain be't, and, by my feggs,
  Gif ye will be my mate,
Wi' you I'll screw the cheery pegs,
  Ye shanna find me blate;   40
We'll reel an' ramble thro' the sands,
  And jeer wi' a' we meet;
Nor hip the daft and gleesome bands
  That fill Edina's street
              Sae thrang this day."   45

Ere servant maids had wont to rise
  To seeth the breakfast kettle,
Ilk dame her brawest ribbons tries,
  To put her on her mettle,
Wi' wiles some silly chiel to trap,   50
  (And troth he's fain to get her,)
But she'll craw kniefly in his crap,
  Whan, wow! he canna flit her
              Frae hame that day.

Now, mony a scaw'd and bare-ars'd lown   55
  Rise early to their wark,
Enough to fley a muckle town,

Wi' dinsome squeel and bark.
"Here is the true an' faithfu' list
   O' Noblemen and Horses;   60
Their eild, their weight, their height, their grist,
   That rin for Plates or Purses
               Fu' fleet this day."

To whisky plooks that brunt for wooks
   On town-guard soldiers faces,   65
Their barber bauld his whittle crooks,
   An' scrapes them for the races:
Their stumps erst u'sd to filipegs,
   Are dight in spaterdashes
Whase barkent hides scarce fend their legs   70
   Frae weet, and weary plashes
               O' dirt that day.

"Come, hafe a care (the captain cries),
   On guns your bagnets thraw;
Now mind your manual exercise,   75
   An' marsh down raw by raw."
And as they march he'll glowr about,
   'Tent a' their cuts and scars:
'Mang them fell mony a gausy snout
   Has gusht in birth-day wars,   80
               Wi' blude that day.

Her *Nanesel* maun be carefu' now,
   Nor maun she pe misleard,
Sin baxter lads hae seal'd a vow
   To skelp and clout the guard: 85
I'm sure Auld Reikie kens o' nane
   That wou'd be sorry at it,
Tho' they should dearly pay the kane,
   An' get their tails weel sautit
               And sair thir days.   90

The tinkler billies i' the Bow
   Are now less eidant clinking,
As lang's their pith or siller dow,

They're daffin', and they're drinking.
Bedown Leith-Walk what burrochs reel   95
  Of ilka trade and station,
That gar their wives an' childer feel
  Toom weyms for their libation
            O' drink thir days.

The browster wives thegither harl   100
  A' trash that they can fa' on;
They rake the grounds o' ilka barrel,
  To profit by the lawen:
For weel wat they a skin leal het
  For drinking needs nae hire;   105
At drumbly gear they take nae pet;
  Foul water slockens fire
            And drouth thir days.

They say, ill ale has been the deid
  O' mony a beirdly lown;   110
Then dinna gape like gleds wi' greed
  To sweel hail bickers down:
Gin Lord send mony ane the morn,
  They'll ban fu' sair the time
That e'er they toutit aff the horn   115
  Which wambles thro' their weym
            Wi' pain that day.

The Buchan bodies thro' the beech
  Their bunch of Findrums cry,
An' skirl out baul', in Norland speech,   120
  "Gueed speldings, fa will buy."
An', by my saul, they're nae wrang gear
  To gust a stirrah's mow;
Weel staw'd wi' them, he'll never spear
  The price o' being fu'   125
            Wi' drink that day.

Now wyly wights at rowly powl,
  An' flingin' o' the dice,
Here brake the banes o' mony a soul,

Wi' fa's upo' the ice: 130
At first the gate seems fair an' straught,
    So they had fairly till her;
But wow! in spite o' a' their maught,
    They're rookit o' their siller
                            An' goud that day.   135

Around whare'er ye fling your een,
    The haiks like wind are scourin';
Some chaises honest folk contain,
    An' some hae mony a whore in;
Wi' rose and lily, red and white,   140
    They gie themselves sic fit airs,
Like Dian, they will seem perfite;
    But its nae goud that glitters
                            Wi' them thir days.

The Lyon here, wi' open paw,   145
    May cleek in mony hunder,
Wha geck at Scotland and her law,
    His wyly talons under;
For ken, tho' Jamie's laws are auld,
    (Thanks to the wise recorder),   150
His Lyon yet roars loud and bawld,
    To had the Whigs in order
                            Sae prime this day.

To town-guard drum of clangor clear,
    Baith men and steeds are raingit;   155
Some liveries red or yellow wear,
    And some are tartan spraingit:
And now the red, the blue e'en-now
    Bids fairest for the market;
But, 'ere the sport be done, I trow   160
    Their skins are gayly yarkit
                            And peel'd thir days.

Siclike in Robinhood debates,
    Whan twa chiels hae a pingle;
E'en-now some couli gets his aits,   165

An' dirt wi' words they mingle,
Till up loups he, wi' diction fu',
　　There's lang and dreech contesting;
For now they're near the point in view;
　　Now ten miles frae the question　　　　　　170
　　　　　　　　In hand that night.

The races o'er, they hale the dools,
　　Wi' drink o' a' kin-kind;
Great feck gae hirpling hame like fools,
　　The cripple lead the blind.　　　　　　　175
May ne'er the canker o' the drink
　　E'er make our spirits thrawart,
Case we git wharewitha' to wink
　　Wi' een as blue's a blawart
　　　　　　　　Wi' straiks thir days!　　　180

ODE TO THE GOWDSPINK

Frae fields whare Spring her sweets has blawn
Wi' caller verdure o'er the lawn,
The gowdspink comes in new attire,
The brawest 'mang the whistling choir,
That, ere the sun can clear his ein,　　　　　　5
Wi' glib notes sane the simmer's green.
　　Sure Nature herried mony a tree,
For spraings and bonny spats to thee;
Nae mair the rainbow can impart
Sic glowing ferlies o' her art,　　　　　　　10
Whase pencil wrought its freaks at will
On thee the sey-piece o' her skill.
Nae mair through straths in simmer dight
We seek the rose to bless our sight;
Or bid the bonny wa'-flowers sprout　　　　　15
On yonder ruin's lofty snout.
Thy shining garments far outstrip

179

The cherries upo' Hebe's lip,
And fool the tints that Nature chose
To busk and paint the crimson rose.   20
    'Mang men, wae's-heart! we aften find
The brawest drest want peace of mind,
While he that gangs wi' ragged coat
Is weil contentit wi' his lot.
Whan wand wi' glewy birdlime's set,   25
To steal far aff your dautit mate,
Blyth wad ye change your cleething gay
In lieu of lav'rock's sober grey.
In vain thro' woods you sair may ban
Th' envious treachery of man,   30
That, wi' your gowden glister ta'en,
Still hunts you on the simmer's plain,
And traps you 'mang the sudden fa's
O' winter's dreary dreepin' snaws.
Now steekit frae the gowany field,   35
Frae ilka fav'rite houff and bield,
But mergh, alas! to disengage
Your bonny bouck frae fettering cage,
Your free-born bosom beats in vain
For darling liberty again.   40
In window hung, how aft we see
Thee keek around at warblers free,
That carrol saft, and sweetly sing
Wi' a' the blythness of the spring?
Like Tantalus they hing you here   45
To spy the glories o' the year;
And tho' you're at the burnie's brink,
They douna suffer you to drink.
    Ah, Liberty! thou bonny dame,
How wildly wanton is thy stream,   50
Round whilk the birdies a' rejoice,
An' hail you wi' a gratefu' voice.
The gowdspink chatters joyous here,
And courts wi' gleesome sangs his peer:
The mavis frae the new-bloom'd thorn   55
Begins his lauds at earest morn;
And herd lowns louping o'er the grass,

Need far less fleetching till their lass,
Than paughty damsels bred at courts,
Wha thraw their mou's, and take the dorts: 60
But, reft of thee, fient flee we care
For a' that life ahint can spare.
The gowdspink, that sae lang has kend
Thy happy sweets (his wonted friend),
Her sad confinement ill can brook   65
In some dark chamber's dowy nook:
Tho' Mary's hand his nebb supplies,
Unkend to hunger's painfu' cries,
Ev'n beauty canna cheer the heart
Frae life, frae liberty apart;   70
For now we tyne its wonted lay,
Sae lightsome sweet, sae blythly gay.
    Thus Fortune aft a curse can gie,
To wyle us far frae liberty:
Then tent her syren smiles wha list,   75
I'll ne'er envy your girnal's grist;
For whan fair freedom smiles nae mair,
Care I for life? Shame fa' the hair:
A field o'ergrown wi' rankest stubble,
The essence of a paltry bubble.   80

TO THE PRINCIPAL AND PROFESSORS OF THE UNIVERSITY OF ST ANDREWS, ON THEIR SUPERB TREAT TO DR SAMUEL JOHNSON

St Andrews town may look right gawsy,
Nae grass will grow upon her cawsey,
Nor wa'-flowers of a yellow dye,
Glour dowy o'er her ruins high,
Sin Samy's head weel pang'd wi' lear,   5
Has seen the *Alma Mater* there:
Regents, my winsome billy boys!
'Bout him you've made an unco noise;

Nae doubt for him your bells wad clink
To find him upon Eden's brink,   10
An' a' things nicely set in order,
Wad kep him on the Fifan border:
I'se warrant now frae France an' Spain,
Baith cooks and scullions mony ane
Wad gar the pats an' kettles tingle   15
Around the college kitchen ingle,
To fleg frae a' your craigs the roup,
Wi' reeking het and crieshy soup;
And snails and puddocks mony hunder
Wad beeking lie the hearth-stane under,   20
Wi' roast and boild, an' a' kin kind,
To heat the body, cool the mind.
    But hear me lads! gin I'd been there,
How I wad trimm'd the bill o' fare!
For ne'er sic surly wight as he   25
Had met wi' sic respect frae me.
Mind ye what Sam, the lying loun!
Has in his Dictionar laid down?
That aits in England are a feast
To cow an' horse, an' sican beast,   30
While in Scots ground this growth was common
To gust the gab o' man and woman.
Tak tent, ye Regents! then, an' hear
My list o' gudely hamel gear,
Sic as ha'e often rax'd the wyme   35
O' blyther fallows mony time;
Mair hardy, souple, steive an' swank,
Than ever stood on Samy's shank.
    Imprimis, then, a haggis fat,
Weel tottled in a seything pat,   40
Wi' spice and ingans weel ca'd thro',
Had help'd to gust the stirrah's mow,
And plac'd itsel in truncher clean
Before the gilpy's glowrin een.
    Secundo, then a gude sheep's head   45
Whase hide was singit, never flead,
And four black trotters cled wi' girsle,
Bedown his throat had learn'd to hirsle.

What think ye neist, o' gude fat brose
To clag his ribs? a dainty dose!   50
And white and bloody puddins routh,
To gar the Doctor skirl, O Drouth!
Whan he cou'd never houp to merit
A cordial o' reaming claret,
But thraw his nose, and brize and pegh   55
O'er the contents o' sma' ale quegh:
Then let his wisdom girn and snarl
O'er a weel-tostit girdle farl,
An' learn, that maugre o' his wame,
Ill bairns are ay best heard at hame.   60
    Drummond, lang syne, o' Hawthornden,
The wyliest an' best o' men,
Has gi'en you dishes ane or mae,
That wad ha' gard his grinders play,
Not to *roast beef*, old England's life,   65
But to the auld *east nook of Fife*,
Whare Creilian crafts cou'd weel ha'e gi'en
Scate-rumples to ha'e clear'd his een;
Than neist whan Samy's heart was faintin,
He'd lang'd for scate to mak him wanton.   70
    Ah! willawins, for Scotland now,
Whan she maun stap ilk birky's mow
Wi' eistacks, grown as 'tware in pet
In foreign land, or green-house het,
When cog o' brose an' cutty spoon   75
Is a' our cottar childer's boon,
Wha thro' the week, till Sunday's speal,
Toil for pease-clods an' gude lang kail.
Devall then, Sirs, and never send
For daintiths to regale a friend,   80
Or, like a torch at baith ends burning,
Your house 'll soon grow mirk and mourning.
    What's this I hear some cynic say?
Robin, ye loun! its nae fair play;
Is there nae ither subject rife   85
To clap your thumb upon but Fife?
Gi'e o'er, young man, you'll meet your corning,
Than caption war, or charge o' horning;

Some canker'd surly sour-mow'd carline
Bred near the abbey o' Dumfarline,   90
Your shoulders yet may gi'e a lounder,
An' be of verse the mal-confounder.
   Come on, ye blades! but 'ere ye tulzie,
Or hack our flesh wi' sword or gulzie,
Ne'er shaw your teeth, nor look like stink,   95
Nor o'er an empty bicker blink:
What weets the wizen an' the wyme,
Will mend your prose and heal my rhyme.

THE ELECTION

Nunc est bibendum, et bendere Bickerum magnum;
Cavete Town-guardum, Dougal Geddum atque Campbellum.

Rejoice, ye Burghers, ane an' a',
   Lang look't for's come at last;
Sair war your backs held to the wa'
   Wi' poortith an' wi' fast:
Now ye may clap your wings an' craw,   5
   And gayly busk ilk' feather,
For Deacon Cocks hae pass'd a law
   To rax an' weet your leather
              Wi' drink thir days.

"Haste, Epps," quo' John, "an' bring my gez,   10
   Tak tent ye dinna't spulzie;
Last night the barber ga't a friz,
   An' straikit it wi' ulzie.
Hae done your paritch lassie Liz,
   Gi'e me my sark and gravat;   15
I'se be as braw's the Deacon is
   Whan he taks affidavit
              O' faith the day."

"Whar's Johnny gaun," cries neebor Bess,
   "That he's sae gayly bodin   20
Wi' new kam'd wig, weel syndet face,
   Silk hose, for hamely hodin?"
"Our Johnny's nae sma' drink you'll guess,
   He's trig as ony muir-cock,
An' forth to mak a Deacon, lass;   25
   He downa speak to poor fock
          Like us the day."

The coat ben-by i' the kist-nook,
   That's been this towmonth swarmin,
Is brought yence mair thereout to look,   30
   To fleg awa the vermin:
Menzies o' moths an' flaes are shook,
   An' i' the floor they howder,
Till in a birn beneath the crook
   They're singit wi' a scowder   35
          To death that day.

The canty cobler quats his sta',
   His rozet an' his lingans;
His buik has dree'd a sair, sair fa'
   Frae meals o' bread an' ingans: 40
Now he's a pow o' wit and law,
   An' taunts at soals an' heels;
To Walker's he can rin awa,
   There whang his creams an' jeels
          Wi' life that day.   45

The lads in order tak their seat,
   (The de'il may claw the clungest)
They stegh an' connach sae the meat,
   Their teeth mak mair than tongue haste:
Their claes sae cleanly dight an' feat,   50
   An' eke their craw-black beavers,
Like masters mows hae found the gate
   To tassels teugh wi' slavers
          Fu' lang that day.

The dinner done, for brandy strang   55
    They cry, to weet their thrapple,
To gar the stamack bide the bang,
    Nor wi' its laden grapple.
The grace is said – its no o'er lang;
    The claret reams in bells;   60
Quod Deacon let the toast round gang,
    "Come, here's our noble sel's
            Weel met the day."

"Weels me o' drink," quo' cooper Will,
    "My barrel has been geyz'd ay,   65
An' has na gotten sic a fill
    Sin fu' on handsel-Teysday:
But makes-na, now its got a sweel,
    Ae gird I shanna cast lad,
Or else I wish the horned de'el   70
    May Will wi' kittle cast dad
            To hell the day!"

The Magistrates fu' wyly are,
    Their lamps are gayly blinking,
But they might as leive burn elsewhere,   75
    When fock's blind fu' wi' drinking.
Our Deacon wadna ca' a chair,
    The foul ane durst him na-say;
He took shanks-naig, but fient may care,
    He arselins kiss'd the cawsey   80
            Wi' bir that night.

Weel loes me o' you, souter Jock,
    For tricks ye buit be trying,
Whan greapin for his ain bed-stock,
    He fa's whare Will's wife's lying.   85
Will coming hame wi' ither fock,
    He saw Jock there before him;
Wi' master laiglen, like a brock
    He did wi' stink maist smore him
            Fu' strang that night.   90

186

Then wi' a souple leathern whang
   He gart them fidge an' girn ay,
"Faith, chiel, ye's no for naething gang
   Gin ye man reel my pirny."
Syne wi' a muckle alshin lang   95
   He brodit Maggie's hurdies;
An' 'cause he thought her i' the wrang,
   There pass'd nae bonny wordies
                        'Mang them that night.

Now, had some laird his lady fand,   100
   In sic unseemly courses,
It might hae loos'd the haly band,
   Wi' law-suits an' divorces:
But the niest day they a' shook hands,
   And ilka crack did sowder,   105
While Megg for drink her apron pawns,
   For a' the gude-man cow'd her
                        Whan fu' last night.

Glowr round the cawsey, up an' down,
   What mobbing and what plotting!   110
Here politicians bribe a loun
   Against his saul for voting.
The gowd that inlakes half a crown
   Thir blades lug out to try them,
They pouch the gowd, nor fash the town   115
   For weights an' scales to weigh them
                        Exact that day.

Then Deacons at the counsel stent
   To get themsel's presentit:
For towmonths twa their saul is lent,   120
   For the town's gude indentit:
Lang's their debating thereanent;
   About *protests* they're bauthrin,
While Sandy Fife, to mak content,
   On bells plays *Clout the caudron*   125
                        To them that day.

Ye lowns that troke in doctor's stuff,
  You'll now hae unco slaisters;
Whan windy blaws their stamacks puff,
  They'll need baith pills an' plaisters;   130
For tho' ev'now they look right bluff,
  Sic drinks, 'ere hillocks meet,
Will hap some Deacons in a truff,
  Inrow'd in the lang leet
              O' death yon night.   135

ELEGY ON JOHN HOGG,
LATE PORTER TO THE
UNIVERSITY OF ST ANDREWS

Death, what's ado? the de'il be licket,
Or wi' your stang, you ne'er had pricket,
Or our auld *Alma Mater* tricket
          O' poor John Hogg,
And trail'd him ben thro' your mark wicket   5
          As dead's a log.

Now ilka glaikit scholar loun
May dander wae wi' duddy gown;
Kate Kennedy to dowy crune
          May mourn and clink,   10
And steeples o' Saint Andrew's town
          To yird may sink.

Sin' Pauly Tam, wi' canker'd snout,
First held the students in about
To wear their claes as black as soot,   15
          They ne'er had reason,
Till death John's haffit ga'e a clout
          Sae out o' season.

When regents met at common schools,
He taught auld Tam to hale the dules,   20

And eidant to row right the bowls
            Like ony emmack;
He kept us a' within the rules
            Strict academic.

Heh! wha will tell the students now,   25
To meet the *Pauly* cheek for chow,
Whan he, like frightsome wirrikow,
            Had wont to rail,
And set our stamacks in a low,
            Or we turn'd tail.   30

Ah, Johnny! aften did I grumble
Frae cozy bed fu' ear' to tumble;
When art and part I'd been in some ill,
            Troth I was sweer,
His words they brodit like a wumill   35
            Frae ear to ear.

Whan I had been fu' laith to rise,
John than begude to moralize:
"The tither nap, the sluggard cries,
            And turns him round;   40
Sae spake auld Solomon the wise
            Divine profound!"

Nae dominie, or wise mess John,
Was better lear'd in Solomon;
He cited proverbs one by one   45
            Ilk vice to tame;
He gar'd ilk sinner sigh an' groan,
            And fear hell's flame.

"I hae nae meikle skill," quo' he,
'In what you ca' philosophy;   50
It tells that baith the earth and sea
            Rin round about;
Either the Bible tells a lie,
            Or you're a' out.

Its i' the psalms o' David writ,   55
That this wide warld ne'er shou'd flit,
But on the waters coshly sit
          Fu' steeve and lasting."
An' was na he a head o' wit
          At sic contesting!   60

On einings cauld wi' glee we'd trudge
To heat our shins in Johnny's lodge;
The de'il ane thought his bum to budge
          Wi' siller on us:
To claw het pints we'd never grudge   65
          O' *molationis*.

Say ye, red gowns! that aften here
Hae toasted bakes to Kattie's beer,
Gin e'er thir days hae had their peer,
          Sae blyth, sae daft;   70
You'll ne'er again in life's career
          Sit ha'f sae saft.

Wi' haffit locks sae smooth and sleek,
John look'd like ony antient Greek;
He was a Naz'rene a' the week,   75
          And doughtna tell out
A bawbee Scots to straik his cheek
          Till Sunday fell out.

For John ay lo'ed to turn the pence,
Thought poortith was a great offence: 80
"What recks tho' ye ken mood and tense?
          A hungry weyme
For gowd wad wi' them baith dispense
          At ony time.

Ye ken what ails maun ay befal   85
The chiel that will be prodigal;
When wasted to the very spaul
          He turns his tusk,

For want o' comfort to his saul
        O hungry husk!"   90

Ye royit lowns! just do as he'd do;
For mony braw green shaw and meadow
He's left to cheer his dowy widow,
        His winsome Kate,
That to him prov'd a canny she-dow,   95
        Baith ear' and late.

THE SITTING OF THE SESSION

Phœbus, sair cow'd wi' simmer's hight,
Cours near the yird wi' blinking light;
Cauld shaw the haughs, nae mair bedight
        Wi' simmer's claes,
They heeze the heart o' dowy wight   5
        That thro' them gaes.

Weel lo'es me o' you, business, now;
For ye'll weet mony a drouthy mou',
That's lang a eisning gane for you,
        Withouten fill   10
O' dribbles frae the gude brown cow,
        Or Highland gill.

The Court o' Session, weel wat I,
Pitts ilk chiel's whittle i' the pye,
Can criesh the slaw-gaun wheels whan dry,   15
        Till Session's done,
Tho' they'll gie mony a cheep and cry
        Or twalt o' June.

Ye benders a', that dwall in joot,
You'll tak your liquor clean cap out,   20
Synd your mouse-wabbs wi' reaming stout,

While ye ha'e cash,
And gar your cares a' tak the rout,
        An' thumb ne'er fash.

Rob Gibb's grey gizz, now frizzl'd fine,   25
Will white as ony snaw-ba' shine;
Weel does he lo'e the lawen coin
        Whan dossied down,
For whisky gills or dribbs of wine
        In cauld forenoon.   30

Bar-keepers now, at Outer Door,
Tak tent as fock gang back and fore:
The fient ane there but pays his score,
        Nane wins toll-free,
Tho' ye've a cause the house before,   35
        Or agent be.

Gin ony here wi' canker knocks,
And has na lous'd his siller pocks,
Ye need na think to fleetch or cox;
        "Come, shaw's your gear;   40
Ae scabbit yew spills twenty flocks,
        Ye's no be here."

Now at the door they'll raise a plea;
Crack on, my lads! – for flyting's free;
For gin ye shou'd tongue-tacket be,   45
        The mair's the pity,
Whan scalding but and ben we see
        Pendente lite.

The lawyer's skelfs, and printer's presses,
Grain unco sair wi' weighty cases;   50
The clark in toil his pleasure places,
        To thrive bedeen;
At five-hour's bell scribes shaw their faces,
        And rake their ein.

The country fock to lawyers crook,   55
"Ah! Weels me on your bonny buik!

The benmost part o' my kist nook
             I'll ripe for thee,
And willing ware my hindmost rook
             For my decree."   60

But Law's a draw-well unco deep,
Withouten rim fock out to keep;
A donnart chiel, whan drunk, may dreep
             Fu' sleely in,
But finds the gate baith stay and steep,   65
             'Ere out he win.

TO MY AULD BREEKS

Now gae your wa's – Tho' anes as gude
As ever happit flesh and blude,
Yet part we maun – The case sae hard is,
Amang the writers and the bardies,
That lang they'll brook the auld I trow,   5
Or neibours cry, "Weel brook the new;"
Still making tight wi' tither steek,
The tither hole, the tither eik,
To bang the birr o' winter's anger,
And had the hurdies out o' langer.   10
    Sicklike some weary wight will fill
His kyte wi' drogs frae doctor's bill,
Thinking to tack the tither year
To life, and look baith haill an' fier,
Till at the lang-run death dirks in,   15
To birze his saul ayont his skin.
    You needna wag your duds o' clouts,
Nor fa' into your dorty pouts,
To think that erst you've hain'd my tail
Frae wind and weet, frae snaw and hail,   20
And for reward, whan bald and hummil,
Frae garret high to dree a tumble.

For you I car'd, as lang's ye dow'd
Be lin'd wi' siller or wi' gowd:
Now to befriend, it wad be folly,   25
Your raggit hide an' pouches holey;
For wha but kens a poet's placks
Get mony weary flaws an' cracks,
And canna thole to hae them tint,
As he sae seenil sees the mint?   30
Yet round the warld keek and see,
That ithers fare as ill as thee;
For weel we lo'e the chiel we think
Can get us tick, or gie us drink,
Till o' his purse we've seen the bottom,   35
Then we despise, and ha'e forgot him.
    Yet gratefu' hearts, to make amends,
Will ay be sorry for their friends,
And I for thee – As mony a time
Wi' you I've speel'd the braes o' rime,   40
Whare for the time the Muse ne'er cares
For siller, or sic guilefu' wares,
Wi' whilk we drumly grow, and crabbit,
Dowr, capernoited, thrawin gabbit,
And brither, sister, friend and fae,   45
Without remeid of kindred, slay.
    You've seen me round the bickers reel
Wi' heart as hale as temper'd steel,
And face sae apen, free and blyth,
Nor thought that sorrow there cou'd kyth;   50
But the niest mament this was lost,
Like gowan in December's frost.
    Cou'd Prick-the-louse but be sae handy
To make the breeks and claise to stand ay,
Thro' thick and thin wi' you I'd dash on,   55
Nor mind the folly of the fashion:
But, hegh! the times *vicissitudo*,
Gars ither breeks decay as you do.
Thae Macaronies, braw and windy,
Maun fail – *Sic transit gloria mundi*!   60
    Now speed you to some madam's chaumer,
That butt an' ben rings dule an' claumer,

Ask her, in kindness, if she seeks
In hidling ways to wear the breeks?
Safe you may dwall, tho' mould and motty,   65
Beneath the veil o' under coatie,
For this mair faults nor yours can screen
Frae lover's quickest sense, his ein.

   Or if some bard in lucky times,
Shou'd profit meikle by his rhimes,   70
And pace awa', wi' smirky face,
In siller or in gowden lace,
Glowr in his face, like spectre gaunt,
Remind him o' his former want,
To cow his daffin and his pleasure   75
And gar him live within the measure.

   So Philip, it is said, who wou'd ring
O'er Macedon a just and gude king,
Fearing that power might plume his feather
And bid him stretch beyond the tether,   80
Ilk morning to his lug wad ca'
A tiny servant o' his ha',
To tell him to improve his span,
For Philip was, like him, a man.

HORACE, ODE XI. LIB. I

Ne'er fash your thumb what gods decree
To be the weird o' you or me,
Nor deal in cantrup's kittle cunning
To speir how fast your days are running.
But patient lippen for the best,   5
Nor be in dowy thought opprest,
Whether we see mare winters come
Than this that spits wi' canker'd foam.
   Now moisten weel your geyzen'd wa'as
Wi' couthy friends and hearty blaws;   10
Ne'er lat your hope o'ergang your days,

For eild and thraldom never stays;
The day looks gash, toot aff your horn,
Nor care yae strae about the morn.

THE AUTHOR'S LIFE

My life is like the flowing stream
That glides where summer's beauties teem,
Meets all the riches of the gale
That on its watry bosom sail,
And wanders 'midst Elysian groves   5
Thro' all the haunts that fancy loves.
    May I, when drooping days decline,
And 'gainst those genial streams combine,
The winter's sad decay forsake,
And center in my parent lake.   10

ON NIGHT

Now murky shades surround the pole;
Darkness lords without controul;
To the notes of buzzing owl
Lions roar, and tygers howl.
Fright'ning from their azure shrine,   5
Stars that wont in orbs to shine:
Now the sailor's storm-tost bark
Knows no blest celestial mark,
While, in the briny troubled deep,
Dolphins change their sport for sleep: 10
Ghosts, and frightful spectres gaunt,
Church-yards dreary footsteps haunt,
And brush, with wither'd arms, the dews
That fall upon the drooping yews.

NOTES

Poems by Allan Ramsay

The date of the first extant printing is given in each case, but the texts followed
for most of the poems are those of Ramsay's *Poems* of 1721 and 1728 (STS
Volumes I and II). A few poems noted here are from STS Volume III, and being
transcripts of Ramsay's MSS, have been edited to conform with the presenta-
tion usual in his printed works.

P. 3. Elegy on Maggy Johnston, who died Anno 1711. 1718. Ramsay's own
annotations to this and the three poems following have been reproduced. This
one is first referrred to in 'The Journal of the Easy Club' (STS Volume V),
under entries for June and July of 1712.

P. 7. Elegy on John Cowper, Kirk-Treasurer's Man, Anno 1714. 1718. There
was one Kirk Session for the whole of Edinburgh. Its Treasurer took charge of
fines for immorality and offences against Church discipline, his position being
comparable with that of Chaucer's Summoner. 2. **Ohon!** (Ochane!): a Gaelic
expression of sorrow, 'alas!' 10, 12. **Fleed, dead:** Scots 'dead' has the same
sound as 'deed'. 32. **lang hame:** grave (*Ecclesiastes*, xii, 5). 79. **Stinking Stile:**
an entry or passage through the Luckenbooths, in the High Street of Edinburgh
(see Fergusson, 'Auld Reikie', 53n), leading to the three churches into which
St. Giles was then divided. John Cowper may have combined his post as Kirk-
Treasurer's Man with that of beadle in one of these churches.

P. 10. Elegy on Lucky Wood in the Canongate, May 1717. 1718.

P. 13. Lucky Spence's Last Advice. 1718. This mock elegy was inspired by
William Hamilton of Gilbertfield's 'The Last Dying Words of Bonny Heck'.
(See 'Familiar Epistles, Answer I', 12, 27). 13. **black-ey'd Bess** etc.: see 'The
Marrow Ballad', 9–10. 41. **hale the dools:** see Fergusson, 'Leith Races', 172n.;
'Elegy on John Hogg', 20n. 51. **Hangy's taz:** the 'taz' was the tawse or leather
whip which the hangman used at public floggings.

Familiar Epistles between Lieutenant William Hamilton and Allan Ramsay.
1719. Ramsay added his own notes to each. William Hamilton of Gilber-
field near Cambuslang (1670–1751), a retired army officer, was the author of
an abridged version (1722) of Hary's *Wallace*, which later inspired Burns with
patriotic fervour. He also contributed to Ramsay's *The Tea-Table Miscellany*.

197

P. 17. Epistle I. 5. **Tamtallon:** Tantallon Castle, a formidable fortress near North Berwick, scene in 1528 of one of the last great sieges. 49. **crambo:** cleverly informal, sometimes doggerel verse.

P. 20. Answer I. 8. **Gossy Don's:** a tavern in Don's Close, opposite the Lucken-booths; William Don, vintner, lived there in 1704, and the reference may be to his widow. 12, 27. **Bonny Heck:** 'The Last Dying Words of Bonny Heck', published in Watson's *Choice Collection*, was a mock elegy on a renowned Fife greyhound. It was modelled on the 'Habby Simpson' elegy to which Ramsay refers in his own note to l. 36. 36. **Standart Habby:** 'standard' because so often used. The name came from its use by Robert Sempill of Beltrees in the humorous elegy 'The Life and Death of Habbie Simpson, the Piper of Kilbar-chan' (c. 1640), one of Ramsay's models for his own elegies. The stanza came to be used extensively by Fergusson and Burns. 49. **Cam, and Ox:** Cambridge and Oxford. 51: refers to Pope's *The Rape of the Lock*, Tassoni's *Secchia Rapita* (The Stolen Bucket). 59. The comic poems *Peblis to the Play* and *Christ's Kirk* were attributed respectively to James I and James V of Scotland.

P. 22. Epistle II. 102. **Trough of Clyde:** Clydesdale.

P. 26. Answer II. 12. **scull-thacker:** Ramsay was a periwig-maker. 33. **Kairnamount:** Cairnamount, a hill in Kincardineshire. 55–58. 'Whoever calls us . . . than bad manners, many great men . . . it has been shown, for example, Horace . . . ' 72. **Beltan:** Beltane, an ancient festival celebrated in Scotland on the first of May.

P. 28. Horace to Virgil, on his taking a Voyage to Athens. 1720. A rendering of Horace, *Odes* I, iii. 2. **Helen's brithers:** Castor and Pollux, the stars. 5. **King Eol:** Aeolus, represented in Homer as having dominion over the winds. 37. **Daedalus:** in Greek legend Daedalus escaped from the labyrinth at Crete by means of wings which he had constructed for himself and his son Icarus.

P. 30. To the Phiz an Ode. 1720. This is the best known of all Ramsay's free versions of the Odes, based on Odes I, ix. "The Ph-" of the text is probably the Phiz Club, an Edinburgh club of which Ramsay's friends Duncan Forbes of Culloden and Dr John Clerk were members. They were accustomed to address each other as 'Phiz Forbes' and 'Phiz Clerk'. 1. **Pentland's:** the Pentland Hills may be seen from Edinburgh, just as the Soracte of the original ode may be seen from Rome, though 26 miles away.

P. 32. An Ode to Mr. Forbes. 1720. This rendering of Odes, I, iv is addressed to John Forbes of Newhall, a cousin of Duncan Forbes of Culloden, Lord Presi-dent of the Court of Session. John Forbes was a patron and friend of Ramsay's, and his estate of Newhall is traditionally held to be the scene of 'The Gentle Shepherd'. In the title his name was disguised as 'Mr. F–'. 13. **Paphian:** of Paphos on Cyprus sacred to Venus. 19. **rinnen down:** eyes watering. 25. **Forbes:** is dissyllabic. **tutor time:** keep time under your tutorship.

P. 33. Horace: Book I, Ode V. The text is from STS Vol. III (1961), from MS. 2233 f. 38 in the National Library of Scotland. Spelling and punctuation have been modernised. 11. **belivest-na,** MS. 16. **frosted nails:** nails prepared against the ice.

P. 34. Horace: Book I, Ode VI. To His Grace John, Duke of Argyle. The text in STS Vol. III (1961) is from MS. 2233 f. 38v. in the National Library of Scotland. The Duke of Argyle commanded the royal troops against the Earl of Mar at Sheriffmuir in 1715, and was present at Marlborough's victory at Malplaquet in 1709. 1. **Harmonious Pope:** Pope's translation of the *Iliad* appeared in 1715–20. 8–10. **King Fergus . . . Corbredus Gald . . . Caractatus:** all three are mentioned as early Scots kings in George Buchanan's *History of Scotland*, of which a scholarly edition had appeared in 1715, by Ramsay's friend Thomas Ruddiman. Caractatus, King of Scots in AD 27, is said to have quelled a rebellion in the Hebrides; Corbredus Galdus is said to have been the first King of Scots to have encountered the Romans ("Some think he is the same who is called Galgacus by Tacitus"); Fergus was the first of the Dalriadic or Scottish kings. 22. **drink . : . hans:** drink to the expected child.

P. 35. The Vision. Ramsay's old-style imitation came out in *The Ever Green* 1724 but may have been written just before the 1715 rebellion. Its main reference is to the unpopular 1707 incorporation of the Scottish parliament in the London parliament and the consequent hurt to Scotland's pride and economy. For reasons of space only a selection is given here. The poem influenced Burns's *Vision* and was admired by Scott. The stanza is from Alexander Montgomerie's *The Cherrie and the Slae*, and the patriot's dream while sheltering from the weather is suggested by Lindsay's *Dreme*. The signature disguises 'Allan Ramsay, Scotsman'. 1. **Banquo:** the mythical ancestor of the Stewart kings. 11. **feidom:** from 'fey'; here strange behaviour that seems to invite destruction. 103. **Langshanks:** the Scots derisive nickname for Edward I. 116. **cloysters:** the Church suffered interference, for example, in the restoration of patronage. 171. **schoil:** she'll. 177. **Saxon gold:** it was believed that Unionists had been bribed. 195. **schois:** she is. 201. **tak the feild neir Forthe:** another Bannockburn is prophesied. 207. **a king:** a Stewart king, of course.

P. 40. My Peggy is a young thing: first printed in *The Tea-Table Miscellany* 1729, this was made the opening song when 'The Gentle Shepherd' was made into a ballad-opera, and was to be sung by Patie.

The Gentle Shepherd. 1725. The text is that of the second edition 1726, which differs slightly and was the version printed in *Poems* 1728, but the play originated in two eclogues, 'Patie and Roger' and 'Jenny and Meggy', probably written in 1720, 1723, and both incorporated in the finished drama. There were originally four songs; later editions have twenty-one, making the play into a ballad-opera. The time of action is the end of the Commonwealth; the scene is not far from Edinburgh and by the North Esk; a map is published in the

Works, ed. George Chalmers, 1848, vol. 2, facing p. 148. On the song-titles mentioned see Notes in the forthcoming sixth and last volume of *Ramsay*, Scottish Text Society.

P. 43. Act I, Scene I: has a note at the end: "The first scene is the only piece in this volume that was printed in the first. Having carried the pastoral the length of five acts at the desire of some persons of distinction, I was obliged to reprint this preluding scene with the rest." It was originally the eclogue 'Patie and Roger'. 78. **shellycoat or cow:** as in the original eclogue, was later misprinted 'shelly-coated kow'. Ramsay supplies a footnote (STS I, 144): "**Shellycoat:** One of these frightful Spectres the ignorant People are terrified at, and tell us strange Stories of; that they are clothed with a Coat of Shells, which make a horrid rattling, that they'll be sure to destroy one, if he gets not a running Water between him and it; it dares not meddle with a Woman with Child, &c.". Scene II: originally the eclogue 'Jenny and Meggy'. 108. **the bonny lass of Branksome:** a song-title. 116. **The deel gaes o'er John Wobster:** a phrase, 'things are in a devil of a mess'. 180. cp. *The Cotter's Saturday Night*, ll. 23–4.

P. 54. Act II, Scene I. 29–31: General Monk declared for Charles II in 1660 and expelled the so-called Rump Parliament. 100. **bobbit bands:** knotted neckcloth. Scene II. 32. **Plotcock:** a name for the devil. 100: this song first appeared in *Poems* 1721.

P. 67. Act III, Scene II. 112. **Lyon:** the armorial lion of the Scottish kings. Scene IV. 75. Drummond of Hawthornden and William Alexander, Earl of Stirling, a poet as well as statesman. 76. **Cowley:** Abraham Cowley.

P. 80. Act IV, Scene I. 72. **sae gray a gate:** so disastrous a course. 77. **the haly band:** the kirk session.

P. 91. Act V, Scene I. 37. **Upon me fast the witch** etc.: cf. *Tam O' Shanter*. The last execution of a witch in Scotland was in 1722, in England 1727. The Witchcraft Act was repealed 1736.

P. 105. The Monk and the Miller's Wife: A Tale. 1728. The idea for this tale was taken from an anonymous late 15th-century poem 'The Freiris of Berwik', which can be read in editions of Dunbar. The original is in the Bannatyne and Maitland MSS, and Ramsay may have come upon it when he was compiling his *Ever Green*. 'The Miller and his Man' (STS III, 203) was written as a sequel to this tale. 218. **Rosiecrucian:** cf. Epistle II, note to 49. 223. **Albumazor:** (805–885) an Arabian astronomer, consulted by students of astrology. 230. **Pacolet:** a dwarf in the romance of Valentine and Orson, whose magical horse of wood could convey him wherever desired. 251. **Radamanthus** etc.: names of farm dogs, as in Henryson's fable, *The Cock and the Fox*.

Pp. 112–13. Polwart on the Green. Up in the Air. I'll never leave Thee. These three songs were first printed in 1720. The text is as given in *Poems* 1721.

Polwarth is in Berwickshire; marriages were celebrated there with a dance round the hawthorn trees on the village green.

P. 115. The Widow. This appeared in Ramsay's Quarto of 1728.

P. 116. The Marrow Ballad. The text is from S T S III, which in turn is taken from MS. 1030 f. 6 in the National Library of Scotland. Punctuation has been modernised. The poem was composed in 1738 and in style and attitude looks forward to Burns's *Holy Fair*. The Marrow controversy was one of the burning issues in the Church of Scotland from 1718 onwards. It centres on Edward Fisher's *The Marrow of Modern Divinity*, 1646 but reissued in Scotland in 1718. The extreme Presbyterians, including such distinguished men as Ralph and Ebenezer Erskine, supported the 'Marrow' doctrines, but the Church as a whole did not approve. The poem is one of Ramsay's most lively satiric attacks and betrays his resentment at the action of the Edinburgh Presbytery, which at that time was trying to have his theatre closed. 9–10. **blinkan eyed Bessy** etc.: see 'Lucky Spence's Last Advice', l. 13. 25. **black stools:** where fornicators did public penance.

POEMS BY ROBERT FERGUSSON

The date of a poem's first printing is given in each case, being mostly that of its appearance in *The Weekly Magazine or Edinburgh Amusement*, referred to here as W M.

P. 121. The Daft-Days. WM, 2 January, 1772. The Daft Days are the holidays at New Year (Yule, Hogmanay, New Year's Day, and Handsel Monday, the first Monday of the New Year). They were characterised by wild sprees and gay abandon. 35. **well of Spa:** Spa is a watering place in Belgium, but by Fergusson's time the word was used of any medicinal spring or well. cf. Ramsay, 'Lucky Spence's Last Advice', l. 77. 37–42. **Then tho' at odds** etc.: cf. Ramsay, 'Familiar Epistles', 'Answer II', ll. 37–42. 45. **vile Italian tricks:** Ramsay, Fergusson and Burns rightly objected to the distortion of native songs by over-elaborate re-arrangements in the Italian style. Ramsay and Fergusson no doubt also had in mind the succession of Italian musicians engaged by the Edinburgh Musical Society. cf. 'Elegy on the Death of Scots Music', ll. 49–54. 48. **Tulloch-gorum:** a tune, later given words by John Skinner, published in W M, 2 May, 1776. 66. **The City-Guard:** the military police force of Edinburgh, largely recruited from veterans of the Highland regiments.

P. 123. Elegy, On the Death of Scots Music. WM, 5 March, 1772. 13–18. **Mourn ilka nymph** etc.: cf. Ramsay, 'Elegy on Lucky Wood', 7–8.

37. **Macgibbon:** principal violinist of the Edinburgh Musical Society, who had died in 1756. See Johnson, *Music and Society in Lowland Scotland*, p. 193. 59. **Birks of Invermay:** in text Indermay; known to be a favourite song of Fergusson's.

P. 125. The King's Birth-Day in Edinburgh. WM, 4 June, 1772. The occasion was George III's 36th birthday, celebrated on 4 June. Drummond of Haw-thornden's *Polemo-Middinia* or 'Midden-Fecht' was a burlesque and macaronic poem. Burns's *A Dream* was indebted to the present poem. 13–18. **O Muse, be kind** etc.: cf. Burns, *Scotch Drink*, ll. 1–7, *Epistle to John Lapraik*, ll. 27–30. 31. **Mons Meg:** the 15th-century iron bombard on the battlements of Edin-burgh Castle. The name suggests it was made in Flanders, but some hold it was of Scots construction. It was listed by Cromwell as "that great iron murderer". Fergusson's reference is to the bursting of the gun when fired in honour of James VII when he visited Edinburgh in 1682 as Duke of York. 49. **blue-gown bodies:** the King's Bedesmen, privileged beggars, paid ceremonially on the monarch's birthday. Edie Ochiltree in Scott's *The Antiquary* was one. 62. **Land of Cakes:** the expression is recorded in *The Lauderdale Papers* under the year 1669, and refers to oatmeal cakes or bannocks. cf. Burns, *On the Late Captain Grose's Peregrinations Thro' Scotland*. 67. **serpents:** fireworks, a species of rocket.

P. 128. Caller Oysters. WM, 27 August, 1772. The motto is from John Philips's *The Splendid Shilling*, a burlesque of Milton in blank verse, ll. 1–4. 35. **simmer roses:** a skin eruption caused by much drinking. 39. **Luckie Middlemist's:** Luckie Middlemass kept a famous oyster tavern in the Cowgate. 65. **pan-dours:** large oysters, "caught at the doors of the (salt) pans" near Prestonpans. 75–6. **Mix caller oysters wi' your liquor:** oysters were thought to keep the drinker sober a little longer.

P. 131. Braid Claith. WM, 15 October, 1772. Reprinted in *The Caledonian Mercury*, 12 June, 1772 with a complimentary foreword: "This poem exhibits so many qualities of true excellence that we quote it entire for our readers, as so many persons of polite taste desired to see it." 7. **fa:** have as his portion. 17. **four quarters:** all parts of him. 23. **Or to the Meadow or the Park:** Hope Park (now called The Meadows) and the King's Park (round Arthur's Seat) were two public promenades.

P. 132. Hallow-Fair. WM, 12 November, 1772. 1. **Hallowmas:** during the first week of November. 5. **Near Edinbrough:** actually at Castle Barns, near the modern Fountainbridge, on the Falkirk road. 37–45. **Here Sawny cries** etc.: the poet is indicating the sound of the Aberdeenshire 'Buchan' dialect. 79. **Lochaber aix:** a long pole with an axe at the end and a hook at the back of it. 93–6. **"She maun pe see":** indicates the Highland pronunciation of the Gaelic warriors of the City Guard. See also note on City Guard to 'The Daft-days'.

P. 136. Elegy, On the Death of Mr David Gregory. Text, 1773 edition. Gregory
was one of the famous Aberdeenshire family which produced generations of
professors in St Andrews, Edinburgh, and Oxford. He died in April, 1765, but
resigned his Chair in 1764 so that Fergusson, who matriculated in 1764, could
not have heard him lecture. The STS editor notes of this poem in 'standart
Habbie', that "It is the first of its kind to have a 'respectable' person for its
subject". 11. **the maist fek:** the most valuable part. 22. **lang head:** his intel-
lectual brilliance. 42. **as sound's a tap:** cf. Ramsay, *Elegy on Maggy Johnston*,
l. 60.

P. 137. An Eclogue. Text, 1773 edition. 1–4. **Twas e'ening** etc.: cf. Gray's
Elegy written in a Country Churchyard. 19. **but:** without. 81–8: tea, at first a
costly drug, was still a luxury. 87. **Apple-bogg:** an invented place-name.

P. 141. The Lee Rigg. *The Charmer: A Collection of Songs . . . In Two Volumes.
Vol. II . . . Edinburgh . . . 1782.* Apart from some convivial verses for the Cape
Club, this is Fergusson's sole attempt at Scots song. In a note in Johnson's
Musical Museum to his own *The lea-rig,* Burns wrote that the words printed
here were "mostly composed by poor Fergusson, in one of his merry humors",
and that before Fergusson's day the original words were:

> I'll rowe thee o'er the lea-rig,
> My ain kind dearie, O,
> I'll rowe thee o'er the lea-rig,
> My ain kind dearie, O,
> Altho' the night were ne'er sae wat,
> And I were ne'er sae weary, O,
> I'll rowe thee o'er the lea-rig,
> My ain kind dearie, O.

Burns took ideas and sentiments from both sources for his song. A version of
the present poem is also to be found in *Songs from David Herd's Manuscripts,* ed.
Hecht, Edinburgh, 1904: this may have been given to Herd by Fergusson, for
they were friends and fellow members of the Cape Club.

P. 141. Auld Reikie. Text is the separate 1773 print, with the addition of the
last 40 lines, which are taken from the 1779, Part II, edition. Auld Reikie is a
popular name for Edinburgh: records of its use go back with certainty to
Charles II's reign, but tradition claims an even greater antiquity. 29. **turnpike
stair:** the narrow spiral staircase connecting the storeys of a 'land' or tenement-
house. 38. **Nore Loch Brig:** the Nor' Loch – where Princes Street Gardens
now are – was drained, and the Lord Provost, George Drummond, laid the
foundation stone in 1763 of a bridge at the east end of it. The bridge, opened
in 1768, collapsed in 1769, killing five people. 53. **Luckenbooths:** Chambers
in his *Traditions of Edinburgh* says: "A portion of the High Street facing St.
Giles's Church was called the *Luckenbooths,* and the appellation was shared with

a middle row of buildings which once burdened the street at that spot. The name is supposed to have been conferred on the shops in that situation as being *close shops*, to distinguish them from the open booths which then lined our great street on both sides; *lucken* signifying closed." In a tenement at the east end of the Luckenbooths Allan Ramsay had had his bookseller's shop and circulating library. 71. **usefu' cadie:** caddies were public servants, officially licensed by the magistrates to run errands, look after strangers and even to act as police informers. 133. **ten-hours drum:** the drum that sounded at ten o'clock as described by Ramsay in Answer I, l. 63n. 143. **Pandemonium:** also known as the Gormandizing Club. 151. **salamanders:** possibly the name of a convivial club. 153. **But chief, O Cape!:** Fergusson was admitted to the Cape Club on 10 October, 1772. This club, known to have existed as early as 1733, was formally constituted in 1764. Like many Edinburgh clubs before and since, it mingled mock ceremonial with witty talk and song. 168. **saulie's face:** the look of the professional mourner. 183. **corp:** coffin. 207. **flow'r-pat:** chamber-pot. 219. **Gillespies' snuff:** John and James Gillespie kept a snuff-shop on the north side of the High Street, east of the Cross. 230. **the Line:** the Equator. 253. **Comely-Garden:** public gardens in the Abbeyhill district, east of Holyrood Palace. **the Park:** King's Park; cf. 'Braid Claith', l. 23. 255. **Canonmills:** then a village north of Edinburgh. 285. **whare debtors daily run:** insolvent debtors could claim the right of sanctuary within the precincts of Holyrood Abbey. Ramsay's comedians fled there in January, 1739, to avoid arrest under the 1737 Licensing Act. 300. **Simon Fraser:** keeper of the Tolbooth prison, the 'Heart of Midlothian'. 303. **St. Mary:** St Mary's Wynd, where were the dealers in old clothes. 314. **Drummond:** George Drummond (1687–1766), six times Lord Provost, largely responsible for the building of the New Town, and for the establishment of the Royal Infirmary in 1729. 325–6: the Glasgow of that day was acknowledged the most attractive city of Scotland. 333. **The spacious brig neglected:** the bridge over the end of the Nor' Loch, which had fallen in 1769.

P. 151. To the Tron-kirk Bell. WM, 26 November, 1772. The original Tron-Kirk bell, hung in 1673, must have had a harsh, unpleasant sound. **Wanwordy,** meaning worn-out, implies that it was in need of repair, and Edinburgh Burgh Records reveal that in August, 1774, the Dean of Guild ordered the bell sent to London and a new one purchased there. The Tron was the public beam for the weighing of merchandise and gave its name to the Kirk nearby. 9. **pig:** chamber-pot. **master-cann:** earthenware vessel into which the 'pig' could be emptied.

P. 153. Mutual Complaint of Plainstanes and Causey, in their Mother-tongue. WM, 4 March, 1773. **Plainstanes** is the pavement, **Causey,** causeway or street. This poem influenced Burns's *The Brigs* of Ayr. 1. **Merlin:** there was a tradition that the first causeway in Edinburgh was laid by a Frenchman called

Marlin. 6. **Fraser:** the contractor who supplied the lamps. 44. **Gallic chairmen:** Highland sedan-chair carriers, noted for their irritability and 'character'. 102. **magnum damnum datum:** to win a case, get damages, and have your opponent fined. 108. **the Guard:** the town guard-house right in the centre of the High Street. 116 **Charlie:** Charles II. 126. **water-hole:** probably the reservoir on Castlehill. 130. **the Robinhood:** a debating society, later known as the Pantheon. 138. **Thetis:** a sea-nymph, hence the sea.

P. 157. The Rising of the Session. WM, 18 March, 1773. The Session is the Court of Session, the highest court of judiciary in Scotland: its winter term ended in March. 3. **Writers:** lawyers or lawyers' clerks, though the term was loosely applied to all clerks. 34. **barley seed:** season for sowing barley. 50. **the pillars:** an arcade skirting the passage leading into Parliament Close. 51. **protests:** a formal procedure of intimation of non-payment of promissory notes and of intention to exact payment. 56. **Robin Gibb:** a tavern-keeper in the Old Parliament Hall. 62. **Indian Peter:** Peter Williamson (1730–99), from Aboyne, Aberdeenshire, a colourful character who had been kidnapped as a boy in Aberdeen and sold to the plantations in America. He was later captured and tortured by Indians. On his return to Scotland, he settled in Edinburgh, and kept a profitable tavern in Parliament Close. He established the first penny post service in Scotland, and published the first Edinburgh Directory in 1773. 69. **He can fell twa dogs wi' ae bane:** cf. Ramsay's *Scots Proverbs*, 'He fells twa dogs with ae stane'.

P. 159. Ode to the Bee. WM, 29 April, 1773. Fergusson addresses this poem from "Broomhouse, East-Lothian, April 26. 1773". Broomhouse was an estate in the parish of Spott, south of Dunbar. 29–32: the plight of poverty-stricken old age could indeed be terrible in Fergusson's day. 55–6. cf. *Tam o' Shanter* 193–4.

P. 161. The Farmer's Ingle. WM, 13 May, 1773. This poem provided Burns with the idea for *The Cotter's Saturday Night*. 1–4. **Whan gloming grey** etc.: cf. Gray's *Elegy*, stanza 1, and *The Cotter's Saturday Night*, stanza 2. 14. **The gudeman, new come hame:** cf. 'The Gentle Shepherd', Act I, sc. II, ll. 177–80. 28–36. **Frae this let gentler gabs** etc.: cf. Thomson, *Castle of Indolence*, Canto II, stanzas lv–lvii. 43. **Laid Denmark's daring sons on yird alang:** at the legendary Battle of Luncarty, in Perthshire, Kenneth III, King of Scots, is said to have defeated the Danes. 59–63. **In rangles round** etc.: cf. Thomson's *Seasons* ('Winter'), ll. 617–20. 68–72. **O mock na this** etc.: cf. Shenstone's *Schoolmistress*, ll. 33–6 and 64–8. 106. **Tacksman and cottar:** farmer holding a lease and a cottager whose house is dependent on his labour on the farm.

P. 165. The Ghaists: A Kirk-yard Eclogue. WM, 27 May, 1773. Watson is George Watson, accountant to the Bank of Scotland, and Herriot is George Heriot, James VI's goldsmith, who both endowed hospital schools in Edinburgh.

(These schools still exist as George Watson's Boys' College and George Heriot's School.) In 1773 these charities were threatened by the Mortmain Bill, which was intended to empower trustees to invest their funds in government securities. It was felt in Edinburgh that such a bill would discourage future benefactors, and that the income of the trusts would be lower than that from their previous investments. There was also strong national feeling against Scots resources being handled in England. 1. **planes:** plane trees. 3. **Geordie Girdwood:** the gravedigger, said to have turned over the earth of Greyfriars Churchyard (on the east side of Heriot's Hospital) seven times in the course of his duties. 21–28: cf. *Hamlet*, I. i. 166–7, *Julius Caesar*, I. iii. 26–8. 37. **Danish Jones:** Inigo Jones, the architect (1573–1652), once employed by Christian IV of Denmark. He was supposed to have designed Heriot's Hospital. 39–40: Heriot's effigy in the court of his Hospital was annually garlanded by the boys on the first Monday of June. 43. **Major Weir:** once commander of the City Guard. He confessed to incest, sorcery, and murder, and was burned at the stake 12 April, 1670; his sister Grizel was hanged in the Grassmarket as an accomplice. Their house in the West Bow was reputed to be haunted by their ghosts until its demolition in 1878. 49. **Adam's tomb:** burial place of William Adam (1689–1748), the architect, father of the famous architects Robert and James Adam. 66. **grassum gift:** fee paid to the landlord by the incoming tenant. cf. Henryson's *Taill of the Wolf and the Lamb*. 125. **wise Mackenzie:** Sir George Mackenzie (1636–91), who founded the Advocates' Library, later the National Library of Scotland. In 1669 he opposed Charles II's proposal to unite the two kingdoms. In Covenanting tradition he was "the bluidy Advocate".

P. 169. On seeing a Butterfly in the Street. WM, 24 June, 1773. 69. **thir ben:** right into the heart, lit. into the inner part. 71–2. **scad their lips:** cf. Ramsay, *Scots Proverbs*; here the proverb expresses anti-Union feeling.

P. 171. Hame Content. A Satire. WM, 8 July, 1773. 4. **plumb:** the sum of one hundred thousand pounds. Here 'a fortune'. 17. **Dog-day:** one of the days when Sirius, the Dog-Star, rises and sets with the sun (3 July–11 August). 60. **second sharger:** a weakling who succeeds to an inheritance. 66. **Spaw:** Spa; cf. *The Sitting of the Session*, note to 35. 68. **far aff fowls hae feathers fair:** cf. Ramsay, *Scots Proverbs*, "Faraway fowls have fair feathers". 89. **Leader haughs an' Yarrow braes:** title of a song. 96. **Tweeda's banks or Cowdenknowes:** well-known songs, 'Tweedside' and 'The Broom of Cowdenknowes'. 107–9: refer to William Hamilton of Bangour (1704–54) Jacobite and poet, author of *The Braes of Yarrow*.

P. 174. Leith Races. WM, 22 July, 1773. The Races were held annually about this time; in 1773 they were held from 20 to 24 July. One of the most important prizes was 100 guineas presented by the King. The races, and the procession that accompanied them, were supported by a fair and drinking stalls. 1–45: the derivation of Burns's Fun, in *The Holy Fair*, from Fergusson's Mirth is plain. 5–9: recall ballads such as *Thomas the Rhymer*. 31. **Late-wakes:** see Pennant's *A Tour In Scotland* (1772) on the festive occasions these could become. 76. **marsh:** the spelling represents Highland pronunciation, as in 'Hallow-Fair', 93–6. 84–5: an Edinburgh baker had died a few days before of wounds inflicted by the City Guard. 89: 'should be severely punished'. 91. **the Bow:** the West Bow, the ancient street connecting the Lawnmarket with the Grassmarket. Fergusson's reference is to the "tinklers" or tinsmiths, whose shops were in the West Bow. 127. **Rowly Powl:** a game, played at fairs, where a stick was thrown at pegs carrying penny cakes of gingerbread. 145. **The Lyon:** the Lord Lyon King of Arms can prosecute for the display of unrecorded coats of arms. 152. **the Whigs:** here a nationalist term of insult, meaning 'factious and unpatriotic people'. 172. **hale the dools:** go the limit. cf. Ramsay, 'Lucky Spence's Last Advice', l. 41.

P. 179. Ode to the Gowdspink. WM, 12 August, 1773. A 'gowdspink' is a goldfinch. 19. **fool:** cause to look foolish or inferior. 76. **girnal's grist:** stored grain, 'extent of wealth'. 78. **Shame fa' the hair:** 'hair' means a very small portion (Jamieson's *Dictionary*), hence, 'My curse on the smallest bit of it!'

P. 181. To the Principal and Professors of the University of St Andrews on their superb treat to Dr Samuel Johnson. WM, 2 September, 1773. The banquet given by the university to Dr Johnson on 19 August, 1773, is mentioned in Boswell's *Journal of a Tour to the Hebrides*. 7. **Regents:** Professors. cf. *Elegy on John Hogg*, l. 18. 10. **Eden's brink:** the river Eden flows into the sea at St Andrews Bay. 27–32. **Mind ye what Sam** etc.: Johnson's oft quoted reference in his *Dictionary* to oatmeal as the diet of horses in England and of the people in Scotland. 60. **Ill bairns are ay best heard at hame:** Ramsay's *Scots Proverbs*. 61–8: allude to the first six lines of Drummond's *Polemo-Middinia*, which describes a mock battle in the East neuk of Fife. 65–6. **roast beef . . . east nook of Fife:** references to tunes. 67. **Creilian crafts:** fishing vessels from Crail, 10 miles from St Andrews. 83–98. Fergusson had recently been challenged to a duel by a native of Dunfermline, angered by his criticisms of Fifan inhospitality and bigotry ('An Expedition to Fife', ll. 107–19). 88. **caption . . . horning:** legal terms for writs issued against a debtor.

P. 184. The Election. WM. 16 September, 1773. From 1583 to 1833 the Town Council of Edinburgh consisted of 33 members, of whom 14 were Deacons elected by the 14 Incorporated Trades of the city. The complicated method of electing the Deacons, which is the subject of the poem, is well described in the STS Vol. II, pp. 301–2. 1–9. **Rejoice, ye Burghers, ane an' a'** etc.: cf. Burns, *The Ordination*, stanzas 1, 6, 13. 2. **Lang look't for's come at last:** cf. Ramsay, *Scots Proverbs*, "Lang look'd for comes at last". 17–18. **affidavit O' faith:** the oath of loyalty to Crown and Established Church required of all holders of public office. 23. **nae sma' drink:** no unimportant person. 43. **Walker's:** a

tavern on the north side of the High Street, west of the Royal Exchange.
94. **Gin ye man reel my pirny:** Ramsay says that to wind someone a "Pirn"
(bobbin) was to "contrive some malicious thing". 123. **protests:** formal
declarations of objection. 124. **Sandy Fife:** probably the bellman of St Giles
Kirk. 125. **Clout the caudron:** the name of a popular tune and song. 132. **'ere
hillocks meet:** quite soon. cf. Ramsay, *Scots Proverbs*, "We'll meet ere hills
meet".

P. 188. Elegy on John Hogg, late Porter to the University of St. Andrews.
WM, 23 September, 1773. John Hogg, according to a note quoted in STS I,
p. 304, was popular with the students. He left property both in houses and
land to his widow, 'His winsome Kate'. 1. **the de'il be licket:** excl., 'it
must be the devil's fault'. 9. **Kate Kennedy:** a bell in the steeple of St Salvator's
College, named after a niece of Bishop Kennedy, founder of the college.
13. **Pauly Tam:** Thomas Tullidelph, the unpopular disciplinarian Principal of
the United Colleges of St Salvator and St Leonard. He died in 1777. Fergusson
had suffered at his hands. 'Pauly' means either 'small, weakly', or, as is more
likely here, 'flat-footed'. 19. **common schools:** a meeting of the whole
college at which the Principal harangued the students and punished offenders,
advised by the Porter. 20. **hale the dules:** hit the mark. cf. 'Leith Races', note
to 172. 66. **molationis:** macaronic Latin for molass, a spirit distilled from
molasses.

P. 191. The Sitting of the Session. WM, 4 November, 1773. The Court of
Session at this period sat for two terms in the year, from 12 November to 12
March, and from 12 June to 12 August. There was a three-week break at
Christmas. 1: Phœbus severely shorn of his strength, summer being past.
25. **Robb Gibb:** cf. 'Rising of the Session', note to 56. 41. **Ae scabbit yew spills
twenty flocks:** cf. Ramsay, *Scots Proverbs*, "A scabbit sheep files all the flock"·
43. **raise a plea:** argue a case. 47. **but and ben:** the outer and inner rooms of
a two-roomed cottage, the joke being that the High Court was divided into
the Outer House, where first instance cases were heard, and the Inner House,
to which appeals were referred. 48. **pendente lite:** a legal phrase meaning
'pending the result of the suit'.

P. 193. To my Auld Breeks. WM, 25 November, 1773. These very human
lines were remembered in Burns's *The Auld Farmer's New Year Morning Saluta-
tion to his Auld Mare Maggie*. 10. **langer:** distress. 46. **Without remeid of
kindred:** without acknowledging the superior rights or claims of relationships.
Cf. Ramsay, 'Elegy on Maggy Johnston', st. 13, and Fergusson's 'Elegy on the
Death of Mr David Gregory', 4. 64. **to wear the breeks:** to rule her husband.

P. 195. Horace, Ode XI. Lib. I. This was printed under 'Posthumous Pieces' in
Ruddiman's 1779 volume. 12. **thraldom never stays:** care never stops coming.
13. **toot aff your horn:** drink off your cup.

P. 196. The Author's Life. Text 1779 as a posthumous piece.

P. 196. On Night. From "A Collection of English Prose and Verse, For the Use of Schools. By Arthur Masson, MA. Late Teacher of Languages in Edinburgh. The tenth Edition", Edinburgh, 1788, p. 332. According to Grosart (Fergusson's *Poems*, 1851), Masson was a friend of Fergusson's. He also published anthologies of French and Italian poetry.

GLOSSARY

Explanations from Ramsay's glossary for his 1721, 1728 *Poems* are marked (R). Fergusson's spellings to indicate the Buchan dialect are noted (Aberdeen).

ablins, perhaps.
aftimes, often.
aik, oak.
air and late, early and late.
airth, airt, direction.
ait, oat, oaten; **ait-strae,** oat straw; **gets his aits,** gets his deserved punishment.
aith, oath.
alshin, shoemaker's awl.
ambrie, cupboard (R).
antrin, different, strange, exceptional.
apen, open.
arle-penny, money given to confirm a bargain.
attour, out-over (R); **by and attour,** over and above.
auld-farran, ingenious (R).
auld-gabbet, sagacious.
ava, at all.
back-gaun, needy.
bagnets, bayonets.
ban, bann, *vb.,* curse.
badrans, baudrins, a cat (R).
bakes, biscuits, small cakes.
bands, collar; **bobbit bands,** decorated neck-tie.
bane-fire, bonfire.
bains, bones.
ban, curse.
bang, a great number (R); *vb.,* overcome, cram.
bangster, a blustering roaring person (R).
barkent, barkit, hardened.
barlick-hood, barlikhood, a fit of passion or ill-humour (R).

barras, cockpit, confined place.
bassend, brindled or streaked.
bassie, an old horse.
batts, colick (R).
baugh, shy, sheepish.
bauk, strip of grassy, untilled land.
bauk, balk, deny; **bawked,** balked.
baum, balm, comfort.
bauthrin, fussing.
bawk, *n.,* bat.
bawk. *See* **bauk.**
baxter, baker.
bear seed, barley sowing time.
bedeen, immediately (R), quickly.
bedoun, down.
beek, beik, to bask (R), warm.
been. *See* **bein.**
beenge, cringe, bow.
beet, kindle.
begoud, began (R).
begunk, trick; *vb.,* cheat.
beild, shelter; **beildy,** sheltered.
bein, wealthy (R); **bien,** prosperous.
beirdly, stalwart.
bellum, force, blow, noise.
ben, benn, the inner room of a house (R); **ben-by,** *adv.,* in the inner room.
bend, drink; **bend the bicker,** empty the wooden cup; **benders,** drinkers.
bennison, blessing (R).
bent, field; **bents,** slopes; **to the bent,** taken flight.
betooch-us-to!, God save us!
beuk, baked.
bield. *See* **beild.**
bicquor, bicker, a wooden dish (R); drinking-cup.

bien. See **bein.**

big, build; **bigging,** building.

bigonet, a linen cap or coif (R).

bikes, bykes, nests or hives of bees or pismires (R).

billy, brother (R), comrade.

bink, shelf.

binna, *imperat.*, be not.

bir, birr, force.

birk, birken-tree, birch-tree.

birle, spend freely.

birn, burden; burnt mark for identification; **birns or briers,** stems of burnt heather or sprouts of grain.

birsel, scorch.

birze. See **briss.**

bittle, a wooden mell for beating hemp (R), a beetle.

biz, buzz, hiss; **bizzing,** parched, burning.

blad, beat, abuse.

blae, pale blue, the colour of the skin when bruised (R).

blae berries, bilberries.

blashy, deluging.

blasting, withering.

blate, bashful (R).

blaw, blow, bloom, drink; **blaw . . . by,** coax away.

blawart, bluebell.

bleer, dim; **bleer-ey'd,** blear-eyed; **bleering,** dimming.

bleeters, sheep.

bleez, rapid growth.

bleirt. See **bleer.**

bleisit, made blaze.

blink, shine, flicker, glance; **blinkit,** tipsy; *n.*, **blinks,** looks, moments of sunshine.

blobs, drops.

boal, bole, a small press or open cupboard.

bobbit. See **bands.**

bode, foretell, signify.

boden, supplied.

bodle, two pennies Scots or one-sixth of a penny English (R).

bog-staker, lout.

bon-grace, large bonnet of coarse straw.

boor. See **bure.**

boord, table.

bouden, bowden, laden, swollen.

bougil, cock-crow.

bouck, bouk, buick, buke, bulk (R), body, self.

bouls, bowls; **byas bouls,** bowls weighted on one side as in bowling.

bourd, *n.*, jest or dally (R); *vb.*, jest, mock.

bourocks. See **burrochs.**

bow, boll.

bowie, little barrel.

bowt, a bolt, shaft; drinking bout.

bra. See **braw.**

brae, the side of a hill (R).

brander, a gridiron (R).

brankan, prancing, a-capering (R).

branks, wherewith the rusticks bridle their horses (R).

brats, rags (R), clothing.

brattling, running.

braw, fine, handsomely dressed.

brawly, in a brave manner.

breeks, breeches.

brigs, bridges (R).

briss, birze, to press (R).

brodit, pricked, pierced.

broe, broth.

brook, bear, enjoy, use; **"weel brook",** "congratulations on".

brose, oatmeal mixed with boiling water.

brown cow, liquor jar.

browsters, brewers.

browster-wives, female ale-sellers.

bruke. See **brook.**

brulzies, fights.

bucky, the large sea snail. A term of reproach when we express a cross-natured fellow by **thrawn bucky** (R).

bught, the little fold where the ewes are enclosed at milking-time (R).

buick, buke. See **bouck.**

buit, must.

bumbaze, to confuse.
bummil, to bungle, blunder.
burachs. *See* **burrochs.**
burd, bird; **burd alane,** bird alone, solitary.
bure, bore; **boor the bell,** took the prize.
burnbank brae, hill with a burn at the foot.
burrochs, burachs, bourochs, groups, crowds.
busk, dress, deck; **buskit,** *adj.*, ready dressed.
buss, bush.
bustine, fustian, cotton fabric.
but, *prep.*, without (R).
butt, but, *adv.*, towards the outer apartment of a house: **ben** referring to the inner apartment.
ca', call, turn, drive; **ca'd,** drove, turned; **ca'd thro',** mixed; **ca't,** drive it.
cadge, carry.
cadgie, cadgy, happy, wanton.
cadie, messenger, one who runs errands.
cairds, vagrants.
caldrife, cauldrife, spiritless, wanting cheerfulness in address (R).
callan, callant, a boy (R).
caller, cauller, cauler, cool or fresh (R).
campsho, camschough, stern, grim, of a distorted countenance (R).
canny, careful, gentle, easy.
cant, tell merry old tales (R).
cantrapes, cantrips, cantraips, cantrups, charms, a witch's tricks.
canty, cheerful and merry (R).
cap and stoup, drinking-cup and flagon; **cap out,** drunk off.
capernoited, capernoity, whimsical, ill-natured (R).
caption, summons to pay debts.
carl, carlie, an old word for a man (R).
carline, an old woman (R).
cassin, cast.
caulrife, cold.

causey, cawsey, street.
cawk, chalk.
chafts, jaws.
champers, teeth.
chandler, candle-stick.
chap, break.
chaping, chappin, an ale measure or stoup, somewhat less than an English quart (R).
chaunter, chanter, or drone of the bagpipe.
chiel, a general term, like fellow (R).
childer, children.
chirm, chirp and sing like a bird (R).
chopies, shops.
chow, jowl; **cheek for chow,** face to face.
chucky, a hen (R).
chuff-cheeked, fat-faced.
claes, claese, clothes.
clag, stick to.
claiking, chattering, gossiping.
clam, climbed.
clamihewit, blow.
clap, fondle.
clarty, dirty.
clashes, chats, gossiping.
clavers, nonsense.
claw, scratch (R), handle.
cleathing, cleeding, clothing.
cleck, gossip.
cleed, clothe.
cleek, catch as with a hook (R).
cleugh, a den betwixt rocks (R).
clever, clover.
clever, quick.
clew, clawed.
clink, hammer, knock, ring.
clink, clinks, coins, money.
clinty, hard, stony (R).
cloit, fall heavily.
clour, batter, beat.
clout, rag of cloth; **clute,** 'single one'; **clouted,** patched.
clungest, hungriest.
coble, small, flat-bottomed boat.
cockernony, the gathering of a woman's hair, when 'tis wrapt or

snooded up with a band or snood (R).

cod, a pillow (R).

codlin, codling.

codroch, clownish.

coft, bought.

cog, a pretty large wooden dish the country people put their potage (porridge) in (R); **coggie.**

connach, devour.

coof, a stupid fellow (R).

cooser, a stoned horse (R); stallion.

corbies, ravens (R).

corning, meet your, get your due punishment.

corp, corpse (perhaps for 'coffin').

corss, corpse.

cosh, comfortable; *adv.,* **coshly.**

couli, fellow (contemptuous).

coup, exchange.

cour, to crouch and creep (R).

couth, couthy, sociable, facetious.

cow, rebuke; **cow'd,** abused; clipped, shorn.

crabbit, perverse, cross, ill-tempered; *adv.,* **crabbitly.**

crack, moment; **cracks,** conversation, boasts; **crack,** *vb.,* to chat (R).

craig, throat, neck.

crambo, clever doggerel verse.

crap, *vb.,* crop, gather.

crap, stomach.

craw'd, crowed.

crazy, worn-out.

creesh, lash.

crish, criesh, grease (R); **crished,** greased; **crishy, crieshy,** oily.

crook, iron hook and chain on which pots are hung over a fire.

crook, twist, bow.

croupin', croaking.

crouse, bold (R); **crously,** *adv.*

crowdy-meal, a kind of porridge.

cruizy, small oil lamp, usually made of iron.

crune, murmur or hum o'er a song (R); *n.,* the lowing of bulls (R).

cuissers, stallions.

culzie, entice or flatter (R).

cunzie, coin (R).

cunzied, acknowledged.

curn, a particle, a small quantity.

cutty, short (R).

cutty-stool, the stool of repentance.

dad, a large piece; *vb.,* thrash, stroke, fall.

dads, forebears.

daffine, daffin, folly, wagrie (R).

daintithes, dainties, delicacies.

dander, to wander; **danert,** wandered.

dang. *See* **ding.**

dantan, deject.

darn'd, hid, hidden.

daut, cocker and caress with tenderness (R); *pret.,* **dauted, dawted.**

dead, death; **dead-deal,** board for measuring and lifting a corpse.

deas, seat, wooden settle, or turf-seat.

deave, stun the ears with noise (R).

deel, deil, devil.

dern, *adj.,* secret, hidden.

devall, cease.

dic'd, in diamond shapes.

dighting, winnowing grain.

ding, to beat, thrust, drive (R); **dings,** wins; **dang,** beat, surpassed; **dung,** struck off, driven.

dinlin, rattling, beating (of a drum).

dirk, slip; **dirk thir ben,** slip deep in, get deeply involved.

dit, to stop or close up a hole (R).

divet, broad turf (R).

dizens, dozens.

doil'd, doilt, *adj.,* exhausted; confused and silly (R).

doited, *adj.,* dozed or crazy, as in old age (R).

dollers, five shilling pieces.

dome, home (*domus*).

dominie, schoolmaster.

doner'd, donnart, stupid, stupefied.

doncie, donsie, affectedly neat. Clean, when applied to any little person (R).

doof, a dull, stupid fellow.

doofart, a dull heavy-headed fellow (R).

dool, grief, trouble.

dorts: tak the dorts, be sullen.

dorty, proud, not to be spoke to, conceited, appearing as disobliged (R).

dosens, declines.

dosin', drowse.

dossied, flung, tossed, paid.

dou. *See* **dow.**

douce, solid, grave, prudent (R); *compar.* **dousser.**

dought, could, would; **doughty,** mighty.

douk, duck, dip, dodge.

doup, dowp, the arse; the small remains of a candle (R); **in a doup,** in a moment.

dow, *vb.,* can, will, allow; **dow'd,** could, would.

dow, wither; **dowed,** *adj.,* (Liquor) that's dead, or has lost the spirits; or withered (Plant) (R).

dowff, mournful, wanting vivacity (R).

dowie, dowy, gloomy.

drap, drop, leave.

draunt, drivel.

dree, suffer.

dreech, dull.

dribs, drops (R).

drie, suffer.

drift, driven snow.

drog, drug, medicine.

droukit, drenched.

drouth, thirst; **drouthy,** thirsty.

drug, rough or violent pull.

drumble, disturb.

drumly, drumbly, muddy, gloomy, troubled.

dubbs, mire, puddles.

duddy, ragged, tattered.

duds, duddies, shabby clothes.

dules. *See* **hale.**

dung. *See* **ding.**

dunk, moist, damp.

durk, a poinyard or dagger (R).

dwall in, subsist on.

dwine, droop, decline; *adj.,* **dwining, dwyning.**

dyver, dyvour, bankrupt.

een, eyes.

eidant, eident, eydent, diligent, laborious (R).

eik, addition, patch.

eild, age.

einow, just now.

eiry, irie, fearful, apprehensive.

eisning, shrinking from dryness.

eistacks, dainties.

eith, easy.

elbuck, elbow.

elf-shot, injured by fairies.

elritch, wild, hideous, uninhabited except by imaginary ghosts (R).

elson, a shoemaker's awl (R).

elvand, rod.

emmack, ant.

ergh, *adj.,* scrupulous, when one makes faint attempts to do a thing without a steady resolution (R); *vb.,* hesitate.

ether-cap, an adder (R), a spider, malicious person.

ettle, etle, aim, design (R), try.

fa, fall, befall, happen to possess.

fa (Aberdeen), who.

fadge, flat loaf or bannock.

fain, *adj.,* eager; *adv.,* gladly.

fairin, present bought at a fair.

fairn-year, last year.

fait, neat, in good order (R).

farl: girdle farl, quarter of an oatcake, baked on a girdle.

fash, vex, trouble; **fash your thumb,** trouble yourself; **fashous,** troublesome (R).

faugh, a colour between white and red (R); fallow.

faught, fight.

faun, *pret.,* found.

fause, false.

faush'd. *See* **fash.**

fear, frighten.

feat, smart, neatly dressed.

feck, a part, quantity (R); **maist feckly,** for the most part.

feckless, weak, powerless, worthless.

feed, feud, hatred, quarrel (R).

feg, fig, thing of no account.

fegs, feggs, *interj.*, truly, in truth.

feidom. *See note.*

fek. *See* **feck.**

fell, serious, great; *vb.*, supply.

fenzying, pretending, feigning.

ferlie, wonder.

ferra cow, cow not with calf, not yielding milk. *See also* **forrow.**

ferst, at first.

fettle, attend to business.

fient, devil; **the fient ane,** the devil a one.

fier, healthy.

figmaliries, whims.

fike, fuss, give trouble. *See* **fyke.**

file, defile or dirty (R).

filipegs, filibegs, kilt.

findrums, small smoke-dried haddocks.

fireflaught, lightning.

fire-shools, fire shovels.

firlot, a corn measure, quarter of a boll.

fistle, *vb.*, stir; *n.*, a stir, fuss.

fitsted, the print of the foot (R).

flaes, fleas.

flaff, flap, flutter.

flaw, to lie or fib (R).

flead, flayed.

fleetch, cox (*sic*) or flatter (R).

fleg, to frighten.

flet, scolded.

fleuk, flounder.

flewet, a smart blow on the head (R).

fley, frighten, drive away; **fleid, fley'd,** frightened.

flie, affright (R).

flighter, flutter; *hence* **flightering,** fluttering.

flipe, flype, flyp, wrinkle, to pull off anything, like a stocking, by turning it inside out.

flit, move.

flite. *See* **flyte.**

flung, deceived.

flyp. *See* **flipe.**

flyte, flite, scold, chide (R).

foggy, mossy.

fool, mock.

forfairn, abused, bespattered (R).

forfoughen, wearied, worn out.

forrow, not with calf; **forrow nowt,** cows which have not calved but yet are giving milk.

forseeth (Aberdeen), forsooth.

fou, *adj.*, full; *adv.*, very.

fouk, folk.

fousom, nauseous.

fouth, abundance, plenty (R).

foy, farewell feast.

frase, fraise, *vb.*, make a noise; *n.*, a noise. "We use to say one **makes a frais,** when they boast, wonder, and talk more of a matter than it is worthy of, or will bear" (R).

freath the graith, make the soap-suds (or other lather) foam.

fremit, strange, not a kin (R).

furthy, *adj.*, forward (R).

fyke, be restless, uneasy (R).

ga', gall.

gab, mouth; *vb.*, prattle, talk foolishly.

gabby, a ready and easy talker. The same with **auld gabbet** (R), fluent in speech. **Shevelling-gabit,** having a distorted mouth.

gadge, talk impertinently.

gads, rods, spears.

gaff, talk loudly or merrily.

gait, way, style; goat.

gallows-face, rascal.

gamphrell, fool.

gantry, wooden stand for barrels.

gar, to cause, make, or force (R); *pret.*, **gart.**

gardies, arms.

gare, greedy, rapacious, earnest to have a thing (R).

gash, solid, sagacious. One with a long out chin we call **gash gabbet** or gash-beard (R); bright, talkative; *vb.*, chat.

gate, way, road; **tak the gate,** be on one's way; **tine the gate,** lose the way.

gauds, See gads.

gaunt, yawn.

gaw, gall.

gawky, idle, staring, idiotical person (R).

gawsy, stately.

geck, slight, mock.

geed, went.

get, brat, a child, by way of contempt or derision (R); Belzi's get, a limb of Beelzebub.

geyzan'd, adj., past part., when the wood of any vessel is shrunk with dryness (R); geyz'd, gizzand, dried out.

geyz'd. See geyzan'd.

gez, gizz, wig.

gezy-makers, wig-makers.

ghaist, ghost.

giglit, girl.

gillygacus, gilly-gawpy, a staring, gaping fool (R).

gilpy, rascal.

gimmer, a young sheep (R); gim-mers, gossips.

gird, strike, pierce (R).

girn, grimace, jeer.

girnal, meal-chest, granary.

girsle, gristle.

gizz. See gez.

gizzen, go thirsty; dried up, thirsty. See geyzan'd.

glaikit, glakit, silly, foolish.

glar, mire, mud.

gleds, kites.

gleg, sharp, quick.

glent, gleam.

gleyb, glebe.

glomin, gloaming.

glore, glory.

glowr, glowre, stare, look stern (R); (usually) gaze, look.

gousty, ghastly, large, waste, desolate and frightful (R).

gowans, daisies; gow'ny, daisied.

gowd, gold; gowden, golden.

gowdspink, goldfinch.

gowff, golf: hence gowfer, golfer.

gowk, cuckoo, simpleton.

gowl, howling; vb., bellow and cry (R).

gowpin, handful.

grain, grane, groan.

graith, gear, stuff, outfit.

grassum, a tenant's payment on entering a farm.

gravat, cravat, scarf.

greapin, groping.

gree, prize; to bear the gree, to carry off the prize.

green, grein, grien, long for.

greet, weep.

grist, size.

grit, great.

groat, (obsolete) coin: drunken groat, fine for drunkenness.

grouf, lie flat on the belly (R); a-grouf, on one's belly.

gruntles, grunting sounds.

gryce, gryse, pig.

gudame, grandmother.

gueed (Aberdeen), good.

gudeman, master of the house, hus-band.

gudewife, mistress of the house.

guly. See gulzie.

gulzie, large knife.

gumption, good sense (R).

gusts his gabb, pleases his palate; gustit, flavoured.

gusty, savoury, tasty.

gutcher, grandfather.

gyte, beside one's self, mad.

gyzen'd. See geyzan'd.

haffet, haffit, the cheek, side of the head (R).

haflen, halflin, not fully grown.

haflins, hafflins, partly.

hagabag, coarse napery (R).

haggies, haggise, a kind of pudding made of the lungs and liver of a sheep and boiled in the big bag (R). There are other ingredients.

hags, hacks, peat-pits, or breaks in mossy ground (R).

haiks, hackneys.

hain, save, manage narrowly (R); *n.*, **haining,** saving.

hair, a very small portion.

hair-kaimers, barbers.

hair-mould, mouldy.

haith, *excl.*, faith!

hales, drives away; **hale the dools,** 'go all out', hit the mark.

hallan, halland, hallon, partition between cottage door and fireside.

haly, holy.

hamel, hameil, hamelt, hameld, domestic (R), home-bred, home-made.

handsel-Teysday, the first Tuesday of the New Year.

hantle, a considerable number; *also* **hantla,** a considerable number of.

haps, hops, leaps.

hap-warms, wraps.

harigalds, heart, liver, and lights.

harl, drag, trail.

har'st, harvest.

hash, damage.

haughs, valleys, or low grounds on the sides of rivers (R).

hause, haws, the throat, or fore-part of the neck (R).

haveril, foolish fellow; *adj.*, silly.

havins, manners.

hawkie, cow with a white face; affectionate name for a cow.

hawslock, finest wool, the lock that grows on the throat of the sheep.

heartscad, heartburn.

heese, heeze, lift, help, hurry; **heisit,** raised.

heezy, a good lift (R).

heffs, dwells.

heghts, promises.

herried, plundered.

het, hot.

heuchs, crags, hollows.

hidlings, lurking, hiding-places (R).

hinny, honey.

hip, miss, omit, avoid.

hirsle, move as with a rustling noise (R).

hissel, flock of sheep.

hissy, hissie, hizzy, woman (contemptuous).

hobble, move.

hobbleshew, hobleshew, confused racket, noise (R).

hodden-gray, cloth with the natural colour of the wool; **hodin.**

hool, husk, body.

hool'd, enclosed (R).

hooly, slowly.

horning, declaring a person to be a rebel.

hotches, jolts.

hou, roof-tree.

houff, howff, haunt, meeting place.

hought, hoed.

houk, howk, dig.

how, low ground, a hollow (R).

howder, swarm.

howdy, midwife (R).

howms, plains on river-sides (R).

how-towdy, a young hen (R).

humdrums, dejection.

hych, high.

iceshogles, icicles.

ingans, onions.

ingle, fireside; **ingle cheek,** fireside.

inlakes, deficiencies; *vb.*, lacks.

irie. *See* **eiry.**

jad, jade, abuse.

jaws, dashes.

jee, incline to one side (R); **a jee,** to one side.

jink, avoid.

joes, sweethearts.

joot. *See* **jute.**

jouk, a low bow (R); *vb.*, escape.

jow, toll.

jute, joot, sour or dead liquor (R); liquor.

jyb, mock; **jybe, gibe,** *n.*, taunt (R).

kail, colewort; broth from colewort and other greens.

kail-worm, caterpillar.

kail-yard, cottage garden.

kain, a part of a farm-rent paid in fowls (R); rent in kind, payment.

kame, kaim, comb.

kebuck, kebbuck, cheese.

keckling, laughing noisily.

keek, peep, glimpse; **keeking-glass,** mirror.

ken, know; **ken'd, kent,** known.

kent, a long staff, such as shepherds use for leaping over ditches (R).

keytch, toss, drive backwards and forwards.

kickshaws, novelties.

kill, kiln.

kimmer, a female gossip (R).

kiples, rafters.

kirn, churn.

kist, chest; **kist-nook,** corner of a chest.

kitchen, all sorts of eatables, except bread (R).

kittle, difficult, mysterious, knotty (writings) (R); *vb.,* stir.

kniefly, vigorously.

knit up, burst.

knoit, beat or strike sharply (R).

knoost, a large lump (R).

know, a hillock.

kow, goblin, or any person one stands in awe to disoblige, and fears (R).

kyte, the belly (R).

kyth, show.

laidin, laiding, load, burden.

laigh, low.

lair, lear, learning; *vb.,* learn, teach.

lair'd, buried; **lairs,** lies.

laith, loath.

laits, tricks.

lammer-bead, amber bead.

landart, landwart, the country, or belonging to it, rustic (R).

landlouper, vagabond.

lang, long.

langer, distress.

lapper'd, curdled.

late-wake, watch beside the dead, but could become a festive occasion.

lave, the rest or remainder (R).

lavrock, lark.

lawin, lawen, a tavern reckoning (R).

leal, true, truly.

lear. *See* **lair.**

leem (Aberdeen), loom.

leen, cease.

lee-rig, ley-rig, ridge or stretch of grassy, uncultivated land.

leesh, lash, whip.

leet, list of candidates.

leg-bail, flight without waiting for the course of justice.

leglen, a milking pail with one lug or handle (R).

lerroch, appointed place.

leugh, laughed.

lick, blow; **licket,** beaten.

lift, the sky or firmament (R).

lightlyin, despising, slighting.

ligs, lies.

limmer, wench (pejorative).

ling, quick career in a straight line; *vb.,* gallop (R).

lingan, lingle, cord, shoemakers' thread (R).

linkan, walking briskly.

lintie, linnet.

lippen, expect, trust.

lith, a joint (R).

loan, milking park near a village.

loof, the hollow of the hand (R).

loot, let.

loun, lown, rogue, whore, villain (R); boy.

lounder, a sound blow (R).

loup, lowp, leap, spring.

lout, stoop.

low, flame; **lowan,** flaming (R).

lown, calm; **keep lown,** be secret (R).

lucky, familiar address to an elderly woman.

lug, ear, handle of a pot or vessel (R).

luggie, a dish of wood with a handle (R).

lum, chimney.

lyart, hoary or grey-haired (R).

lyther, more sheltered.

maik, make, match, equal (R); partner.

mail, meal.

mailen, mailin, a farm that is rented; the rent for a farm.

mail-payers, payers of rent or taxes.

mair, more.

make. *See* **maik.**

makes na, doesn't matter.

mane, moan, lament.

mant, maunt, stutter, stammer in speech.

mark, dark; *superl.,* **markest.**

mask, mash, in brewing; **masking-loom,** mash-vat.

master, *n. as adj.,* able.

master-cann, vessel for holding urine.

maught, strength.

maun, must; **mauna,** must not.

maut, malt.

mavis, song-thrush.

meikle, muckle, much, big, great, large (R); **muckle maun,** very big.

mell, maul, heavy mallet.

meltith, meal.

mennin-pool, minnow-pool.

mense, discretion, sobriety, good breeding (R); **mensfowly,** *adv.*

menzie, crowd, companions.

mergh, marrow, strength, power.

merl, blackbird.

messen, a little dog, lap-dog (R).

Mess John, common name for a priest or minister.

mest, a master.

mett, measured.

milane, by myself, alone.

mint, aim, endeavour (R).

mirk, dark.

mirlygoes, illusions, fancies.

mishanter, mishap.

miskend, neglect or not to take notice of one; also, let alone (R).

mislear'd, unmannerly.

mony, many.

mool in, copulate.

mools, the earth of the grave (R).

motty, spotted, full of motes.

mou, mouth; large rick of hay or corn.

mouse-wabbs, phlegm in the throat.

mows, jests (R); **nae mows,** no joke.

muckle. *See* **meikle.**

muddy, dark, troubled.

muisted, perfumed.

multer, multure, the miller's toll of meal for grinding.

mundungus, bad tobacco.

mutchken, an English pint (R).

mutton-bouk, carcase of a sheep.

nacky, clever, active in small affairs (R).

nanesel, her, her own self (Highland).

nappy, ale.

near-gawn, mean.

nebb, nose.

neist, next.

newcal, cow newly calved.

nicked, cheated (R).

nicksticks, tallies.

nigher, nicker, neigh; **nighering,** neighing.

nignyes, nignays, trifles (R).

nive, the fist (R); length of a hand.

nodle, head.

noggans, noggins.

nowt, cows, kine.

obtemper'd, fulfilled.

o'ercome, surplus.

oolie. *See* **ulie.**

orp, weep with a convulsive pant (R).

orro, orrow, spare.

ourlies, owrlays, cravats (R).

owk, week (R).

owsen, oxen.

oxter, the arm-pit (R).

oy, grandchild.

padock, puddock, a frog.

pakes, strokes.

pale, cut into a cheese.

pandour, large oyster.

pang, squeeze, press or pack one thing into another (R).

paritch, porridge.

partans, crabs.

paten, patten, wooden shoe.

paughty, proud.

pauky, pawky, witty or sly in word or action, without any harm or bad designs (R).

pe (Highland **p** for **b**), be.
pea-hools, pea-pods.
pease-clods, coarse rolls made of peasemeal.
pech, pegh, pant.
pensily, affectedly.
pet, a favourite, fondling; **to take the pet[t],** to be peevish or sullen (R).
pettle, dandle, feed, cherish, flatter (R).
peuther, pewther, pewter.
pig, jar.
pingle, contend, strive, or work hard (R); a contention.
pirny, bobbin on which yarn or thread is wound.
pit-mirk, darkness of a pit; *adj.*, very dark.
pith, strength, might, force (R); **pithless,** lacking strength.
plack, Scots copper coin worth one-third of a penny sterling.
plaiding-coat, coat made of tartan plaiding.
playfair, plaything.
plea, case.
plet, plait, fold.
pleys, quarrels (with the law).
plook, pimple; **plouky,** covered with pimples.
pluck, feed, grazing.
plumb, £100,000, *hence* 'a fortune'.
pock, poke, wallet, purse.
poind, to distrain.
pomet, pomatum.
poortith, poverty.
pople, paple, the bubbling, purling or boiling up of water (R); **popilan,** bubbling.
poses, stores of money.
poutch, a pocket.
pow, head.
prick-the-louse, the tailor.
prie. *See* **prive.**
priggin, entreating.
prin, pin.
prive, prove or taste (R); **prie; prieven,** a taste.
propine, gift or present (R).

protty (Aberdeen), pretty.
purpie, purple, deep red: **purpie-smiles,** blushes.
quat, quit, give over; **quat the grip,** died.
quean, lass.
queff, quegh, quaich, small shallow cup.
quey, a young cow (R).
rackless, careless (R).
raffan, merry, roving, hearty (R).
raggit clay, untidy, untilled soil.
raiking, running, hurrying.
rair, roar.
rangles, clusters.
rant, romp, make merry; **rantin,** cheering.
rary-shows, raree-shows, peep-shows.
rax, stretch (R); reach, grow.
ream, cream; **reaming,** creaming.
reath, quarter of a year.
redd: I'm redd, I'm afraid.
redd, to rid, unravel.
reek, reik, smoke, steam, smell; *n.*, reach.
reesle, clatter.
reest, rust, or dry in the smoke (R).
remead, remedy.
restit, burnt out.
revel'd, tangled.
rift, belch.
rig, rigg, ridge between furrows.
rigging, the back or rig-back, the top or ridge of a house (R); back.
ring, reign.
rive, *n.*, break; *vb.*, rob, spoil.
rokelay, rokely, mantle.
rook, hindmost, 'last farthing'.
roose, commend, extol (R).
roset, rub with resin or cobbler's wax.
roudes, old, ill-natured woman.
roun'd, whispered.
roup, hoarseness.
roust, cry, bellow in a loud voice.
rousted, rusted, dry.
rout, blow.
row, roll, enroll; **rowan, rowing,** rolling.

rowly powl. *See note.*
rowt, roar, especially the lowing of bulls and cows (R).
rowth, plenty (R).
royit, riotous, wild.
rubs, vexations, difficulties.
rucks, ricks, hay-stacks.
rug, rugg, pull, take away by force (R); tak a rug, pick a bargain.
rumblegare, disorderly.
rung, cudgel.
runkle, wrinkle; *vb.*, ruffle (R).
rype, search, rake.
sae, so.
saebeins, since, if it be so.
sain'd. *See* sane.
sair, *n.*, *vb.*, sore, hurt.
sair, *vb.*, serve, supply.
sakeless, saikless, guiltless, free (R).
sane, bless; sain'd, blessed, crossed.
sappy, sweet.
sark, shirt.
saugh, willow.
saul, soul.
saulie, hired mourner at funerals.
saut, salt.
scad, scald.
scald, scauld, scold, scolding; scauldin, scolding.
scancing, shining.
scantlins, scarcely.
scape, bee-hive.
scar, bare place on the side of a hill.
scart, scrape.
scate, skate; scate-rumples, hinder parts of skate.
scauld. *See* scald.
scaw'd, worthless.
scoug, flee for shelter; screen.
scoup, scowp, leap or move hastily from one place to another (R).
scowder, scorch, scorching.
scowry, showery.
screed, play in a lively way.
scrimp, narrow, straitened, little (R); *vb.*, stint.
scrog, stunted bush or shrub.
scud, quaff; scuds, runs.

scuds, ale, a late name given it by the benders (R).
scug. *See* scoug.
seenil, seldom.
seeth, to boil.
servite, table napkin.
sey, try; sey-piece, show-piece.
seything. *See* seeth.
shan, pitiful, silly, poor (R).
shank, leg, stocking; *vb.*, walk.
shape and shew, cut out and sew.
sharger, weakling.
shaw, wood; *vb.*, show.
she-dow, she-dove.
shekelbane, wrist.
shelly-coat, sheriff's officer (in Fergusson, but see Ramsay's note to 'The Gentle Shepherd', Act I, scene 1, l. 78).
shevelling-gabit. *See* gabby.
shew, sew.
shoars, warns, threatens.
shog, shogan, wag, shake.
shoon, shoes.
shotle, shottle, drawer (R).
sic, siccan, sicken, such.
sicker, firm, secure.
siller, silver, money.
simmer, summer; simmer roses, *see note.*
skair, share; scare.
skaith, hurt, damage, loss (R); effort.
skelf, shelf.
skellum, rascal.
skelp, run, used when one runs barefoot (R).
skreed. *See* screed.
slae-black, sloe-black.
slaister'd, greased.
slaisters, mixtures, prescriptions.
slap, narrow gap between hills, *or* gap in a dyke.
sled, cart without wheels.
slee, sly, skilful; *adv.*, sleely; slee-gabet, slyly spoken.
slid, slippery, smooth.
slocken, quench; slock'ning, allaying thirst.

sloughs, skins, coats.

smeek, smoke.

smirky, smiling.

smoor, smother.

snack, nimble, ready, clever (R).

snaw, snow; **snaw-tapit,** snow-covered.

snell, sharp, smarting, bitter, firm (R).

snifter, snuff or breathe through the nose a little (R).

snishing, snuff; **snishing mill,** snuff mill.

snod, neat, trim.

snool, dispirit by chiding (R).

snoovs, moves smoothly.

snug, neat.

snurl, ruffle or wrinkle (R).

sock, ploughshare.

soden, boiled.

soger, soldier.

sole, sill.

sonse, good luck.

sonsie, sonsy, happy, fortunate, lucky; sometimes used for large and lusty (R).

sorn, spunge, live off others.

souce, oatmeal porridge, or brose.

soucht, breathed deeply as in sleep.

sough, moaning of the wind, murmur.

soum, swim, drown.

soup, quantity, mouthful.

souter, shoemaker, cobbler.

sowder, solder.

sowens, flummery, or oatmeal soured amongst water for some time, then boiled to a consistency and eaten with milk or butter (R).

sowf, whistle to one's self.

spae, foretell.

spaeman, fortune-teller.

spain, wean; **spaining-time,** weaning time for lambs.

spang, leap or jump (R).

spats, spots.

spaul, bone shoulder, arm; **to the very spaul,** to the bone.

speal, holiday.

spean. *See* **spain.**

spear, speer, ask, enquire.

speel, climb.

spelding, small fish (often haddock) split and sun-dried.

spells, spill, cast; **spill ye'r dice,** throw the dice.

spill, ruin, spoil.

spink, the pink, primrose.

spoolie, spulzie, spoil, booty, plunder (R).

spraings, stripes of different colours (R); **sprangit,** various-coloured.

spring, tune.

sprush, spruce, neat.

spulzie, plunder, ruin.

spung, rob.

squeel, make an outcry.

stairhead, at the top of a flight of stairs.

staker, stagger.

stammer, blunder.

stamack, stomach, appetite.

stang, sting.

stap, stop; **stappit,** filled full.

stap your wa's, step your way.

starns, stars.

staw, stole.

staw'd, stuffed.

stay, hard to climb.

steek, shut, close; *n.,* stitch.

steer, touch, meddle with.

steeve, firm.

stegh, cram (R).

stend, sten, stent, move with a hasty long pace (R).

stent, lot, allowance of grazing land; tax, assessment; *vb.,* tax.

stirk, steer or bullock (R).

stirrah, fellow.

stoiter, stagger; **stoited,** staggered.

stoo, nibble.

stoup, flagon.

stoup and roup, completely.

stov'd, stewed in a pot.

stow'd, stole.

straik, stroke.

stramp, trample.

stravaig, wander.

streek, stretch, speed.

streich, draw out, argue the fine points of.

stringing, hanging; ornament.

strute, stuffed full, or drunk (R).

study, studdy, anvil, stithy.

suck, *vb.*, fine.

sucker, sugar.

sumph, blockhead.

sung, singed.

sunkots, something (R); provision of some kind.

swankies, clever young fellows (R).

swash, squat, fuddled (R).

swats, small ale.

sweel, swill.

sweer, lazy, slow (R); reluctant.

swith, quickly.

sybous, young onions.

synd, wash down, rinse; *n.*, rinse, draught.

syne, then, afterwards.

tabby, watered silk.

taiken, token.

tangs, tongs.

tap, top.

tape, use anything sparingly (R).

tappit-hen, the Scots quart-stoup (R).

targets, targits, pieces, tatters.

tass, cup.

tassels, tussles.

tate, teat, small lock of hair, or any little quantity of wool, cotton, etc. (R).

tawpie, idle, stupid girl.

taz, tawse, whip or scourge.

teem. *See* **toom.**

teen, anger.

tent, attend; heed, attention; **tenty,** watchful.

thack, thatch; **theekit,** thatched.

thae, thay, these, those.

thievless, thowless, wasted, unprofitable.

thir, these.

thir ben, *adv.*, deep in.

thirle, pierce.

thirling, binding; **thirling mill,** mill where the tenant is bound to have his grain ground.

thole, to endure, suffer.

thorn, hawthorn; **thornie dike,** fence of hawthorns.

thow, thaw.

thowless, spiritless.

thrang, crowd; crowded.

thrapple, windpipe.

thrave, throve, prospered.

thrawart, perverse, hostile.

thrawn, thrawin, stern and crossgrained (R); **thrawn gabbed,** quarrelsome.

threap, threep, aver, allege, urge and affirm boldly (R).

threave, twenty-four sheaves.

thristles, thistles.

tick, credit.

tids, fits of temper.

tift, good order, health (R).

tight, good-looking.

timmer, timber, wood; wooden cup.

tine, lose; **tint,** lost.

tingle, tinkle, ring.

tip, tippony, ale sold for twopence the Scots pint (R).

tirl, tirle, tir, uncover, strip.

titty, sister.

tocher-good, marriage dowry.

tod, fox; **Tod Lawrie,** name for the fox.

todling, gently sounding.

tongue-tackit, with an impediment of speech.

tooly, tulzie, fight, quarrel.

toom, empty; **teem** (Aberdeen).

toot aff your horn, drink off your cup.

tottled, boiled.

tousle, touse, touzel, rumple, tease.

tout, toot, drink; **toutit aff the horn,** drained the cup.

tout, sound of a horn or trumpet (R).

towin'd. *See* **twin.**

towmand, towmond, towmonth, year or twelve month (R).

223

tree'n, wooden.

trees, barrels.

treit, deal with.

trig, neat, handsome.

trinckling, flowing.

trock, troke, deal, do business, exchange.

tron, market.

trough, valley, dale.

trow, true, believe.

truf, truff, steal (R); truffer, thief.

truf, turf.

trunchers, wooden platters.

tulzie. *See* tooly.

turners, copper coins worth two pennies Scots.

turnpike stair, spiral staircase of a tenement.

twafald, double.

twalt, twelfth.

twin, part with, or separate from (R).

ugsome, hateful, nauseous (R).

ulie, ulzie, oil, oily; ulie pig, vessel for holding oil.

umquhile, umwhile, the late, or deceased some time ago. Of old (R).

unclowr'd, without bumps and bruises.

uncanny, dangerous.

unco, unka, unko, uncouth, strange (R).

unfald, unfold.

unfleggit, undismayed.

unsonsy, unlucky.

usquebae, whisky.

vallie, valet.

vaut, vault.

virles, rings.

vissyt, examined, viewed.

vogie, vougy, elevated, proud (R); glad.

wae, woe; wae worth, woe become.

waefou, woeful.

waesuck, alas!

waff, waif, strayed, solitary.

wag, shake, wave.

wairn, warn.

wald, wield.

wale, pick and choose (R); hand-waild, hand-picked; the wale, the best.

walie, wally, chosen, beautiful, large (R). bonny wallies, gewgaws, finery.

wame, weym, weyme, wyme, stomach, womb.

wanchancy, dangerous.

wanruly, unruly.

wanwordy, worthless.

wanworth, a mere nothing.

war, waur, worse.

wat, know.

waught, deep draught.

waus, waws, walls.

wawking, watching; wawking o' the fauld, watching the sheepfold at weaning time.

weans, we'ans, children.

weary, accursed, vexatious.

weeks, corners of the mouth.

weelfardly, with a good grace, pleasantly.

weels me on, blessings on.

weid, dress.

weigh-bauk, balance.

weir, war.

weirlike, warlike.

westlin, westerly.

wether-gammond, leg of mutton.

weym. *See* wame.

weyr (Aberdeen), wire, knitting needles.

whang, slice, thong.

whauk, whip, beat, flog (R).

whid, spring; fly quickly (R).

whilk, which.

whilliwhaw, unreliable person, cheat.

whindging, whining.

whitens, the young of the salmon-trout.

whittle, knife.

whumble, turn down.

wierds, fates, destinies.

wile, select.

will-fire, wild-fire.

willawins, alas!

wimple, wind (of a road or river);
  wimpling, winding.

win, winn, reside, dwell.

windocks, winnocks, windows.

winnelstrae, stalk of withered grass, 'a
  straw'.

winnock. *See* **windock.**

wirricow, wirrikow, bug-bear or
  goblin (R).

wisent, wissened, parched, dried,
  withered (R).

withershins, motion against the sun
  (R); in a contrary direction.

wizen, gullet.

woo, wool.

wood, mad.

woody, woodies, gallows.

wordy, worthy.

writers, clerks, lawyers.

wumill, gimlet.

wylie, wily, cunning.

wyse, guide; **wysing a-jee,** directing
  in a bending course.

wyson. *See* **wizen.**

wyte, blame.

yae, one.

yap, eager.

yarkit, bruised.

yate, yett, gate.

yeard, garden.

yed, contend, wrangle (R).

yellowchin, screaming.

yence, once.

yesk, hiccup (R).

yett. *See* **yate.**

yird, earth; **yird-laigh,** as low as
  earth.

yole, yawl.

youdith, youth.